EXODUS–JOSHUA

The Storyteller's Companion to the Bible

Michael E. Williams, editor

VOLUME TWO

EXODUS–JOSHUA

Abingdon Press
Nashville

EXODUS–JOSHUA

Copyright © 1992 by Abingdon Press

This book is printed on recycled, acid-free paper.

Library of Congress Cataloging-in-Publication Data
(Revised for volume 2)

The Storyteller's companion to the Bible.
  Includes indexes.
  Contents: v. 1. Genesis — v. 2. Exodus–Joshua.
  1. Bible—Paraphrases, English.   2. Bible—Criticism, interpretation, etc.
I. Williams, Michael E. (Michael Edward), 1950-
BS550.2.S764   1991   220.9'505   90-26289
ISBN 0-687-39671-9 (v. 2)
ISBN 0-687-39670-0 (v. 1 : alk. paper)

Scripture quotations in "The Story" section of each chapter are from The Revised English Bible. Copyright The Delegates of the Oxford University Press and the Syndics of the Cambridge University Press 1989. Used by permission.

Scripture quotations in the "Comments on the Story" section of each chapter are the author's own translations.

MANUFACTURED IN THE UNITED STATES OF AMERICA

As always
for
Margaret
and now
for
Sarah

Contributors

James C. Howell earned his Ph.D. in Old Testament from Duke University and is presently serving as pastor of Davidson United Methodist Church in North Carolina.

Beth A. Richardson, a storyteller, earned her M.Div. from Vanderbilt Divinity School. She is associate editor of *alive now!* a contemporary devotional magazine published by The Upper Room. She also is a resident at the Penuel Ridge Retreat Community in Nashville, Tennessee.

Edward P. Wimberly a storyteller, is the author of *African American Pastoral Care* and is Assistant Professor of Pastoral Care and Counseling at Gammon Theological Seminary in Atlanta, Georgia.

John Jamison, a storyteller, is pastor of Carthage United Methodist Church in Carthage, Illinois.

Michael E. Williams earned his Ph.D. from Northwestern University and is Associate Pastor of Belle Meade United Methodist Church in Nashville, Tennessee, and former Director of Preaching for The United Methodist Church. He presently is establishing the Center for Religious Imagination as a network for educators and pastors who seek to spread the good news through story.

Contents

A Storyteller's Companion

Michael E. Williams

This volume, like the last in the Storyteller's Companion to the Bible Series, is for anyone interested in telling Bible stories. Now we focus our attention on a number of the stories from Exodus through Joshua. Pastors who have preaching responsibilities will find this book particularly helpful as they prepare to tell one of these stories as part of a sermon. If preaching is to help the listener to participate in the world of the biblical narrative, then telling stories from the Bible is imperative.

In addition, leaders of Bible studies and teachers of church school classes will invariably be called upon to tell Bible stories as part of their lessons. The story recounted here is already a part of the Seder meal in Jewish households. It may be that parents and grandparents will want to tell portions at other times, too.

Every culture, indeed each person, has a story or collection of stories that shape its very character. For the Jewish people, it is the story of slavery in Egypt, of God's choosing Moses to lead the people out of bondage, of wandering in the wilderness and finally coming to the promised land. Along the way we encounter many stories that are very familiar: the burning bush, the dividing of the sea, the golden calf, the giving of the commandments, and the fall of Jericho. There may be some stories here that are less familiar or virtually unknown to many people.

In addition to forming the core of the Jewish tradition, these stories have offered hope to numerous other communities who found themselves in bondage. The images find their way into the spirituals and preaching that was forged in the slave camps of the antebellum South. They are currently shaping the conversation about God's role in the liberation of the oppressed in base communities of Latin America. These stories are not simply ancient history. Like so many biblical narratives the stories from Exodus–Joshua continue to live and touch the lives of people across the centuries.

The Stories

This volume offers an overview of the journey that took a people from slavery to freedom to the promised land. Obviously, we could not deal in detail with every verse of all the books between Exodus and Joshua. In the first place, this literature is not entirely narrative, nor does every description fit a narrative presentation. Much of the legal material is simply left out. We have included the passages that appear in the lectionaries (including the proposed revisions of the *Revised Common Lectionary 1992*). Beyond these texts we included those stories that seemed to make a significant contribution to the narrative as a whole.

If you do not happen to find one of your favorite stories in this collection, there is no need to despair. Much of the information that you will learn from the comments on the stories that are included can be transferred to other portions, especially repeated tellings of the same story, of the Exodus and wilderness narrative. This will allow you to use your creativity even more fully.

The translation from which the printed texts in this companion are taken is *The Revised English Bible*. You may wish to compare the readings here with your favorite translation or several others. It enriches the telling of biblical stories, especially for those who do not read the original language, to work from various translations.

Comments on the Stories

James C. Howell is pastor of Davidson United Methodist Church in Davidson, North Carolina, and emphasized study of the Hebrew Bible in his Ph.D. work at Duke University. He provides information about the history, geography, social structure, culture, and theology that shape the stories collected here. He does not tell you how you must tell the stories, but rather provides you with the information you need to choose how you will tell the stories.

The specific contribution that you will make to the preparation for telling one of these stories is knowing your audience. You can take the information James Howell offers and shape a telling of the story that will be appropriate to the ages and life experiences of your listeners. Only you can know where in the lives of those in your congregation, class, or family a story will strike a chord, turn on a light, or heal a hurt. For more information on how to prepare a story for a specific group of listeners, refer to "Learning to Tell Bible Stories: A Self-directed Workshop" on pages 21-22.

Retelling the Stories

As a storyteller you will contribute something of your own personality and understanding of the Bible and your listeners to the telling of a Bible story. There is no one right way to accomplish this. While this companion includes sample retellings for each story, these are only examples of one way a story may be told. You may choose to tell it very differently.

The retellings are intended to free your imagination for telling and not limit you to any one form. Some retellings here are fairly straightforward recountings of a text. Others choose a character or characters from whose point of view to tell the story. Some retellings place the story in the modern world. We hope these will offer you a sample of the vast ways Bible stories can come to life in storytelling.

The goal of each retelling is to help our listener to hear the story as if for the first time and to see the world of the story as something new and fresh. We are grateful for the imaginations of the three storytellers who provided the retellings in this volume: Beth A. Richardson, associate editor of *alive now!* retold the first third of our stories. Edward P. Wimberly, who teaches pastoral care at Garrett-Evangelical Theological Seminary, wrote retellings of the second third. The Reverend John Jamison, pastor of Carthage United Methodist Church, Carthage, Illinois, wrote our final third of the retellings. In the midst of these I did the retelling for Exodus 20 (The Ten Commandments).

Midrashim

If you ask a rabbi a question, you are very likely to get a story for an answer. This reflects a wisdom that knows truth to be irreducible to a one-two-three answer. Truth is embodied in events as they happen and in persons as they relate to each other and to God. This kind of truth is best experienced in stories and concrete images. Perhaps no book is a better example of this storied truth telling than the Bible.

The most unique contribution this companion makes to the art of biblical storytelling is to include the stories and sayings of the ancient rabbis related to the Exodus–Joshua narrative. These are called midrashim (the singular is midrash), from a Hebrew word that means "to go in search of." When the rabbis went in search of the relevance of these already "old, old stories" for their time, they returned with questions. Those questions generated stories that stand alongside the scripture passages and interpret them in ways that children and adults alike can understand.

The midrashim included here came from several sources, and I have retold and adapted them for inclusion here. These midrashim appear in boxed text in the retelling of each story, placed near the part of the story to which it most closely relates. As you retell the story, you may wish to include one of the midrashim at these points in the story or at other appropriate places. For more information, refer to "What Are Midrashim, and What Are They Doing Here?" on pages 17-19.

You will probably not want to read this companion from front to back as you would most books. It was not designed to be read that way. One way to make effective use of it would first be to read James Howell's introduction to his comments on the stories and the introduction to midrash. Then choose a story that you wish to tell from the table of contents. This may be a story from an upcoming Sunday of the lectionary or the church school curriculum or it may simply be a story that captures your interest. Once you have chosen the story, work through the short workshop on storytelling using the story you chose as your content.

Use the retelling provided with the story as a guide, but do not feel obligated to simply repeat it. Tell the story for your hearers in your own way. You may choose to include the midrashim with your retelling, or you may tell them afterward. In any case, you are about to take part in one of the most ancient experiences people do in community: offering the gift of God's story so that it touches our story today.

Reading the Narratives of Exodus–Joshua

James C. Howell

Of all of Israel's stories, the narrative about the Exodus-Sinai wilderness and occupation are preeminent. The very identity of the Hebrew people is forged in these stories. Even through scholars try to identify the pieces, the stories of this volume are but one story, resisting division. Each episode is but a vignette in the broader drama. The story deftly threads origin and destination through almost every scene.

Biblical storytelling is an act of both imagination and fidelity. We begin with the inexhaustible mine of the text itself. Trust the text! The unadorned story has "worked" for centuries. We fiddle with it only with discretion. Keep an eye trained on what the text does not say. These gaps are crucial. As we do our filling in, we need to honor the text's intention so that we do not get diverted into every conceivable matter. The comments in this second volume of the Storyteller's Companion to the Bible are designed to stimulate creativity and to lay some boundaries. We remember that Hebrew narrative moves, not by description and personality, but by action and dialogue. We never know what Moses looks like; we are never told how he feels. But we watch where he goes. We hear what he says. Perhaps the storyteller is wise to stick to these items, which tantalize the listeners who can make their own deductions.

At the same time, this volume of the Storyteller's Companion shares "facts," grist for the creative mill. Joshua knew what "the Jordan" looked like, but we need some help. Scholars have tackled the text from every conceivable angle.

1. *Geographical.* The story pinpoints specific locations. In the wilderness "wanderings," the people moved from one named place to another; they weren't "lost." A skillfull storyteller needs to know whether the trek from Kadesh Barnea to Shittim is 100 yards or 100 miles. A craggy overhang (if there in fact was a craggy overhang) or the adjective *uphill* can transform a story. Keep an atlas within reach.

2. *Archaeological.* Excavators have zealously uncovered physical "stuff" that tells its own story of real life in the days of Moses and Joshua. We have paintings of a Pharaoh whipping an Asiatic bricklayer; we see Pharaoh's impressive building remains as well as Jericho's not so impressive walls; we can hold in our hands ancient lamps and dishes. For the storyteller, archaeolo-

gy is not a tool to establish historicity. Instead the archaeologist provides a concrete detail or two that can enrich any story.

3. *Historical.* A story is not a history lecture. But we know some dates; the events of the Exodus are roughly contemporary with the Trojan War! We know what the pharaohs were up to when they weren't dickering with Moses. We know a good bit about who lost the land of Canaan.

4. *Sociological.* Recent studies have helped us to grasp the depth of the socioeconomic turbulence that shaped Israel's birth. Listeners are keenly aware of tension between haves and have-nots in the real story "between the lines" in Exodus through Joshua. What do the Exodus, the Boston tea party, the storming of the Bastille, the Montgomery bus boycott, and Mao's "long march" have in common?

5. *Rhetorical.* The biblical text has been crafted with skill. The storyteller will revel in the hyperbole, inclusions, puns, and allusions found here; a raconteur will discern irony and surprises in the plot. Images (bondage, thirst, wilderness) abound and "speak" at many levels. A storyteller can learn to tell these stories with the same depth and skill as those whose artistry appears in the text.

6. *Liturgical.* These stories come to us via the worship life at ancient sanctuaries (Gilgal, Shiloh, Jerusalem). At the great festivals, the people congregated to hear their story, a story only later congealed into ink on parchment. Liturgical rites (meals, sacrifices, litanies), well-known to us, were the medium through which biblical people experienced their story. A clever storyteller could set the stage of a Temple celebration to great advantage.

7. *Canonical.* So generative was this story that the rest of the Bible can be said to be a commentary upon it. Within the Bible itself, this story is told and retold in more than one kind of narrative, in more than one kind of song, in varieties of prophetic preaching. New Testament storytellers recast the Hebrew narrative in the light of Christ's advent. Attend to these canonical connections! The Bible expects us to recognize patterns, allusions, and fulfillments. A well-schooled Bible student (like a hearer in biblical times) will make the connections mentally; the storyteller needs to state these aloud, partly to affirm the well-schooled, partly to assist those who aren't.

8. *Traditional.* What afterlife has this story had? Preachers (e.g., Augustine, Luther) have plumbed its depths; a residue of musical tradition ("Go Down, Moses," "Joshua Fit the Battle of Jericho") lingers. We hear the story most clearly from those who embody the plot in real life. Just consider what impact the Exodus story had on Cromwell and the Puritans, America's founders, the Civil War, Third World "liberation" theologies, and anti-Apartheid thought (see Michael Walzer, *Exodus and Revolution,* New York: Basic Books, 1985).

9. *Theological.* The ultimate intent of the biblical story is not to entertain or to psychologize, but to glorify God and to instill faith and obedience. Early on,

the story took on symbolic dimensions. But it was a long time before a narrator could say, "Moses led them through the figurative sea of anxiety and fear." All language is metaphorical. If we trust it and let it stand, it will evoke its own images. But this story will continue to spawn very tangible readings (see Walzer, whose political applications may make Americans squirm). Second, don't try to explain the "mysterious." The burning bush should be allowed to burn without being consumed by verbiage. Moses was mystified, as we must be.

If the storyteller is a "stage director," then these approaches offer camera angles to look into the action. For each story, more than one approach is offered. Play around, find which one is most comfortable, which is most daring. In subsequent retelling, try another angle.

Space does not allow discussion of every story in Exodus–Joshua. All the stories found in the *Common Lectionary* (read on Sunday in church) are here, but imagine churchgoers' never hearing about the reconnaissance of Canaan or the tumbling walls of Jericho or the plagues or even Balaam's talking donkey—none of which appear in that lectionary! They are here. Legal texts (in the lectionary or not) are regretfully omitted (but see Exod. 19 and Deut. 26); there is plenty of action even in the ordinances (oil poured over heads, rams succumbing to the knife, waving of sheaves, and the mysterious red heifer parading out of camp). The biblical legal codes clearly have a narrative feel, and they are set in a narrative framework. The laws of Sinai are inextricably yoked to the stories of deliverance and guidance; many laws find their rationale in the story (e.g., Deut. 15:15).

Beware the "fig leaf"! For centuries, interpreters tried to hide Moses' black wife in the closet. While we may relish this detail, we will stumble upon our own little embarrassments; we may wish to "ban" the violence. Heed the detail you'd rather leave out. Learn from those that make you or your listeners uncomfortable.

Capitalize on dialogue. The Bible is no account of how "this happened, then that happened." Dialogue drives the plot and gives the story its depth. Be inventive, with sensitivity. Surely the Bible itself fleshes out a few conversations that no one had gotten on cassette.

Remember fondly, but warily, the "prism-like" personality of Moses. Each generation recreates Moses in its own image. Before his death, Rabbi Daniel Jeremy Silver favored us with a historical survey of representations of Moses in his useful book *Images of Moses*. How pliable Moses proved to be in Greek culture, as he was transformed into Plato's teacher, model Stoic, mathematician, inventor, navigator, codifier of laws. In the Middle Ages he became a mystic philosopher. Cecil B. DeMille cast a rugged Charlton Heston, ideally heroic, of "commanding presence," deliberately framing his silhouette to mimic Michelangelo's famous sculpture in Rome's S. Pietro in Vincoli. In children's books, Moses is god-like, gray, wizened, with uplifted gaze. Rabbi

Silver put it best: "I have yet to see any children's book or any popular movie depict Moses as a small, dark, hollow-chested man, though, given his stock and background, Moses would most likely have inherited such a body type" (*Images,* p. 5).

The rest of the Bible is strangely silent about Moses; nobody carved a bust or painted his portrait. Perhaps this gap tells us something about leadership, about human life, about service. A Moses alien to what we deem to be "leader" may in fact mold and even evoke new "leader" images. The fact that Moses turns out to be something of a cipher may call into question the promethean achievements we proudly list on our resume; his two forays into assertiveness fail miserably. The storyteller who refrains from embroidering Moses' "person" will serve the hearer (and God) well.

What a privilege to tell this story! What a cloud of witnesses you will join! Just a few of the wonderful resources available are mentioned below; this Companion's dependence on them is evident on every page.

A SHORT BIBLIOGRAPHY

Boling, Robert G., and G. Ernest Wright. *Joshua.* Garden City: Doubleday, 1982. Chock-full of archaeology and history, yet remarkably in tune with the narrative and its power.

Childs, Brevard S. *The Book of Exodus.* Philadelphia: Westminster Press, 1974. Still the definitive commentary on Exodus, with sensitivity to the storyteller's agenda.

Mann, Thomas W. *The Book of the Torah: the Narrative Integrity of the Pentateuch.* Atlanta: John Knox Press, 1988. Deft handling of the narrative flow of Genesis through Deuteronomy.

Milgrom, Jacob. *Numbers.* The JPS Torah Commentary. Philadelphia: JPS, 5750/1990. Vigorous, thorough discussion by a great Jewish scholar.

Miller, Patrick D. *Deuteronomy.* Louisville: John Knox Press, 1990. Insightful commentary on the retellings in Deuteronomy.

Sarna, Nahum M. *Exploring Exodus.* New York: Schocken Books, 1986. A vibrant recreation of the biblical world, a sympathetic handling of academic issues.

Citations to these books in the "Comments on the Story" sections will be by author's last name and page number.

What Are Midrashim, and What Are They Doing Here?

Michael E. Williams

Midrash (the plural in Hebrew is *midrashim*) comes from a Hebrew word meaning "to go in search of" or "to inquire." So midrashim resulted when the ancient rabbis went in search of (inquired into) the meaning of the Scriptures for their lives. Midrash is also the name for the process of inquiring into the Scriptures for their meaning.

We might say that midrash is both our encounter with the biblical stories as we seek their meaning for our lives and times and the stories that emerge to express that meaning. Often midrashim do take the form of stories or pieces of stories (at least the ones we will focus on here do). These stories seek to answer questions about and to fill gaps in the biblical stories.

The midrashim drawn from for this volume come from the period 400–1200 C.E. (what is sometimes called A.D.). They were told, in part, to make the stories of Exodus–Joshua relevant to a Jewish community that had no homeland, could not hold citizenship in other countries, and experienced hostility and persecution from the outside, including from Christian authorities. Most of these midrashim originated in sermons preached in synagogues, based on the prescribed weekly readings from the Torah (the first five books of the Bible). Others emerged from the popular folk traditions of the Jewish communities. Though they were collected and written during that eight-hundred-year period, there is no way of knowing how long the midrashim had been circulating by word of mouth before someone wrote them down. Some are attributed to rabbis living at the time of Jesus. In fact, certain scholars find evidence that this way of interpreting the Bible has its roots intertwined with the texts of the biblical stories themselves.

I see three basic functions for the midrashim I have selected to be included in this book. The first might be called "filling the gaps." These stories and story fragments answer questions about the biblical stories that the Scripture leaves unanswered. For example, how did Moses become a part of Pharaoh's household? How did manna in the wilderness taste? When the rabbis answered such questions, they revealed both their fertile imaginations and their own understanding of God and human beings. Sunday school teachers and college professors will also have encountered these imaginative questions.

The second function of midrash is to draw an analogy. These stories begin with "This may be compared to. . . ." Then the rabbi would tell a contemporary story that exhibited a situation and characters like the biblical story under consideration. You may notice that these stories sometimes bear a resemblance to the parables of Jesus and the *mashal* (parable) form of Jewish teaching.

The third function is to describe an encounter. In these stories someone comes to a rabbi with a question, and the rabbi's response interprets both the biblical story and the situation from which the question emerged. For example, when someone asked a rabbi why Moses broke the tablets containing the Ten Commandments, the rabbi described how Moses and the elders wrestled over whether or not to present the Commandments to a people who would not keep them.

Why did I choose a predominantly Jewish form of interpretation in this book? First, Christians have too often ignored this ancient and time-honored way to interpret the Bible. Given our Jewish roots and Jesus' heritage, midrash is at least as directly related to our tradition as the Greco-Roman philosophy on which we have depended so heavily for ordering our questions and structuring our theological doctrines.

Second, midrashim provide us with a way of interpreting the Bible that involves the imagination and speaks to our experience. It is also, according to certain scholars, the way the Bible interprets itself.

Third, midrashim provide a model for a community-based, inclusive (even children can imaginatively participate in stories), nonprofessional (you don't have to be a trained theologian) way of interpreting the Bible for our times. In short, we can learn the stories the rabbis told about the scriptures to interpret them for their time. In addition, we can follow the example of the rabbis and learn to tell stories about Bible stories that interpret them for our time.

This is just the first step to reclaiming midrashim for modern tellers of Bible stories, but it is a step. If you want to learn more about midrashim related to the stories of Exodus–Joshua, you may wish to read the volumes from which those included here were chosen.

Midrash Rabbah, translated by H. Freedman (London: Soncino Press, 1939), is a ten-volume translation of midrashim on a variety of books of the Bible. The references here, which have been paraphrased and adapted, are to chapter and section. The third edition of this work was published in 1983.

Volume one in Louis Ginzberg's classic collection of stories related to biblical texts, *The Legends of the Jews,* translated by Henrietta Szold (Philadelphia: The Jewish Publication Society, 1909 and 1937), still in print, draws from a wide number of sources, including Christian and Islamic traditions. Here this work, again paraphrased and adapted, is listed as Ginzberg, followed by the volume and page number.

A good general Jewish commentary on the Torah is Gunther Plaut, ed., *The Torah: A Modern Commentary* (New York: Union of American

Hebrew Congregations, 1981). Here this work is listed as Plaut, followed by the page number.

One more word on midrash: For any given passage of Scripture, several stories or interpretations of various rabbis are presented side by side in collections of midrashim. Those who collected these stories saw no reason to decide which was the one right interpretation. This is also true, we might mention, of those who assembled the canon of the New Testament, who saw no reason to choose among the four very different stories about Rabbi Jesus. The understanding behind these choices is that there need be no single correct interpretation. The Bible is viewed as being so inclusive that it could apply to a range of possible life situations. Therefore, we would expect a variety of interpretations to speak to a variety of life situations. Not only the Bible, but also all of its many possible interpretations, are encompassed by the expansive imagination of God. In fact, Solomon, the wisest of all humans, is reputed by the rabbis to have known three thousand stories for every verse of Scripture and one thousand and five interpretations for every story.

Learning to Tell Bible Stories

A Self-directed Workshop

1. Read the story aloud at least twice. You may choose to read the translation included here or the one you are accustomed to reading. I recommend that you examine at least two translations as you prepare, so you can hear the differences in the way they sound when read aloud.

Do read them *aloud.* Yes, if you are not by yourself, people may give you funny looks, but this really is important. Your ear will hear things about the passage that your eye will miss. Besides, you can't skim when you read aloud. You are forced to take your time, and you might notice aspects of the story that you never saw (or heard) before.

As you read, pay special attention to *where* the story takes place, *when* the story takes place, *who* the characters are, *what* objects are important to the story, and the general *order of events* in the story.

2. Now close your eyes and imagine the story taking place. This is your chance to become a playwright/director or screenwriter/filmmaker because you will experience the story on the stage or screen in your imagination. Enjoy this part of the process. It takes only a few minutes, and the budget is within everybody's reach.

3. Look back at the story briefly to make sure you haven't left out any important people, places, things, or events.

4. Try telling the story. This works better if you have someone to listen (even the family pet will do). You can try speaking aloud to yourself or to an imaginary listener. Afterwards ask your listener or yourself what questions arise as a result of this telling. Is there information you need about the people, places, things, or language in the story? Is it appropriate to the age, experiences, and interests of those who will be hearing it? Does the story capture your imagination? One more thing: You don't have to be able to explain the meaning of a story to tell it. In fact, those of the most enduring interest have an element of mystery about them.

5. Read the "Comments on the Story" that James Howell has provided for each passage. Are some of your questions answered there? You may wish also to look at a good Bible dictionary for place names, characters, professions, objects, or words that you need to learn more about. *The Interpreter's Dictionary* *of the Bible* (Nashville: Abingdon Press, 1962) is still the most complete source for storytellers.

6. Read the "Retelling the Story" section for the passage you are learning to tell. Does it give you any ideas about how you will tell the story? How would you tell it differently? Would you tell it from another character's point of view? How would that make it a different story? Would you transfer it to a modern setting? What places and characters will you choose to correspond to those in the biblical story? Remember, the retellings that are provided are not meant to be told exactly as they are written here. They are to serve as springboards for your imagination as you develop your telling.

7. Read the midrashim that accompany each retelling. Would you include any of these in your telling? You could introduce them by saying, "This is not in the original story, but the rabbis say. . . ." Do these midrashim respond to any of your questions or relate to any of your life situations or those of your listeners? If so, you might consider using them after the retelling to encourage persons to tell their own stories, which hearing the Bible story has brought to mind. You may even wish to begin creating some modern midrashim of your own or with your listeners.

8. Once you have gotten the elements of the story in mind and have chosen the approach you are going to take in retelling it, you need to practice, practice, practice. Tell the story aloud ten or twenty or fifty times over a period of several days or weeks. Listen as you tell your story. Revise your telling as you go along. Remember that you are not memorizing a text; you are preparing a living event. Each time you tell the story, it will be a little different, because you will be different (if for no other reason than that you have told the story before).

9. The "taste and see" that even the stories of God are good—not all sweet, but good and good for us and for those who hunger to hear.

Pharaoh and the Israelite Midwives

Pharaoh fears the Israelite slaves and wants their newborn males killed, though their lives are spared by clever midwives.

The Story

In course of time Joseph and all his brothers and that entire generation died. The Israelites were prolific and increased greatly, becoming so numerous and strong that the land was full of them. When a new king ascended the throne of Egypt, one who did not know about Joseph, he said to his people, 'These Israelites have become too many and too strong for us. We must take steps to ensure that they increase no further; otherwise we shall find that, if war comes, they will side with the enemy, fight against us, and become masters of the country.' So taskmasters were appointed over them to oppress them with forced labour. This is how Pharaoh's store cities, Pithom and Rameses, were built. But the more oppressive the treatment of the Israelites, the more they increased and spread, until the Egyptians came to loathe them. They ground down their Israelite slaves, and made life bitter for them with their harsh demands, setting them to make mortar and bricks and to do all sorts of tasks in the fields. In every kind of labour they made ruthless use of them.

The king of Egypt issued instructions to the Hebrew midwives, of whom one was called Shiphrah, the other Puah. 'When you are attending the Hebrew women in childbirth,' he told them, 'check as the child is delivered: if it is a boy, kill him; if it is a girl, however, let her live.' But the midwives were godfearing women, and did not heed the king's words; they let the male children live. Pharaoh summoned the midwives and, when he asked them why they had done this and let the male children live, they answered, 'Hebrew women are not like Egyptian women; they go into labour and give birth before the midwife arrives.' God made the midwives prosper, and the people increased in numbers and strength; and because the midwives feared God he gave them families of their own. Pharaoh then issued an order to all the Egyptians that every new-born Hebrew boy was to be thrown into the Nile, but all the girls were to be allowed to live.

Comments on the Story

Genesis ends on a high note, Joseph's family secure, even successful in Egypt. Exodus 1:1-7 portrays the partial fulfillment of the Lord's promise to

Abraham's progeny (see also Gen. 12:1-4). They have become "great" indeed, but they are dislocated, out of place, not yet in the land; the prospect of blessing the nations is fading from the horizon.

Exodus 1:6-9 simplifies a complex web of events stretching over centuries. Can we fill in some background to Pharaoh's paranoia? Between 1780–1570 B.C.E., Asian invaders ("the Hyksos") controlled Egypt, dominating the eastern delta. The rise of Joseph fits this era neatly. But Amose and Kamose, co-founders of the eighteenth dynasty, overthrew the invaders and probably conscripted them into labor camps in retaliation. It is little wonder, then, that Pharaoh would clamp down on such foreigners lest they again "become masters" (as the REB insightfully interprets *we'alah*; the NRSV sticks with "escape," although surely Pharaoh would rather them just leave than seize his throne!). But just how "shrewdly" (NRSV) does Pharaoh deal with his anxiety?

Can we identify this nameless Pharaoh? The leading candidate, Rameses II (1290–1224 B.C.E.), was an extraordinary builder. We grasp for words to describe his endeavors: colossal, massive, breathtaking. In the late 1980s, Rameses went on tour in America; thousands glimpsed the awesome display that represents only a tiny fraction of his legacy. Folks who have never been to Egypt have mental snapshots of pyramids, sand, and sphinxes. Worth noting is Rameses' egomaniacal habit of scrawling his name on the monuments of others. Most of his construction was in the eastern delta, the home of the Hebrews. Our story uses "local color," by anchoring the events in specific places (Pithom, modern tell el-Maskhuta; Pi-Rameses, near Qantir). The storyteller is wise to convey the "feel" of Egypt, and may do so with confidence. Photographs and drawings of both the region and the actual monuments of Rameses are easily obtained. Egypt "feels" pristine, sunny, hot, sandy, with scaffoldings framing a beehive of activity. For the "haves," the feel is splendor, luxury, progress, a cultural zenith. For the "have-nots," the feel is anonymity, exhaustion, misery, a bottomless pit. Palaces, temples, and monuments mandated massive (and preferably cheap) labor; pyramid paintings depict foreign captives laying bricks. While forced labor was business as usual in Egypt, Israelite ways were violated.

Foreigners dug irrigation ditches and canals; the travails of working in the "fields" were proverbially harsh. The brickmaking assembly line comprised water carrying, stubble collection, pushing alluvial clay into wooden molds, carrying, and lifting. A pyramid required millions of bricks; a single brickmaker's daily quota might be 3,000 bricks! A leather scroll from Rameses' day specifies 40 men's daily assignment of 2,000 bricks apiece (80,000 bricks daily from just one gang!). The log also indicates that the quota was rarely met. The consequences? Punishment: a rod across the back, verbal abuse, deprivation. Degrading, brutal conditions were calculated to take the spirit out of the people. In Exodus 5, after recoiling from a request for a long weekend for worship (and we have evidence of other groups being granted such leaves), the Pharaoh only tightens his grip with a puerile "That'll show them" tactic that really only slows his own building efforts.

Note well the escalation of oppression. The Israelites, once honored guests, see their fortunes plummet from feudal peasants to slaves, deeper into harassment and the worst kind of pogrom against defenseless infants. Even the words grate—"ground down," "bitter," "harsh." This is not chattel slavery, but state slavery, based on class and race. By abusing power, tyrants stumble into self-destructiveness. By mistreating his labor force, the supposedly incarnate son of the sun-disk god Re exhibits little wisdom. And he limits population by getting rid of the males, not the females! One paranoid hypothesis is piled upon another: "If war comes . . . if they rise up . . . "). Not surprisingly, the Egyptians come to loathe the Israelites; power and fear are the genuine roots of prejudice.

It is at this juncture that the story has "spoken" so profoundly to countless oppressed persons. Oliver Cromwell's oratory imaged for the Puritans an exodus from regal bondage. America's founders sensed that they were entering the promised land, only to discover just a few decades later that they could be lambasted as children of Pharaoh by black Americans. A Pulitzer Prize winning narrative of the civil rights movement was not accidentally entitled "Parting the Waters." In Latin America, storytellers understand fully what state oppression is all about. Sociologically, the oppressed don't read Exodus 1 so much as Exodus 1 reads them! The text simply tells the truth, and in so doing it inflames the passions and hopes of the marginalized.

Hearers inevitably make mental jumps. The storyteller has two options: tell the story and let the hearers do the work, or tantalize your hearers through some identification with current persons and groups. The Bible calls the oppressor Pharaoh. Perhaps, considering the various Herods of the New Testament, it makes no difference from the perspective of the chosen people what the oppressor is called; Pharaohs, Herods, and modern tyrants are all the same. This facelessness invites the storyteller to name modern-day Pharaohs. We may bristle at any hint of class struggle here, claiming, "It sounds Marxist!" The Third World doesn't know Marx, but they experience daily the reality that he named. The sociological dynamics may upset even an otherwise pleasant storytelling session. Just by having the luxury of reading this book, you may well find yourself (sociologically speaking) among the modern-day Egyptians out from under whose unwitting oppression the poor might like to escape.

In the opening scene, God does not seem to be among the stage players. For Israel, as Pharaoh's grip tightens, God seems to have gone on vacation. But the hearer is invited to perceive subtle glimpses of God's mysterious workings in the seemingly God-forsaken story. Wryly we might ask, "Is the Lord hiding in the bulrushes?" Theologically, Exodus makes no abstractions about the eternal nature of the Godhead. Rather, a storied contest is played out between Pharaoh (with pretensions to divinity) and the Lord (the true God). Mere escape from Pharaoh will not suffice; he must be judged. Mysteriously, ironically, surprisingly, and even humorously, the Lord bests and even mocks the mocker. For any hearers tempted to be impressed by his might, the pharaoh is duped, made a laughingstock, the butt of the joke.

The first glimmer of resistance comes from the midwives (one of few professions open to women), who have been ordered (threatened?) by Pharaoh to conduct a holocaust, abhorrent to the very nature of their calling. We know their names: Shiphrah ("beautiful") and Puah, ("fragrant flower"). The fact that we know their names is itself a subtle affront to the nameless pharaoh. Are the midwives Hebrews? Could the pharaoh possibly expect their cooperation? If they are Egyptians, why did they refuse? The storyteller cannot answer these questions, but may well raise them. These women dupe Pharaoh in what might be history's first recorded instance of civil disobedience. Rahab and Esther later in the story will be their true sisters. Even we are left befuddled: Are Shiphrah and Puah lying? The midwives combine "fear of God" with "spunkiness," a vital mix in the remainder of the story.

The stage is now set for the second act. In the midst of all the death comes life—against the odds.

Retelling the Story

"Kill all the boy babies."

I could not believe what I was hearing. I raised my eyes just enough to see his face. He was smiling a dark, angry smile. I knew he was serious.

I could feel Puah, my friend, standing next to me. Her body was tense, and I heard her sharp intake of breath as we listened to Pharaoh's words.

"Yes, kill the boy babies when you go as midwives to the Hebrew women. If the baby is a girl, she may live. But if it is a boy, kill him."

I looked at my dusty toes and sandals against the gold inlay of Pharaoh's floor. He continued to speak, as though we were not present.

"Those people are continuing to grow in large numbers. We cannot allow them to overrun our stores. If we were attacked by our enemies, they could join with them in war and escape from our land. This will show them that I am the ruler of all in this land." He spoke slowly, "Yes. Kill all their boy babies."

> The rabbis say that God accused Pharaoh of being stupid as well as wicked. If a shrewd king wanted to get rid of a whole nation of people, he would kill all the female babies rather than the males. After all, it is the women who give birth to and nurture any nation. (*Exodus Rabbah* 1.14)

Puah and I were shaking as we left Pharaoh's palace. To disobey his orders would mean our deaths.

But who can kill a newborn child? So delicate, so fragile, still wet from leaving his mother's womb. These tiny ones bless the name of the Holy One as they fill their lungs with breath and cry out that they are alive. Who can kill one of these innocents? But who can choose to sacrifice her own life? When I arrived back at my house, a young woman was waiting for me. "Shiphrah the midwife?" she asked me.

"Yes, I am Shiphrah," I answered.

"It is my mother, Leah's time. Can you come?"

I felt fear and still I heard myself saying, "Yes, I will come."

I gathered my basket of linens and herbs and followed the young woman to her house. The streets were filled with Egyptian overseers and Hebrew workers. I saw one worker beaten for stumbling with his load of bricks, and I remembered the face of the Pharaoh.

When we arrived, Leah was laboring with the effort of giving birth. It was dark and cool within the walls of the house, but Leah was sweating. The family women surrounding her drew back to let me next to Leah.

> The two midwives, Shiphrah and Puah, not only refused to harm the Hebrew babies, but they actually acted with greater kindness toward them than before. They would ask for food and water from the members of the community who had more and would give it to the poorer families with new babies. In this way the midwives not only saw to it that the children were *born* alive, but they made sure that the youngsters were *kept* alive as well. (*Exodus Rabbah* 1.15)

The birth was a difficult one. I prayed to the Holy One that her life would be spared . . . that the baby would be healthy . . . that it would be a girl.

Finally, I held in my hands a tiny, wet, squirming baby boy. He was shaking from the shock of the birth, but he was breathing the breath of life.

"Kill all the boy babies," Pharaoh's words spoke in my mind.

"I cannot," I said aloud as I laid the baby boy on his mother's chest. "The Holy One has given you life, little one. Who can take that life away but the Holy One? Not Shiphrah the midwife."

I knew that we would be called again before Pharaoh. As I walked back to my house, I thought that we would say to him: "Pharaoh, the Hebrew women are not like your Egyptian women. Because of all the hard work they do, they are healthy and strong and give birth before we arrive." What does Pharaoh know of the ways of women? I paused and stood outside my house. And I prayed, "Praise be to you, O Holy One, who has created us, who feeds us, and who has given the gift of breath to Leah's son. May his life bless your name. Amen."

When assisting the mother with a delivery, the midwives would pray for a safe birth and that the child be born whole and healthy. They would pray to God: "You have heard what Pharaoh commanded us to do, but we will follow your commands instead. If a child would normally be born lame or without sight or hearing, let it be born whole so that no one can say we tried to take its life. And if one would otherwise be born dead, let it live so that no one can accuse us of ending its days on earth prematurely." The rabbis say that God granted their request. (*Exodus Rabbah* 1.15)

The Birth of Moses

*A Hebrew boy, Moses, is saved by being placed in a basket afloat in the
Nile, where he is discovered by Pharaoh's daughter.*

The Story

A certain man, a descendant of Levi,
married a Levite woman. She con-
ceived and bore a son, and when she
saw what a fine child he was, she kept
him hidden for three months. Unable
to conceal him any longer, she got a
rush basket for him, made it water-
tight with pitch and tar, laid him in it,
and placed it among the reeds by the
bank of the Nile. The child's sister
stood some distance away to see what
would happen to him.

Pharaoh's daughter came down to
bathe in the river, while her ladies-in-
waiting walked on the bank. She
noticed the basket among the reeds
and sent her slave-girl to bring it.
When she opened it, there was the
baby; it was crying, and she was
moved with pity for it. 'This must be
one of the Hebrew children,' she said.
At this the sister approached
Pharaoh's daughter: 'Shall I go and
fetch you one of the Hebrew women to
act as a wet-nurse for the child?'
When Pharaoh's daughter told her to
do so, she went and called the baby's
mother. Pharaoh's daughter said to
her, 'Take the child, nurse him for me,
and I shall pay you for it.' She took the
child and nursed him at her breast.
Then, when he was old enugh, she
brought him to Pharaoh's daughter,
who adopted him and called him
Moses, 'because', said she, 'I drew
him out of the water'.

Comments on the Story

In Genesis 12, as if by zoom lens, our focus narrows from the mass of
humanity to a single chosen individual, Abraham. In Exodus 2, the storyteller's
lens deftly zeroes in on just one of the mothers facing the trauma of birth, fearing for her own life, fearing for her child, fearing for her people. Here is a story
to cast out fear. It works, in part because of its verbal dexterity, biting irony,
and rhetorical artistry.

The *Revised English Bible* (REB) calls Moses a "fine" child; how else could
he have been hidden away for three months? The Hebrew *tov* ("fine," "good")
echoes God's verdict on creation in Genesis 1: It was fine. Jochebed (so named
in Exod. 6:20; she was her husband's aunt, although the Septuagint—a Greek
translation—improves this to "cousin") saw her child, and behold, he was *tov*; a

new creation, a new beginning is intimated. She put this *tov* boy in a "rush basket," thatched, caulked with pitch and tar. But instead of using a normal word for "basket," the writer calls it a *tevah*. *Tevah* is used here and only once more in all of Scripture—to label the ship Noah built! Moses floats down the Nile in a well-built ark! A Hebrew listener would nod appreciatively, savoring this delicious word choice.

The text withholds answers to so many questions. These gaps are stimulating. Has Jochebed abandoned her child in resignation? Is exposure her only hope? Has she cast her bread upon the waters, entrusting the infant to a God who just may be hiding in the bulrushes? The basket is, after all, placed among the "reeds"; the relatively rare word *suf* is precisely the name of the sea (*yam suf,* "sea of reeds"), which will stand back at attention when the day of deliverance dawns.

The storyteller must play upon the ironies in the text. Miriam's debut is a surprise, since Moses has a "firstborn" feel about him; yet, even if she was "just a girl," she becomes a key player in the drama. This greatest baby sitter of all time negotiates for Moses' very own mother to be hired as the wet nurse; hilariously, Pharaoh's household pays Jochebed to mother her own child! How is the daughter of Pharaoh able to converse in Hebrew? Didn't Pharaoh notice one of the loathed Hebrews under his own roof? How ironic it is that into Pharaoh's house is welcomed the very one who will bring its downfall. Even the water plays its part: Pharaoh turns the Nile, the very source of life in Egypt, into a grave; the deliverer, snatched from that same water, will wield a rod over water that will become the grave of Egypt's finest. What a clever stage director is the Lord, pulling so many invisible strings to ensure the outcome.

One more word needs exploration. Even though the name "Moses" is given a Hebrew explanation (linked either to his own being as one "drawn out" of the Nile, or to Israel's being, which is "drawn out" through the sea), "Moses" is an Egyptian name, well-attested among the Pharaohs (Thut-mose, A-mose, Ka-mose). But "Moses" by itself isn't really a full name at all; it means "born to/son of" (Ka-mose would be the son of Ka). Moses has only half a name, only half an identity! Whose son is he really? Only in the course of the story does Moses' true identity unfold. Only in the course of the story does Moses himself discover his own identity. He will return to Egypt not as an adopted son of Pharaoh and not as a fugitive, but as the instrument of the Lord; the question "Who set you over us?" (2:14) will be decisively answered.

Rameses had fifty-nine daughters! Egyptian records prove that several non-Egyptians (including Asiatics) were reared in Pharaoh's household (which must have been teeming with hundreds of kids). The Gospels favor us with but one vignette from Jesus' boyhood, but from Moses' we have not a shred. The storyteller often cannot refrain from inferring too much from Moses' Egyptian rearing. The rabbis found the imaginative urge irresistible, regaling us with tales of romance and military acumen to fill in the minute gap between verses

10 and 11. It is interesting that Gandhi, Ho Chi Minh, Lenin, and others were separated from their people for a time of education, only to return to lead a revolution. We may also resist the urge to guess the daughter's motives. The whole story portrays women sympathetically; she is said to have "pity." Formal adoption would occur only after weaning, probably due to the high infant mortality rate.

How many ancient heroes got off to such a start? Hercules was abandoned by Alcmene; Oedipus was exposed on a mountain; Romulus and Remus were thrown into the Tiber; Sargon, ancient ruler of Akkad, was reputed to have been abandoned in a waterproof basket. Moses' story, though, will not be rags to riches, but riches to rags to the most surprising sort of riches.

But where is the Lord, conspicuously unmentioned in the story? Is the Lord peeking through the bulrushes with Miriam? The *tevah* has no rudder, no pilot. Has God entrusted the future of this people, and thus the future of God's promise for all creation, to a rush basket floating aimlessly down the river? How did it drift to just the right spot? Is it mere chance that the pharaoh's daughter happens to be at the right spot at the right time? Did the Lord (as one Midrash surmises) afflict her with an insatiable itching, so that she would seek relief in the river at the proper moment?

The storyteller must manage this "settled suspense." Moses is not lost; he's far from helpless. From such a mustard-seed beginning, the future hangs not on human ingenuity, but on the Lord, who indeed must be hiding in the bulrushes. The text has no interest in magnifying Moses into a folk hero. The wise storyteller will follow pace. On the whole, the text is at pains to keep Moses' personality out of the picture. When a "trait" peeks through in the fight (vv. 11-15; see also Num. 20), the outcome is unhappy. Moses' sorry attempt at justice, however well-intended, is set in bold relief by the sarcastic (and ironic) question: "Who set you up as an official and judge over us?" Who indeed! For the moment Moses has not yet been commissioned by the Lord for the task; little wonder he flops. As the chapter closes, the closest thing to a hero is (rather unheroically) on the run. When will God's silence finally be broken?

This story's images are so fraught with meaning that they spill over into the New Testament. The joy of Matthew's birth narrative is tainted by Herod's slaughter of the "holy innocents." Can you hear "Rachel weeping" (Jer. 31:15; Matt. 2:18) even in the land of Goshen? The narrative pattern shows how tragedy stalks the advent of redemption. Salvation is not welcomed, but is fanatically expelled. The slaughter cannot be glossed over and can hardly be explained; the story must simply relate the cold facts. As the Moses birth story is heard, Christian ears will resonate with another surreptitious escape from a pharaoh-like Herod. After all, where did the holy family find refuge? Egypt! Some fulfillment of a mystery is afoot here, better told in story form than analyzed in abstraction.

The rabbis amplified tiny details into explanatory narrative. Didn't Moses lead Egyptian troops into Nubia? And what of his romantic life? Most likely Moses was tutored in standard Egyptian curricula—arithmetic, geometry, poetry, and music—but wouldn't he have outstripped even his teachers (as Philo said)? And those hieroglyphics (later thought to bear occultic mysteries)— surely Moses comprehended them! But the timing was all wrong when Freud wrote (*Moses and Monotheism* [New York: Knopf, 1939]) that Moses' good character derived from his Egyptian, not his Hebrew, background.

According to one legend, Pharaoh once playfully set his crown on Moses' head, and Moses cast it to the floor! A test was proposed by a court magician, who held the Hebrew in suspicion: offer the boy a jewel and a hot coal. If he chooses the burning coal, he will prove his innocence. God guided his hand to the coal, which he put into his mouth, saving his life, yet impeding his speech (see Daniel J. Silver, *Images of Moses* [New York: Basic Books, 1982], pp. 207f; Elie Wiesel, *Messengers of God: Biblical Portraits and Legends* [New York: Summit Books, 1976], p. 184).

Retelling the Story

> The Egyptians developed a technique for discovering the newborn infants among the Hebrews. They would walk past the Hebrews' houses, taking an Egyptian infant with them. Then they would make the Egyptian baby cry in the hope that any newborn in the vicinity would hear and cry out, too.
> (*Exodus Rabbah* 1.20)

"Mother, tell me the story again." Mosheh ran to his mother's side as she shaped the loaves of bread she was making for their meal.

"You have heard it so many times that you can tell it yourself," she said as she smiled. "But I will tell you again, because you must never forget this story."

Mosheh sat on the ground and looked up at the woman. His eyes sparkled with excitement, even though he already carried the story in his heart.

"Many years ago, your ancestors were chosen by God to be a great nation. The Holy One blessed Abraham and Sarah, Isaac and Rebekah, Jacob and Rachel and Leah. God was their shepherd and shield and promised to increase their numbers and give the Lord's land to their offspring. Then there was a famine in the land, and the people would have died from hunger. But the Holy One had sent a servant, Joseph, to the land of Egypt to prepare a place for God's people to live until that time when they could return to the land God had given them.

"The people lived in Egypt and prospered in numbers. But Joseph died, and after a time a new ruler of Egypt rose who did not know Joseph. This ruler did not know the Hebrew people, and he treated them as slaves. This ruler was afraid of their numbers, so he decreed that every boy that was born to the Hebrews should be thrown into the Nile and drowned."

"And it was a very sad time for the Hebrew people," Mosheh added quietly.

"Yes, a very sad time. Many innocent children were killed, and the people were very sad," she continued.

"And then a baby boy was born to a Hebrew woman who could not allow him to be killed. She hid him for three months, but then he was too big to be hidden in her house. She got a papyrus basket and covered the bottom with tar so that it would float. And she put the baby in the basket and floated it in the river among the reeds. The baby's sister stayed near enough to see what would happen."

"That was Miriam," Mosheh called out.

"Yes," she said. "Do you remember what happens next in the story?"

Mosheh nodded, "One of Pharaoh's daughters came down to the river to bathe, and she saw the basket. Miriam was afraid, but she did not run away. I was crying when they picked up the basket, and when Pharaoh's daughter looked inside, she saw that I was just a little baby." Mosheh leaned down as if he were picking up a baby in his arms.

Mosheh's mother continued, "Then Miriam stood before Pharaoh's daughter and said to her, 'I can find you a Hebrew woman to nurse the child until he is grown.' And Pharaoh's daughter said, 'Yes, bring me that woman.' So Miriam ran to get me, and I came to the river. Pharaoh's daughter hired me to nurse you so that some day you can go to live in the house of Pharaoh.

"That was five harvests ago. Soon you must leave this house and go to live with the one who found you in the

> The rabbis tell that Pharaoh's daughter suffered from leprosy, which is the reason she had come to the river to bathe. But as soon as she touched the basket in which tiny Moses lay she was healed. So she took pity on the baby and took him into her father's household. (*Exodus Rabbah* 1.23)

> Miriam is insistent that she can find a Hebrew to nurse the child, Moses. The rabbis say that this was because young Moses refused the breasts of all the Egyptian wet nurses. Why? Will the mouth that will one day speak for God be filled with non-kosher milk? (*Exodus Rabbah* 1.25)

river." The woman reached over and stroked Mosheh's black hair. Mosheh leaned his head against her knee and looked up at her face.

"But I must never forget the story," he said solemnly.

"No, you must never forget this story," his mother answered. "You must remember your people and the God who saved your life. You will live as Moses among the Egyptian people, but you must carry this story close to your heart. You must respect and obey your Egyptian family, for the Holy One has used Pharaoh's daughter as an instrument of life. They will be your family, but we will be your people. Remember the story. Carry it close to your heart."

Mosheh jumped to his feet, "I remember the story. They will be my family, but you will be my people. Some day my people will return to the land God has given us. I carry the story close to my heart." He put his hand on his chest. Then he touched his mother's hair and ran to his friends. "Let's go to the river and gather some reeds," Mosheh called to them. They raced toward the river to see who would get there first.

Mosheh's mother took the bread out of the stone oven. She watched the children and said softly, "Remember the story, Mosheh."

EXODUS 3:1-15

Moses and the Burning Bush

While keeping sheep for his father-in-law, Moses hears the call of God from a burning bush.

The Story

While tending the sheep of his father-in-law Jethro, priest of Midian, Moses led the flock along the west side of the wilderness and came to Horeb, the mountain of God. There an angel of the LORD appeared to him as a fire blazing out from a bush. Although the bush was on fire, it was not being burnt up, and Moses said to himself, 'I must go across and see this remarkable sight. Why ever does the bush not burn away?' When the LORD saw that Moses had turned aside to look, he called to him out of the bush, 'Moses, Moses!' He answered, 'Here I am!' God said, 'Do not come near! Take off your sandals, for the place where you are standing is holy ground.' Then he said, 'I am the God of your father, the God of Abraham, Isaac, and Jacob.' Moses hid his face, for he was afraid to look at God.

The LORD said, 'I have witnessed the misery of my people in Egypt and have heard them crying out because of their oppressors. I know what they are suffering and have come down to rescue them from the power of the Egyptians and to bring them up out of that country into a fine, broad land, a land flowing with milk and honey, the territory of Canaanites, Hittites, Amorites, Perizzites, Hivites, and Jebusites. Now the Israelites' cry has reached me, and I have also seen how hard the Egyptians oppress them. Come, I shall send you to Pharaoh, and you are to bring my people Israel out of Egypt.' 'But who am I', Moses said to God, 'that I should approach Pharaoh and that I should bring the Israelites out of Egypt?' God answered, 'I am with you. This will be your proof that it is I who have sent you: when you have brought the people out of Egypt, you will all worship God here at this mountain.'

Moses said to God, 'If I come to the Israelites and tell them that the God of their forefathers has sent me to them, and they ask me his name, what am I to say to them?' God answered, 'I AM that I am. Tell them that I AM has sent you to them.' He continued, 'You are to tell the Israelites that it is the LORD, the God of their forefathers, the God of Abraham, Isaac, and Jacob, who has sent you to them. This is my name for ever; this is my title in every generation.'

Comments on the Story

The stage and the dramatic cast are set. Finally we hear the overture to the symphony "Exodus–Joshua," interweaving its varied melodies, teasing us to the edge of our seats.

The mountain, Moses, fire, the villain, the impossible dream, the destination, even the surly named "giants" before whom Israel would tremble as grasshoppers are all voiced. The dramatic dialogue on Horeb continues unabated through 4:17.

This summit meeting follows a pattern recognizable from the likes of Gideon, Jeremiah, Isaiah, and even Mary.

- God calls by name (doubled when God was getting really serious);
- The surprised addressee is basically at a loss for words;
- God proposes a plan (here evidently after shedding the angel disguise);
- The mortal objects (usually with good reasons);
- God reassures (often with a tangible sign).

In chapter 4 a trio of wonders are granted to build Moses' trust in the Lord and the people's trust in Moses. But what is the antecedent of "this" in 3:12? The bush? Returning to the mountain? Was Moses to infer from the bush that a mighty power was being unleashed that could bring about a return to this very mountain?

The storyteller must play on the dynamics of such admittedly lopsided negotiations. But the excuse motif is often overplayed. At one level, it was simply good form in the ancient world (and probably in our own) when summoned to a great task to dissemble, even to impress the superior with one's deep humility. On the other hand, Moses does go to greater lengths than usual. As Robert McAfee Brown put it, "Moses ducks and weaves in every possible way to avoid the body blow of the assignment" (*Unexpected News: Reading the Bible with Third World Eyes* [Philadelphia: Westminster Press, 1984], p. 38). It is not the fact of Moses' resistance, but the persistence of the resistance that tells the tale. All five objections are answered patiently but firmly.

Popular caricature impersonates Moses' answer: "W-w-w-why me?" But did Moses stutter? In the text Moses simply says, without stammering, "I have never been a man of ready speech; I am slow and hesitant" (NRSV: "I have never been eloquent" [4:10]; compare 6:12). He is inexperienced as a speaker. But who, after all, has any experience at uttering God's own words in the courts of the mighty Rameses? Understandably Moses is hesitant; his "heaviness" (*kbd*) of tongue will be matched by the pharaoh's "heaviness" (*kbd,* "hardness") of heart. His words to Pharaoh will be brief and simple, but will precipitate violent calamity. The Lord doesn't say, "I will heal your speech," but "I will be with you" (probably in the fashion of I Pet. 3:15 or Mark 13:11). The pattern demonstrates that God uses unpromising and even unwilling material.

Horeb (Sinai) is the very mountain to which Israel will be led by Moses once the people are free from Pharaoh's grasp. Although St. Catherine's monastery is nestled at the foot of *jebel musa,* allegedly on the very spot at which the bush burned, the location of the original mountain remains an enigma. A delightful Haggadah suggests that when God decided that the time had come for revelation, several tall mountains vied for the honor, all taller than Sinai. God chose Sinai because of its relative modesty. God is not restricted to breathtaking vistas! The mountain is modest enough. Shepherding is modest enough. One caveat, though: We may wish to expound on the lowly status of the shepherd, but Moses keeps pretty good company if we recall that Hammurabi, David, Amos, and Philip of Macedon all honed their leadership skills on sheep! Yet, it is the Lord's surprise invasion of the ordinary that makes this story. Moses is no seeker, no discoverer. He is, rather, discovered, sought out, unwittingly co-opted by the divine plan.

Reductionists explain away the bush as being of a bright red-flowering variety well-known in the region. But why Moses would be so awe-struck by a common bush is unexplainable. As Joseph Heller put it, Moses took off his shoes and "there went the rest of his life" (*God Knows* [New York: Dell, 1984], p. 51). The storyteller will let the bush blaze, trusting the hearer to be as mystified as Moses was. The image may be embroidered via the traditional. The synagogue (or later the church) saw itself in the bush, sorely oppressed but not destroyed. God often appears in a fiery guise. As poignant as the couplets of Elizabeth Barrett Browning may be,

> Earth's crammed with heaven,
> and every common bush afire with God;
> And only he who sees takes off his shoes,
> The rest sit round it and pluck blackberries.
> ("Aurora Leigh")

we must remember that this is no common bush.

Normal people went barefoot; the affluent wore sandals, as did those who worked in rugged terrain. Out of respect, sandals would be removed before entering any house (to leave dust and mud at the door). Egyptians by custom removed footwear in the presence of a superior. Israelite priests performed their cultic duties barefoot (even on frigid pavement!). Most of us have a mental picture of Muslims entering a mosque or of Japanese people removing their shoes out of hospitality. The gravity of Moses' gesture is weightier; to stand in the direct presence of God is not often survived (see Gen. 32:31; Exod. 33:20; Judg. 6:22-23.; 31:22). For Moses, private/family life is over; his public life, hardly a glamorous one, begins. "Who, me?" will be answered in the rest of the story. As God's identity is disclosed, Moses discovers his own.

God has been silent since Genesis 46:4. Through Exodus 1–2 we wondered whether the Lord would be silent forever. Finally in Exodus 3:4 the long silence is shattered, and the news is good. God has been watching, listening, caring, and is now mobilizing to change things. This God takes sides. This God never says, "Religion and politics don't mix." Mann put it shrewdly: "The exodus from Egypt will occur because of an exodus from heaven" (Mann, 82). Of course, Moses must (according to the lyrics of the old spiritual) "go down" to Egypt as well. The sarcastic question, "Who set you up over us?" (2:14) is answered. Who indeed!

God seems to suffer a baffling identity crisis in this repartee. A crucial twist in this drama revolves around God's name, a name little understood by intelligent theologians through the centuries. God begins with a familiar name, "God of your father." In the ancient Near East, many deities were so dubbed. What did Moses know of Abraham, Isaac, and Jacob? Perhaps the roll call rekindled in him a passion for his heritage. For the hearer, a rich texture of associations leaps to mind, most gloriously the old promises that, against all odds, must somehow be on the brink of fulfillment. How tidily Exodus 3:16 ("I have watched over [*pqd*] you") clinches Joseph's deathbed promise (Gen. 50:24, "God will not fail to come to your aid [*pqd*]").

Now a new name is pronounced. Or is it new? Moses doesn't know the name "Yahweh." Does he ask out of curiosity or out of a desire to get back in control of things? To avoid looking foolish or to legitimize his mission? Do the Israelites know the name "Yahweh"? If so, isn't it surprising that only one person (Moses' own mother) back in Egypt bears a compound name using the abbreviation of Yahweh? The Lord doesn't even say it right! "Yahweh" is a third-person verbal form. The Lord speaks in the first person: *ehyeh-asher-ehyeh,* which philologically means something like "I will be what I will be," "I am what I will be," or "I will be there."

What sort of answer is that? Metaphysical theologians have plumbed the name in search of being and essence. But this God isn't very metaphysical. Revelation never satisfies human curiosity, but is an invitation to trust, to move out into the future with this God who will be there. The storyline intimates that the Lord needs to introduce (or reintroduce) himself, for amnesia has infiltrated Goshen. In this reintroduction, God is not about to be pinned down to any single name, to any neat definition or expectation. The verbal form, however translated, is profoundly open-ended. God will, over time in the story, demonstrate God's character. Yahweh walks on stage in Exodus 3, but the complexities of the Lord's character become evident only as the play unfolds. Even in encore performances, God will continue to be master of the name.

Far too much is made of the "hush-hush" mystique of the name. Early on, before priests got persnickety and territorial, people knew the name, invoked the name, rejoiced in the name, spoke with God by name.

Retelling the Story

When Israel was in Egypt's land, let my people go;
Oppressed so hard they could not stand, let my people go.
Go down, Moses, way down in Egypt's land;
Tell old Pharaoh to let my people go!

Well, the Lord God Almighty looked down on the Hebrew people and saw that they were toiling and moaning under the hand of Pharaoh. The Lord God said, "I hear their crying, and I know they are hurting. I'm going to send someone to lead them out of Egypt."

And the Lord looked down and saw his servant, Moses, tending sheep on Mount Horeb. "That's who I'll send," said the Lord God. "I'll send Moses."

Once Moses had become a part of Pharaoh's household, the rabbis say, the king became quite fond of the young Hebrew, playing games with him and hugging him. Sometimes Moses would take Pharaoh's crown off the king's head and place it on his own. When the magicians of Egypt saw this they told Pharaoh that it was a very bad sign, that it meant Moses would one day rebel and attempt to rule Egypt. They recommended that the boy be killed. But Jethro was present and suggested a test for the child. He told them, "This Moses is just a baby and doesn't know what he is doing. Put before him a gold cup and a glowing coal from the fire, and he will as likely reach for the coal as the cup. In fact, if he reaches for the cup, you may do whatever you want with him, but if he reaches for the burning coal, you will know that he doesn't realize what he is doing and let him live."

So they arranged the test just as Jethro suggested. Just as Moses was about to reach for the glittering cup (as most babies would) the angel Gabriel took his hand and thrust it around the coal. Moses jerked his hand away and placed the burning fingers in his mouth. Not only did he live, but he also burned his tongue and was "slow of speech" from that time forward. (*Exodus Rabbah* 1.26)

When Moses was in Midian keeping sheep for his father-in-law, Jethro, one of his young sheep ran away. Moses left the rest of the flock to run after the lamb that fled. The faster Moses ran and the more he shouted, the faster the sheep ran ahead of him. Finally, the sheep found a quiet pool in a shady spot and stopped to drink. When Moses saw this, he said, "How foolish I was. You only wanted a drink, and by chasing after you I made the situation even worse. You must be tired by now." So he placed the lamb on his shoulders and carried it back to the flock. Seeing Moses' compassion for the sheep, God said, "This is the one I want to lead my people out of slavery in Egypt." (*Exodus Rabbah* 2.2)

Go down, Moses, way down in Egypt's land;
Tell old Pharaoh to let my people go!

Well, Moses was watching over his father-in-law, Jethro's, sheep. They'd been out wandering here and there for a long time, and just now they were over at Mount Horeb. It was a nice day, and Moses had sat down on a big rock to rest for a while. Out of the corner of his eye, he thought he saw a bush on fire. He jumped up to his feet and took a step closer to the bush. He could see that the bush was on fire, but it was not burning up.

"Oh, Lord," he said to himself. "Why in the world isn't that bush being burned by the fire?"

And then he heard a voice coming from the direction of the bush, saying, "Moses, Moses." And Moses jumped back about two feet and said, "Here I am." But he was thinking, *Oh, my Lord, who said that?*

And then the voice said, "Don't come any closer. Take your shoes off your feet because you are standing on holy ground." Moses rubbed his eyes and shook his head, and he took off his shoes. Then the voice said, "I am the God of your ancestors. I am the God of Abraham and Sarah, of Isaac and Rebecca, of Jacob and Rachel and Leah."

Well, about then, Moses started shaking and turning and covering up his face. He said to himself, "Oh, Lord, if this is really God, what am I going to do?"

Then the voice of God said, "I've been hearing the moans and cries of my people over in Egypt. They are suffering terribly under the hand of the Egyptians. I have decided to bring them out of Egypt and into a land flowing with milk and honey. And I want you to lead them out."

Go down, Moses, way down in Egypt's land;
Tell old Pharaoh to let my people go!

Well, Moses looked really startled and said to the voice, "Goodness! Who am I to tell Pharaoh to let the Israelites out of Egypt?"

And the Almighty said, "Don't worry. I'll be right there with you the whole time. And not only that, I'll give you a sign that it was really I who sent you. When you lead my people out of Egypt, you will come to this very mountain to worship me."

"Uh-huh," Moses said. "I have to wait until then for a sign? Oh, Lord." And then Moses took a deep breath and stood up really straight and asked the Lord God, "Well, say I go to the Israelites and tell them that I've been sent by the God of their ancestors. And say they ask me, 'So what's that God's name?' Then what do I say to them?"

When Moses attempted to excuse himself from speaking for God, saying, "Words do not come easily for me," God responded very simply, "Am I not the one who created mouths in the first place?" (*Exodus Rabbah* 3.15)

And the voice of God said, "I AM WHO I AM. You'll say to them that you are sent by I AM. You're sent by the God of Abraham and Sarah, the God of Isaac and Rebekah, the God of Jacob and Rachel and Leah. And tell them that I haven't forgotten them. I'm sending you to lead them out of their bondage and suffering. I don't want them to hurt. You will tell them that I AM has sent you to them."

So Moses and God talked for a long time. Moses knew that he'd been chosen to do just what the Lord God Almighty had said, but he wasn't too happy about it.

> When Israel was in Egypt's land, let my people go;
> Oppressed so hard they could not stand, let my people go.
> Go down, Moses, way down in Egypt's land;
> Tell old Pharaoh to let my people go!

Moses and Aaron Confront Pharaoh

*Moses and Aaron attempt to convince Pharaoh to allow the slaves to
leave by showing him a sign, which his court magicians match.*

The Story

After this, Moses and Aaron came to Pharaoh and told him, 'These are the words of the LORD the God of Israel: Let my people go so that they may keep a pilgrim-feast in my honour in the wilderness.' 'Who is the LORD,' said Pharaoh, 'that I should listen to him and let Israel go? I do not acknowledge the LORD: and I tell you I will not let Israel go.'

The LORD said to Moses and Aaron, 'If Pharaoh demands some portent from you, then you, Moses, must say to Aaron, "Take your staff and throw it down in front of Pharaoh," and it will turn into a serpent.' When Moses and Aaron came to Pharaoh, they did as the LORD had told them; Aaron threw down his staff in front of Pharaoh and his courtiers, and it turned into a serpent. At this, Pharaoh summoned the wise men and the sorcerers, and the Egyptian magicians did the same thing by their spells: every man threw his staff down, and each staff turned into a serpent. But Aaron's staff swallowed up theirs. Pharaoh, however, was obstinate; as the LORD had foretold, he would not listen to Moses and Aaron.

The LORD said to Moses, 'Pharaoh, has been obdurate: he has refused to let the people go.'

Comments on the Story

After the elusive encounter with the "bloody bridegroom" (4:19-26), Moses (with sidekick Aaron) comes to Pharaoh. In stunning panavision, Cecil B. DeMille cast a rugged Charlton Heston against a pompous Yul Brenner. The storyteller will do well to paint the dramatic tensions at least as sharply! While the Bible generally avoids simplistic characterizations in favor of the realistic (shades of virtue appear even in Pilate's court), this pharaoh is the epitome of villainy, and Moses is the epitome of goodness.

The plague cycle resists being diced into small pericopes. The ten plagues are a single unit, spanning seven chapters. But when the curtain goes up in 7:8, we are clearly in the middle of things already. The duel of words in 5:1-2 is simply assumed as the summary of each of the ever-escalating ten rounds; each round is not fully fleshed out. In a departure from much biblical narrative, with its proclivity for repetition, the plague cycle economizes on words. God tells Moses to say something; Moses' actual delivery of the speech is assumed.

Is the request to worship a subterfuge? We know that during Rameses' reign such requests from the indentured were granted. Ironically, to worship is their (and God's) intention (fulfilling 3:12); their goal is never just freedom from Pharaoh, but freedom for togetherness with their God. From now on they will "serve" the Lord, not Pharaoh.

There are at least four patterns in the plague cycle that the storyteller must hold in mind. (1) The Egyptian magicians (traditionally named Jannes and Jambres; see II Tim. 3:8 and the pseudepigraphal fragments in Charlesworth) keep pace, matching each "miracle," until folding in the fourth round. In 8:18-19, they not only admit failure and drop out of the contest, reappearing only for a pitiful moment in 9:11, but they even profess their faith! (2) Aaron gradually vanishes from the prominent role he plays in the opening plagues. Increasingly Moses seems to face Pharaoh alone. (3) In the first five plagues, Pharaoh "became obdurate"; it is only with the sixth that "the Lord made Pharaoh obdurate." (4) The first nine plagues are explainable in the light of what we know about climate and custom in ancient Egypt. Only with the tenth do we come to a plague horrifyingly out of the ordinary.

Journalist Ian Wilson is the most recent of many who would debunk the plague cycle, reducing the "miracles" to well-known, "natural" happenings (*Exodus: The True Story* [San Francisco: Harper & Row, 1985]). Relying on maverick theories, he dates the original story earlier than Rameses II, linking the terrors to a volcanic eruption of gargantuan proportions on the island of Thera, near Crete in the Mediterranean. With or without an eruption, each of the first nine plagues is not without precedent.

The serpent/rod was given to Moses by God back in Midian. An appropriate "trick" it was! Pharaohs adopted the stylized headdress featuring a snake, the symbol of power and the looming threat of death for any foe. A serpent staff was toted as a scepter of authority. Archaeologists have found many scarabs, beetle-shaped amulets, depicting magicians duplicating Moses' (actually Aaron's) feat. To this day, snake charmers can rigidify a cobra by touch, to tourists' delight. To the storyteller's delight, the theme of duping the Pharaoh is amplified as Aaron's rod gulps down the Egyptian rods (yes, plural!). Given the well-known custom, it is this swallowing that is the real opening shot of the festivities. Rabbinic speculation notwithstanding, Moses is no magician. What sort of fool would pick up a snake by its tail (see Exod. 4:4)?

The first plague proper, the Nile becoming "blood," is traceable to heavy rains in the African highlands, which commonly pollute with red mud a normally clear river. Many Egyptians claimed to be able to turn this "trick"— among them Prince Khamwas, the fourth son of our very own Rameses! Frogs, maggots, flies, pestilence, and hail are well-documented. In 1889, a two thousand square mile swarm of locusts swooped across the Red Sea. Darkness is attributable not just to a volcanic dust cloud but also to the annual sandstorms *(khamsin)* in that region. One scholar, Greta Hort, has schematized how these phenomena could lead one to another within a twelve month period, even explaining climatically why Goshen in particular would have been spared their severity (see Exod. 8:22; 9:4, 26; 10:23).

Naturalistic explanations and supernaturalistic apologetics miss the point of the story line. At stake is a claim to divinity. The pharaoh is said to be the sun god Re incarnate. In his opening conversation with Moses, Pharaoh has never even heard of this other God, Yahweh, whom he presumes is only a pretender. Dramatically and with a touch of humor, the story unmasks Pharaoh as the pretender; by story's end he has heard much more than he would care to about this Lord!

The impact of the miracles is twofold. First, Pharaoh cannot control this slave; with biting irony, Moses is "obedient" to Pharaoh only once (see 10:27-29). Pharaoh cannot control the weather; as a god, his function is to restrain precisely these sorts of calamities. His inability to keep the Nile pure and the air clear is certain proof that he is no god. As he is delegitimized, his policies, including the unjust enslavement of Israel, are proven to be a sham—good news, indeed, for history will produce more pharaohs to be debunked. Messing with God's people is risky business! Too bad Rameses hadn't heard about the unpleasant consequences a predecessor suffered (see Gen. 12:10-20). The ark narrative (I Sam. 4–6) repeats the pattern: The ark is seized, and plagues infest the wrongful owners, who are only too happy to see it returned.

Second, the story seems at pains to proclaim that God works these miracles to demonstrate who really is God, not just who isn't. The tenth plague is new to Egypt. Even to an Egyptian familiar with hail, flies, muddy water, and sandstorms, the collective impact of so many phenomena hitting the same region all at once would have been perceived as miraculous indeed; even the magicians discern the *'ezbah* (NRSV "finger" [slightly preferable to REB "hand"]), a popular image of God in the ancient Near East (see Luke 11:20). In John's Gospel we discern a pattern of miracles/signs, all "so they will know I am the Lord." The authors are not interested in creating a "thriller." Their concern is to exalt the figure of Yahweh, and perhaps the most important way of doing that is to show that Yahweh is in control of events in the narrative from the outset (Mann, 84).

"If at first you don't succeed, try, try again" is not the Lord's mode of operation. It isn't that it takes God ten times to wear Pharaoh down (in Pss. 78 and 105 there are only seven plagues!). The Lord is not mocked and cannot be denied, even by the likes of Rameses II, power of powers. The secret of real power is made manifest to all, as in the well-focused divine speech voiced by Moses in 9:14-16.

The motif of the hardened heart (see I Kings 22:23; Isa. 6:9-10; Rom. 9:17) has hardly yielded even to the best of theologians. Like so many narrative elements, the "hardening" just stands in the story without explanation. The storyteller cannot omit this agenda, though. Insistently Exodus features the notice that "Pharaoh became obdurate" (and then, "the Lord made him obdurate") as the climax to each round. Note well that Pharaoh does vacillate (8:8, 9:27), only to relent swiftly and stiffen his resolve. This tendency foreshadows his ultimate change of heart after Israel has actually fled (Exod. 14:5).

The outcome of the bout is nowhere more poignantly expressed than in the sonnet penned at Abu Simel by Percy Bysshe Shelley as he pondered a toppled, sixty-foot tall, one thousand-ton statue of Rameses II (dubbed "Ozymandias" in the Greek tradition):

> I met a traveller from an antique land
> Who said: Two vast and trunkless legs of stone
> Stand in the desert. Near them, on the sand,
> Half sunk, a shattered visage lies, whose frown,
> And wrinkled lip, and sneer of cold command,
> Tell that its sculptor well those passions read
> Which yet survive, stamped on these lifeless things,
> The hand that mocked them and the heart that fed:
> And on the pedestal these words appear:
> "My name is Ozymandias, king of kings:
> Look on my works, ye Mighty, and despair!"
> Nothing beside remains. Round the decay
> Of that colossal wreck, boundless and bare
> The lone and level sands stretch far away.

Retelling the Story

Ibrihim was a Hebrew servant in Pharaoh's court. He had served Pharaoh for many years, his father before him had served in Pharaoh's court. Ibrihim's great-great-grandfather had been a young man when Joseph died. When Ibrihim was a child, he listened to the stories of Joseph, of the famine and the Israelites' journey to Egypt to avoid starvation. He learned about the rise of the new ruler of Egypt, who did not know Joseph and who began to enslave the Israelite people, forcing them to build his mighty projects.

Pharaoh was one of four men named by the rabbis who claimed to be divine, and this brought destruction on them. The others were Hiram, Nebuchadnezzar, and Joash, who was king of Judah. (*Exodus Rabbah* 8.2)

Ibrihim was now an old man. He had seen the backs of his people bend and begin to break under the hand of Pharaoh. He saw young Moses raised in

Pharaoh's house, and he saw Moses flee for his life. Recently Moses had returned with his brother, Aaron, and they stood before Pharaoh with a message from the God of Israel that the Hebrew people must be freed.

At first, Pharaoh responded by increasing the suffering of the Israelites. He commanded that the laborers gather their straw for the manufacture of bricks. And the daily quota must be matched, or the laborers would be beaten.

Now Moses and Aaron have appeared before Pharaoh a second time. The servants in Pharaoh's house gather around Ibrihim to hear the story. Izhar is angry, "I wish that Moses had stayed away. Things have never been this bad before. My father-in-law still aches from the beatings of the Egyptians when he refused to gather stubble for straw."

"But wait, my young friend," spoke Ibrihim gently. "Let me tell you of the events of today." The young man looked sharply at Ibrihim, but nodded his head and sat back. Ibrihim looked at the faces around him and began to talk. "It was much like the first time they came before Pharaoh. Moses and Aaron looked old and small before Pharaoh, their plain robes drab against all of the finery of the court.

"They began as before, Aaron speaking the words Moses received from the Lord, 'Let my people go from the land of Egypt.' Pharaoh laughed as if he could not believe their stupidity to stand before him again. Then he said to them, 'If this God of yours is so great, let me see a sign of power. Perform a wonder.' "

Why did God choose a snake as a sign to Pharaoh? The rabbis say that it was because Egypt and its pharaoh were themselves serpentine. They were twisted like snakes, crooked like snakes, and they hissed and killed like snakes. (*Exodus Rabbah* 9.3)

Ibrihim smiled. "Never have I seen such a thing. Aaron and Moses looked at each other and nodded. Their eyes shone like fire. Moses motioned to Aaron to throw down his staff. His staff hit the floor with a loud crack, and as soon as it hit, the staff turned into a snake. Oh, it was a monster of a snake. Pharaoh's court officers stepped back out of the way, but Moses and Aaron stood just where they were.

"Pharaoh looked surprised, and then annoyed. People were rushing around trying to stay out of the snake's path, and Pharaoh shouted for me to summon the magicians to come immediately. I went quickly to the sorcerers and wise ones and relayed Pharaoh's request that they appear before him. When we returned to the court, everything was as we had left it—Moses and Aaron standing in front of Pharaoh, Pharaoh watching angrily as the snake slithered around the uneasy officials in the chamber." Ibrihim paused, took a drink, and sighed, "Oh, what a wonder. Pharaoh and his magicians gathered and talked. I could not hear what was being said, but there was much arm waving and arguing among the sorcerers. Then they separated, and one by one the magicians threw down their staffs. And their staffs turned into snakes! It was not a place for the faint of heart. There were snakes all over the chamber, and I could feel the fear and the wonder of it all. I wondered whether we all would live or be destroyed by such powers. Then I saw that the snake that had been Aaron's staff began to swallow the other snakes. It swallowed all of the snakes that had been the staffs of the magicians. And when all of the other snakes were gone, it turned back into Aaron's staff. It looked just as it had before.

> Pharaoh was so arrogant when Aaron's rod turned into a snake that he called more than his magicians to do the same trick. Oh no! Pharaoh called children from school to do the old rod-into-a-snake trick. Then he called his wife in to repeat that bit of magic as well. (*Exodus Rabbah* 9.6)

"Pharaoh roared in anger and stormed out of the chamber. His sorcerers and advisers followed him out. Soon, the only ones left were Moses, Aaron, and I." Ibrihim looked up at the sky and continued, "I picked up Aaron's staff and handed it to him. He said to me, 'Thank you, old man. May the Holy One bless you and your household.' Moses looked at me and smiled. I think he remembered me from his youth. And then we left the chamber.

"He said that the God of the Hebrews sent him to lead us out of Egypt. He said that we are to go to worship God in the wilderness." The other servants nodded and looked at each other. And one by one they departed to their own quarters.

The Angle Passes Over

The Israelites learn how to protect their households from the angel of death and how to remember this event in future years.

The Story

The LORD said to Moses and Aaron in Egypt: 'This month is to be for you the first of the months; you are to make it the first month of the year. Say to the whole community of Israel: On the tenth day of this month let each man procure a lamb or kid for his family, one for each household, but if a household is too small for one lamb or kid, then, taking into account the number of persons, the man and his nearest neighbour may take one between them. They are to share the cost according to the amount each person eats. Your animal, taken either from the sheep or the goats, must be without blemish, a yearling male. Have it in safe keeping until the fourteenth day of this month, and then all the assembled community of Israel must slaughter the victims between dusk and dark. They must take some of the blood and smear it on the two doorposts and on the lintel of the houses in which they eat the victims. On that night they must eat the flesh roasted on the fire; they must eat it with unleavened bread and bitter herbs. You are not to eat any of it raw or even boiled in water, but roasted: head, shins, and entrails. You are not to leave any of it till morning; anything left over until morning must be destroyed by fire.

'This is the way in which you are to eat it: have your belt fastened, sandals on your feet, and your staff in your hand, and you must eat in urgent haste. It is the LORD'S Passover. On that night I shall pass through the land of Egypt and kill every firstborn of man and beast. Thus I shall execute judgement, I the LORD, against all the gods of Egypt. As for you, the blood will be a sign on the houses in which you are: when I see the blood I shall pass over you; when I strike Egypt, the mortal blow will not touch you.

'You are to keep this day as a day of remembrance, and make it a pilgrimfeast, a festival of the LORD; generation after generation you are to observe it as a statute for all time.'

Comments on the Story

Each spring, Jewish families gather for a three thousand-year-old ceremony, seven times older than America's Thanksgiving. The institution of the Passover, prescribed by a priestly writer more than seven hundred years after the fact, is rooted in the story of the tenth round of the plague cycle. The story, so constitutive of Israel's identity, comes to us in a format designed not for history's sake, but for the sake of those who dutifully observe the celebratory meal each year.

Preeminently the family festival, Passover, surprisingly enough, was ignored for a time until Josiah centralized its revival in Jerusalem (II Kings 23). By New Testament times, Passover was well-attended and very much big business; Josephus does not exaggerate too much when he claims that 255,600 lambs were slaughtered in a single afternoon. But our text opens a window into the most joyful of family settings, long before (and long after) thousands teemed the lanes of Jerusalem.

No better point of view need be sought than in that magical moment when the youngest son rises at table to ask, "Why is this night different from all other nights?" The very foods on the table are object lessons: the bitter herbs (*merorim*) give a taste of Israel's suffering. The *harosset* mixture of apples, cinnamon, and nuts is a curiously happy mnemonic of the mortar. The unleavened bread (*matzot*) are given a storied significance (see below). And, of course, we eat a bit of lamb. Parents fulfill Exodus 13:8 when they share with their children the most momentous and personal of all stories. How fraught with power is our glimpse through the window of Passover, practiced over the millennia, around the globe, at the risk of life itself in sixteenth-century Spain and in the Warsaw ghetto in 1940, spilling over into the Christian Eucharist, Jesus' own Passover night, our own Maundy Thursday. Perennially the *Seder* engages each generation's participation. Truly *we* were slaves, God brought *us* forth, otherwise *we* would still be slaves in Egypt. The storyteller must see the family, taste the food, and sing the songs with sandals and belt fastened on ready, staff in hand, before grasping what this night is all about. Narrative becomes ritual. Ritual reenacts narrative. Identities are forged.

Explainable as the first nine plagues are, the tenth delivered the final blow to Pharaoh. The story, not surprisingly overlaid with the vagaries of a complex oral and literary history, runs from 11:1 through 13:16. In chapter 11 the slaughter of the firstborn is announced with the stunning contrast between the cry of the Egyptians and the silence of the Israelites, who have been crying for many years. But no more tears for Israel! With a wry twist of humor, Moses seals the wonder of this night by silencing the otherwise persistent barking of dogs!

Scholars like to separate the spring festival of husbandry from the historic episode of the passover, but the story insists we do no such thing. Prior to the haunting last night in Egypt, both nomads and herders customarily offered up a lamb in gratitude to the guarantor of life and animal fertility. Such a practice is documented in many cultures. Special sanctity attaches to the firstborn in primitive and modern cultures. Can you not see a clan of nomads, after laboring over the lambing at the vernal equinox, gathered under the lingering light of the full moon, feasting on a lamb of celebration and gratitude to the God upon whom they sensed the most profound dependence?

The feast of unleavened bread (*matzoth*) was certainly separate from passover prior to the Exodus traditions. Agricultural, rather than pastoral, *mazoth* marked the beginning of the spring barley harvest. But "one springtime there had been a startling intervention of God" (Roland de Vaux, *Ancient Israel*, vol. 2 [New York: McGraw-Hill, 1961], p. 493). Henceforth every aspect of life and worship fell under the aegis of this glorious deliverance. The Israel that expresses gratitude to God for the gifts of farm and fold is always the Israel delivered from bondage. Springtime could never be the same.

Leaven is banned in all rituals. The fermentation has a certain negative connotation (see Matt. 16:6). Its omission is picturesquely linked to the haste with which Israel had to flee (Exod. 12:34-39; Deut. 16:3; compare Lot's hasty baking in Gen. 19:3, the witch of Endor's in I Sam. 28:24). Leaven takes too long to knead in and let rise. But the lamb fits the story even better. Blood on the doorposts was a signal to the angel of death to "pass over" (*psh*) an Israelite house. The root *psh* seems to mean "limp" (II Sam 4:4; I Kings 18:21). Does the Lord break step and limp around blood-daubed houses? Is *psh* derived from the Akkadian "to appease" or from an Egyptian root meaning "to strike"? Once at Sinai, Israel learned more about the nature of blood (the norm for sacrifice in most ancient cultures) and its healing significance; somehow hidden in the blood of all those sacrifices is the very life of God, poured out to reconcile, indicative of the costliness of grace. The bloody doorposts are indeed "portals of freedom" (Sarna, 92).

Remarkably enough, the directions for future commemoration of the passover are given even before the first passover occurred! There is always an in-betweenness to Passover. At the first nocturnal meal, Israel is already redeemed—but not yet! It is a "night of watching" (12:42), Israel watching for deliverance, the Lord watching over Israel. The storyteller must somehow capture this sense of incompleteness, the already/not-yetness, a confident urgency, the assured fear of excitement.

Birthing a new calendar is a titanic act of independence. Israel defiantly junks Egypt's solar calendar so that a new "lunisolar" system will be followed. The Canaanites used a lunar calendar with an autumn (harvest) new year. Israel's year opens with the celebration, not of the cycles of nature, but of historical redemption.

Israel's good news is a nightmare for Egypt. In the opening pages of Exodus, Pharaoh dared to slay and imprison the Lord's "firstborn" (1:16; 4:22). With ominous irony, the Lord keeps his word (4:23), "making the punishment fit the crime. The pharaoh sought to destroy God's people, His firstborn, as it were, so the firstborn of Egypt, in whose name he speaks and acts, will suffer the fate that had been planned for Israel" (Sarna, 94). A vignette from another century is fascinating. After the collapse of the Judean state, a band of Jews fled to Egypt, built a temple in Elephantine, and celebrated Passover there. Who could blame the Egyptian priests who had that temple demolished in 411 B.C.E.? Harsh polemic against Moses emerged in Egypt; the "historian" Manetho libeled Moses as a satanic priest who tried to take over Egypt militarily (Silver, *Images of Moses*, pp. 48-60).

Labor supply and the firstborn were not all Egypt lost. Strangely, our story thrice mentions how Egyptian citizens happily gave the impoverished Israelites jewelry and clothing (3:21; 11:2; 12:35). Why were they so willing? Overdue wage compensation (Philo)? Neighborliness (Josephus)? Admiration of Moses and perhaps a subversive sentiment against the tyrant pharaoh? The text is clear: The Israelites don't steal; they "ask." Genesis 15:14 is fulfilled—they leave as victors, with dignity and resources. In later Hebrew ethics, slaves were not to be manumitted empty-handed (Deut. 15:12-13). Of course, Augustine argued that the jewelry would be put to better use by Israel. Apparently, the jewelry would be needed (and used) for the tabernacle appointments, although the potential for fashioning the golden calf (Exod. 32) looms in the background as well.

Retelling the Story

Rachel and Mishael were born in Egypt, as were their parents and generations before them. Mishael's ancestors had come to Egypt to escape starvation in the land where they had lived as shepherds. Rachel did not know where her ancestors had come from, only that they came to Egypt as a place of promise.

Rachel and Mishael are husband and wife. They share a household with Mishael's younger brother and wife, who are childless. Rachel and Mishael have three sons and two daughters.

Mishael works with Pharaoh's herds of sheep. He is grateful that he is able to escape the dust of the city when he takes the sheep out into the grazing land of the countryside. He is also grateful that he is a shepherd rather than a laborer on the building projects of Pharaoh.

Rachel often shares with Mishael the stories she hears in the marketplace as she trades the fabric she has woven from the wool of the sheep. People are afraid of what is happening in Egypt. It is dangerous to be an Israelite. Not long ago, the Egyptians killed every boy child they found. Pharaoh is becoming more cruel to the Hebrew people with every decree. Find your own straw for the bricks—only continue the same daily quota. Israelite laborers are being beaten to death by their overseers.

Then the bizarre occurrences: the waters of the Nile turning to blood, the frogs and insects, the diseases and boils, the thunder and hail, the darkness that fell on the Egyptians for three days. Each of these plagues affected only the Egyptians, but Rachel and Mishael and their household feared greatly. Never had they known of such disasters.

The religious leaders said that the God of the Israelites was punishing the Egyptians because they were mistreating the Hebrew people. They said that the Holy One has sent a deliverer named Moses to lead them out of Egypt. This Moses has performed many wonders and signs before Pharaoh. But Pharaoh does not know the Hebrew God and will not obey God's commands. The religious leaders say to continue doing the work of Pharaoh, but trust in God.

Rachel believes that it is difficult to trust such a God who has watched the people suffering for so many years and has done nothing.

One evening as Mishael is returning home from the grazing lands, he hears people talking of a ritual that every Israelite must perform. He can see fear and excitement in people's faces. Their eyes turn often toward heaven as if they are searching for a sign. Mishael hurries home to his household where his brother is waiting for him to return.

"Mishael, we must select a lamb for the Passover ritual. It is to be a yearling lamb, unblemished. The elders have specified certain things we are to do as a part of the ritual. It must be done tonight. They say it is very important."

Rachel, Mishael, and the others of the household prepared for the ritual. No one spoke much, but their thoughts were busy as they wondered what would happened next. Would the next sunrise bring their deliverance or another decree from the pharaoh?

The lamb was sacrificed, and its blood was smeared on the doorposts and lintel of their house. The meat was roasted for the meal. At the meal they were dressed for a journey—with their shoes on and their staffs in their hands. They ate roast lamb and bread that was unleavened, because they did not have time to prepare leavened bread. They ate bitter herbs to remind them of the bitterness of their bondage. And they offered prayers of thanksgiving and hope for their deliverance.

When the angel of death came to the Egyptian homes, both male and female children died. But one in Pharaoh's household was spared, Bithiah. She was Pharaoh's daughter and Moses' foster mother according to the rabbis. Moses spoke in her favor, and she was spared. (*Exodus Rabbah* 18.3)

Every Hebrew household participated in this ritual. And every household marked with blood was passed over when the angel of death visited the land and struck dead all the firstborn—both humans and animals.

When the sun rose the next morning, people ran through the streets crying out the news that the Hebrew slaves were to leave the land of Egypt. Rachel and Mishael could hear the sounds of weeping and mourning coming from the homes of the Egyptians. Mishael prayed to God as he gathered things to take with them.

They packed as much as they could carry. Rachel gathered some bits of dried meat and fruit, wrapped her dough in her kneading bowl, and put the bundle on her shoulder.

They hurried to be with the others on the important day when they were leaving their bondage. The elders told everyone to hurry before the pharaoh changed his mind.

As they walked out to the desert, Rachel and Mishael remembered the meal they had eaten the night before, when they ate roast lamb, bitter herbs, and unleavened bread, and the angel of death passed over their house and brought God's gift of freedom. And they were very grateful.

Why was God so harsh with the Egyptians? The rabbis tell this story: God was like a king whose son traveled to a far country and the people liked him so well there that he was named king. The father was so pleased that he named that far country after his son. Some time passed, and the people of that distant realm became dissatisfied with their king, driving him from the throne and making him a slave. When his father heard this he declared war on the country in order to save the life of his son. (*Exodus Rabbah* 18.6)

Crossing the Sea

The Israelites make their way to freedom through the Sea of Reeds while the Egyptians pursuing them drown.

The Story

When it was reported to the Egyptian king that the Israelites had gone, he and his courtiers had a change of heart and said, 'What is this we have done? We have let our Israelite slaves go free!' Pharaoh had his chariot yoked, and took his troops with him, six hundred picked chariots and all the other chariots of Egypt, with a commander in each. Then, made obstinate by the LORD, Pharaoh king of Egypt pursued the Israelites as they marched defiantly away. The Egyptians, all Pharaoh's chariots and horses, cavalry and infantry, went in pursuit, and overtook them encamped beside the sea by Pi-hahiroth to the east of Baal-sephon.

Pharaoh was almost upon them when the Israelites looked up and saw the Egyptians close behind, and in terror they clamoured to the LORD for help. They said to Moses, 'Were there no graves in Egypt, that you have brought us here to perish in the wilderness? See what you have done to us by bringing us out of Egypt! Is this not just what we meant when we said in Egypt, "Leave us alone; let us be slaves to the Egyptians"? Better for us to serve as slaves to the Egyptians than to perish in the wilderness.' But Moses answered, 'Have no fear; stand firm and see the deliverance that the LORD will bring you this day; for as sure as you see the Egyptians now, you will never see them again. The LORD will fight for you; so say no more.'

The LORD said to Moses, 'What is the meaning of this clamour? Tell the Israelites to strike camp, and you are to raise high your staff and hold your hand out over the sea to divide it asunder, so that the Israelites can pass through the sea on dry ground. For my part I shall make the Egyptians obstinate and they will come after you; thus I shall win glory for myself at the expense of Pharaoh and his army, chariots and cavalry all together. The Egyptians will know that I am the LORD when I win glory for myself at the expense of their Pharaoh, his chariots and horsemen.'

The angel of God, who had travelled in front of the Israelites, now moved away to the rear. The pillar of cloud moved from the front and took up its position behind them, thus coming between the Egyptians and the Israelites. The cloud brought on darkness and early nightfall, so that contact was lost throughout the night.

Then Moses held out his hand over the sea, and the LORD drove the sea away with a strong east wind all night

54

long, and turned the seabed into dry land. The waters were divided asunder, and the Israelites went through the sea on the dry ground, while the waters formed a wall to right and left of them. The Egyptians, all Pharaoh's horse, his chariots and cavalry, followed in pursuit into the sea. In the morning watch the LORD looked down on the Egyptian army through the pillar of fire and cloud, and he threw them into a panic. He clogged their chariot wheels and made them drag along heavily, so that the Egyptians said, 'It is the LORD fighting for Israel against Egypt; let us flee.'

Then the LORD said to Moses, 'Hold your hand out over the sea, so that the water may flow back on the Egyptians, their chariots and horsemen.' Moses held his hand out over the sea, and at daybreak the water returned to its usual place and the Egyptians fled before its advance, but the LORD swept them into the sea. As the water came back it covered all Pharaoh's army, the chariots and calvalry, which had pressed the pursuit into the sea. Not one survived. Meanwhile the Israelites had passed along the dry ground through the sea, with the water forming a wall for them to right and to left. That day the LORD saved Israel from the power of Egypt. When the Israelites saw the Egyptians lying dead on the seashore, and saw the great power which the LORD had put forth against Egypt, the people were in awe of the LORD and put their faith in him and in Moses his servant.

Comments on the Story

Although the Hebrew text was reworked and touched up over centuries of transmission, the drama set in motion by the bleak note in 1:8 finally reaches its climax. Pharaoh's expulsion order in 12:31 is zealously heeded. Even in the rush, Moses remembers to pack the bones of Joseph! With poignant irony the story has come full circle: vivid memories of dreams, treachery, reconciliation among brothers, the priceless scenario of Joseph tearfully jumping out of his chariot to welcome Jacob to the Egyptian bread basket (Gen. 46:28), and Joseph's tender interment of his father back in Canaan, accompanied by a "great company" of Pharaoh's chariots in lamentation (Gen. 50).

Conjuring a mental image of two million persons stampeding in flight has proven difficult over the centuries. The estimation, "about 600,000 men" (12:37), was deemed so crucial that it is mentioned several times; two census readings in the wilderness yielded 603,550 and 601,730 men respectively. Even if the count of "seventy" in Joseph's entourage is an underestimate, these Hebrews have indeed been astonishingly fruitful (Exod. 1:7-19); Puah and Shiphrah must have had many helpers!

Was the story stretched over the years? Theoretically it is conceivable for a small band to multiply to two million over four centuries; precedent (however exceptional) exists for such explosive growth. But how could the tiny Goshen region sustain such a throng? Just imagine the small Sinai peninsula trampled by so many! If the population of ancient Egypt was in fact five million or so (as scholars surmise), the exit of two million would be devastating. In our day we observe countries where a minority rules over the majority, who lack the means to throw off their oppressors. Imagine the logistics of mobilizing two million in a single day! Some clever person calculated that even in precise formation it would take two hours for a column of one thousand abreast and two thousand deep to get across a half-mile-wide stretch in a clear area. It is puzzling that Egyptian annals are silent about the great escape (perhaps analogously, Roman records know nothing of the birth of Jesus).

But we now know that the Hebrew word translated "thousand" ('elef) originally denoted an extended family unit of perhaps nine to fourteen persons; later, an 'elef was a military contingent of comparable size. So perhaps only eight thousand or so Israelite men made the trek. But the census figures aren't rounded off into thousands ('elefs). The numbers 603,550 and 601,730 are similar to the number of men who lived in the kingdom of Israel in the era of David and Solomon. Did the writer of the old oral story import his own population data into the past in a bold claim of solidarity with and participation in the story? Were they not mystically present, running to their freedom in the ancient story? From the beginning the story took on these massive dimensions. The exodus was no tiny band of fugitives sneaking out unnoticed, but indeed a nation defiantly striding out, flaunting their freedom before a handcuffed pharaoh.

It was a "mixed multitude" (12:38). The movement of liberation, the gift of the covenant, is inclusive. The disgruntled, the marginalized, the hopeless will be jumping on Israel's bandwagon for the balance of this story.

The exact route of Israel's journey (Succoth/Etham/Pihahiroth/Migdol/Baal-zephon) has eluded cartographers. Clearly the Lord does not overdo the miraculous by steering Israel in a beeline for the milk and honey. Well-armed Egyptian outposts (six of which have been excavated) were entrenched along the straight road to Canaan (the ancient thoroughfare was dubbed "the way of the land of the Philistines," the Via Maris of Roman times). We are made privy to God's own rumination on the matter; God makes a remarkable concession to the weakness of the people (13:17). Taking the garrisoned road, the entire Egyptian army could get to Canaan in just over a week. But the itinerary reveals that God has something else in store for these refugees. Their first destination is not Canaan but Mt. Sinai. The throng is hardly in random flight. They follow the cloud by day, the pillar of fire by night. But is the cloud at the vanguard or in the rear?

The miracle is set at the *yam suf*, the "sea of reeds." Pinpointing this *suf* sea is uncertain business. Between the eastern Nile Delta and the Sinai peninsula are several bodies of shallow water that qualify (with *suf*, reeds, peeking above the surface). Since the Vulgate's mysterious rendering, *mare rubrum*, we have imagined the "Red" Sea (which isn't red and has no *suf* at all). At times, the

"Red" Sea is called *yam suf* (I Kings 9:26; Jer. 49:21), so perhaps the whole watery network at Egypt's eastern boundary is designated *yam suf*. Cecil B. DeMille orchestrated towering walls of water, which is not really in keeping with what may have been a more modest wonder. Some critics find in the *J* source a natural cause: a gusting east wind dries the sea bed, a phenomenon that has precedent in the region. It is the *P* source that heightens the "supernatural." And yet, reductionists (including even Josephus, who fingered the parallel in the annals of Alexander the Great) who point to a rather ordinary drying up of a shallow marshy zone cannot explain how Israel would be so gullibly awestruck over such a minor happenstance. With Egyptian forts guarding the passable frontier, the only hope of flight was through a natural (and hence undefended) barrier.

God's blueprint for the escape is no nail-biting cliffhanger. The Lord is said to have chosen the spot in which Israel was bottled up, and even to have urged Pharaoh's change of heart, all in order to make a splashy statement to top off the battle of divinities. The moral problem cannot be erased from the story. Children are chagrined over the deluged Egyptians; the famous rabbinic comment, that the angels did not celebrate after the miracle, underlines the problem (Ginzberg, 6:12). The Bible is less interested in fulfilling some perceived moral code than in exalting the figure of Yahweh. Yahweh's glorification is the unmistakable theme of this story. Happily, while the rescue is retold and dramatized myriad times, there is almost no gloating over the dismal fate of the chariot force. Attention is riveted on God's trustworthiness.

Trust is at issue. Will the people trust Yahweh and his envoy Moses? How swiftly their defiance (14:8) melts away (14:10ff)! No Patrick Henry ("Give me liberty or give me death") appears in this crowd! As has been and will be their habit, they transfer their panic into hostility to Moses. Pharaoh, after all, was a formidable foe; his chariots were the scourge of that corner of the globe. What Israel does not believe is that there will be a battle at all. Faith in this story demands a new perspective. Rather than running as prey from predator, the people are to deploy Israel's historical and laughable battle tactics: "mere words" (Isa. 36) and "waiting" (Isa. 30). God saves not because of good deeds, and not even because of Israel's great faith (Deut. 7:7). How appropriately the church founders saw in this miracle a foreshadowing of baptism! The gospel will henceforth be: When there is no hope, there is hope. And there is dignity! Wiesel vividly captures the moment:

> One could see people running, running breathlessly, without a glance backward; they were running toward the sea. And there they came to an abrupt halt: this was the end; death was there, waiting. The leaders of the group, urged on by Moses, pushed forward: Don't be afraid, go, into the water, into the water! Yet, according to one commentator, Moses suddenly ordered everyone to a halt: Wait a moment.

Think, take a moment to reassess what it is you are doing. Enter the sea not as frightened fugitives but as free men! (*Messengers of God,* p. 193)

It is the pharaoh who has no dignity. In fact, as is the habit of oppressors, he loses his very identity when there is no one to oppress.

The image of the divided sea is indelibly stamped on many cultures. Benjamin Franklin argued that the Seal of the United States should depict Moses, rod uplifted, parting the waters. Diverse appeals have been made to this same moment by Zionists, Anabaptists, South Africans, and even Marxists.

Retelling the Story

Talk Show Host: Welcome back, listeners. And thank you to our sponsor, Promised Land Supply, your outlet for milk, honey, and all the sweet things in life. Our special guest today is Moses, the one who led the Israelites out of Egypt. Welcome to our show.

Moses: Well, it is an honor to be here. Of course, I only did what the Lord told me to do.

The rabbis had many things to say about Moses' crying to God for help. Some suggested that he prayed so long that God became impatient, since God knew what the Israelites needed before they asked. Others say that it was like the friend asking at great length a favor from a powerful ruler. The ruler replied, "Why do you go on and on? Just ask, and your request will be granted." (*Exodus Rabbah* 21.1-2)

Host: You are much too modest, Moses. You are a terrific leader. Before we begin with our primary topic, let me ask you one question: The Israelites have been wandering, under your leadership, for several years now. Do you have any predictions about when we will reach the Promised Land?

Moses: Only the Lord knows that. I would rather not speculate or try to answer that question. I think our task is to trust in the Lord and do what is commanded by the Lord.

Host: Of course. Well, let's get on to the primary focus for today. We are broadcasting live on Wilderness Radio, your station for oral history. We are here talking with Moses about the miraculous crossing of the Red Sea. As you remember, in our last broadcast we heard about the final plague on Egypt and the first Passover. The Israelites had left their homes and were fleeing Egypt. But then the Egyptians began to pursue you. What went wrong, Moses? Why the sudden pursuit of the people?

Moses: Nothing went wrong. The Lord hardened Pharaoh's heart yet one more time in order to show that God is the Lord. I remembered that it was a frightening time when we realized that the Egyptians were pursuing us in their chariots. We could see the dust from their chariots and horses even from far way.

Host: As I recall, you received quite a bit of heat from the people at that point. Did you have doubts?

Moses: During all my years of working for the Lord, I never knew exactly what was coming next. But each time we have faced an obstacle, somewhere inside I knew that the Lord was still in charge. I did feel very sad about the fear of the people. Many of them believed that they were doomed to die there in the wilderness at the hands of the Egyptians.

Host: But you did not. Something very exciting happened. Moses, can you tell our listeners about how you escaped the Egyptian army?

Moses: The Lord, the God of Israel, had promised to bring the people out of the land of Egypt. You've heard us talk about the plagues and the way the Lord hardened Pharaoh's heart in order to show the greatness of the Lord. Some people have said that it was the Lord's plan all along to kill many of the Egyptian leaders. This is not the case. The Lord did not revel in the loss of lives among the Egyptians. In fact, the angels in heaven were sad that day. But the Lord hardened Pharaoh's heart to teach stubborn people that the Lord is God. It was a very somber day, though we were all relieved to have escaped the death that Pharaoh had planned.

Host: Tell us, please, what happened.

Moses: We were camped between the Red Sea and Migdol. That was when we became aware of the Egyptian army coming after us. We were protected for a while by the pillars of cloud and fire, which moved to a position behind us and kept the Egyptians from us. But then it was time for us to move on. But there was no place to move except into the sea.

The Lord told me to tell the people to move forward and to hold out my staff over the sea. I never know what to expect when I get instructions like that. I did just that, and the seas began to part like a seam opening. I have never seen anything like it. The sea bed was dry and firm, even though it had just been covered with water. The people yelled a cry of relief and gratitude, and they began to move across.

The requests of the rich and powerful are listened to in the world while those of the poor are ignored. But it is not so with God, say the rabbis. God hears the prayers of rich and poor, male and female, slave and free alike. How do we know this? Because Moses' prayer is described in the same words as the prayers of the afflicted. (*Exodus Rabbah* 21.4)

Host: Do you have an explanation for that phenomenon?

Moses: The Lord God made it happen. That is the only explanation that I've been able to come up with.

When Moses first attempted to divide the waters of the sea they refused to part. The sea said to Moses, "You mean I'm supposed to divide in two just because you want me to? I am more important than you are. After all, I was created on the third day of creation, and you didn't come along until the sixth." So Moses complained to God about the sea's refusal. Then God placed a divine hand on Moses' hand and the sea parted. (*Exodus Rabbah* 21.6)

Let me continue with the story. The chariots were coming up behind us and started following us into the sea bed. But for some reason, their wheels sank into the ground that we had just crossed. It had turned to mud again. And before they could escape, the walls of water began closing and covering them. Many lives were lost. We expressed our sorrow at their losses. Though we were in bondage to them, the Egyptians saved our people when famine drove us into their land. At that time, we were strangers and they welcomed us.

The water did not roll over onto our people. The sea bed stayed dry and passable until all the Israelites were across.

Host: What a victory for the great God! Well, we're about out of time for this week. In our next program, we'll talk with Moses about the early days in the wilderness and the manna from heaven. Thank you, Moses. And good-bye, listeners.

The Freedom Song

The Israelites celebrate their gift of freedom with singing and dancing.

The Story

Then Moses and the Israelites sang this song to the LORD:
'I shall sing to the LORD, for he has risen up in triumph;
horse and rider he has hurled into the sea.
The LORD is my refuge and my defence;
he has shown himself my deliverer.
He is my God, and I shall glorify him;
my father's God, and I shall exalt him.
The LORD is a warrior; the LORD is his name.
Pharaoh's chariots and his army he has cast into the sea;
the flower of his officers
are engulfed in the Red Sea.
The watery abyss has covered them;
they sank to the depths like a stone.
Your right hand, LORD, is majestic in strength;
your right hand, LORD, shattered the enemy.
In the fullness of your triumph
you overthrew those who opposed you:
you let loose your fury;
it consumed them like stubble.
At the blast of your anger the sea piled up;
the water stood up like a bank;

out at sea the great deep congealed.

'The enemy boasted, "I shall pursue, I shall overtake;
I shall divide the spoil,
I shall glut my appetite on them;
I shall draw my sword,
I shall rid myself of them."
You blew with your blast; the sea covered them;
they sank like lead in the swelling waters.

'LORD, who is like you among the gods?
Who is like you, majestic in holiness,
worthy of awe and praise, worker of wonders?
You stretched out your right hand;
the earth engulfed them.

'In your constant love you led the people
whom you had redeemed:
you guided them by your strength
to your holy dwelling-place.
Nations heard and trembled;
anguish seized the dwellers in Philistia.
The chieftains of Edom were then dismayed,

61

trembling seized the leaders of
Moab,
the inhabitants of Canaan were all
panic-stricken;
terror and dread fell upon them:
through the might of your arm
they stayed stone-still
while your people passed, LORD,
while the people whom you made
your own passed by.
You will bring them in and plant
them
in the mount that is your possession,
the dwelling-place, LORD, of your
own making,
the sanctuary, LORD, which your
own hands established.

The LORD will reign for ever and for
ever.'

When Pharaoh's horse, both chariots and cavalry, went into the sea, the
LORD brought back the waters over
them; but Israel had passed through
the sea on dry ground. The prophetess
Miriam, Aaron's sister, took up her
tambourine, and all the women followed her, dancing to the sound of
tambourines; and Miriam sang them
this refrain:

'Sing to the LORD, for he has risen
up in triumph:
horse and rider he has hurled into
the sea.'

Comments on the Story

Israel is saved, and the throng who have witnessed the glory of God not surprisingly explode with exuberance, celebration, and gratitude. The biblical
story evokes praise and thanksgiving. The Psalms grew out of Israel's sense of
blessing and salvation, but other Psalm-like songs of praise are generously
sprinkled throughout the Bible. Paeans extolling the victories of Rameses II are
etched on monuments that still litter the sands of Egypt. But our song is no
boast. Moses is no warrior. He merely walks through with Israel and they most
assuredly turn in praise and giddy celebration.

Exodus 15 is different from the surrounding narrative because of its poetic
structure, its unmistakable rhythm, and its metaphorical overflow. Even in the
REB, we may revel in its rhythm and its astonishingly rich language (hurled,
the flower engulfed, abyss, sank like a stone/lead, stubble, blast, congealed,
glut). This hymn was indeed a song, never to be merely read, but to be chanted
to what must have been a melody so well-known and so resonant that its
strains alone could touch the deepest, most secret hiding place in every heart.
Not that the hymn was composed long after the story, to be inserted as a way
of responding to the story. In the most distant past, the song was the story! The
epic, the ballad, the expression of praise preceded the narrative. Our story is
contemporary with Homer; the Greek tradition was a chanted, sung epic long
before it was reduced to mere story. The orthography, tenses, and archaic
wordings in the Hebrew lead scholars to date Exodus 15 to perhaps less than a
century after the event itself, much earlier than the biblical narrative.

Exodus 15 is a refined, well-structured poetic piece. But what we must envision on the actual day of deliverance is an effervescent, clamorous, less coherent outburst of song and shouting. No choir queued up to intone a hymn. Songs, cries, and shouts were unleashed. Our scene is better grasped if we start with Miriam (again having to play second fiddle to her brother) and the other women. Her marvelously compact couplet (v. 21) is sung in the context of dancing and "timbrel" (or "drum"). At Luxor, an array of Egyptian women is depicted, each holding a tambourine, a hide stretched over a small wooden ring, tapping rhythmically while dancing. The Hebrew verbs for "dance" involve roots meaning "whirl," "spin," or "writhe"; the dance must have been unreservedly spirited. Other women from Luxor are portrayed as turning somersaults; who wouldn't flip over being snatched from the jaws of Pharaoh? Could Michal restrain David's glee before the ark? Jephthah's daughter (Judg. 11), the cripple who sat at the Beautiful Gate (Acts 3), the swooners at American frontier camp meetings—how could they be still?

At later performances of this epic, the ancient "orchestra" (lyre, harp, pipes, trumpet, castanets, cymbals, and drums) would play. Dancing was commonplace in ancient worship (see I Chron. 25; II Sam. 23; Ps. 47; Ezra 3). In time, professionals played and danced, but in the earliest celebrations, regular folk performed with instruments and body as they were able, and more so as they were moved (see also I Sam. 18:6; Isa. 35:6; Ps. 30:11; Jer. 31:13). This kind of full-bodied response to God's mighty act may strike us as strange. In sanctuary and classroom, people are stiffly perched on pews or in chairs. Bursting into song, jumping up in exuberance would be eyed with suspicion. The mettle of the would-be storyteller is tested by a text like Exodus 15. How can its rejoicing be expressed? How can you help the story to sing and even to dance?

Retelling the Story

The sea was quiet. Bits of debris washed gently to the shore. The people stood on the shore staring at the water. Was it true that they had just walked from the far shore to here? They had camped on the other side of the sea. They had crossed the sea bed safely. The remains of chariots and weapons floating in the sea confirmed that it was true. The Israelites had crossed through the sea, and the Egyptians had been drowned.

The people were quiet. Some wept and wondered why so many had died. Many rocked in prayer to the God who had brought them out of Egypt. Mothers picked up crying children and held them close. They stood there for a long time, each considering his or her own thoughts.

They were the people of God, the Hebrew children who had been set free from bondage in Egypt. They had with them all that they could carry from their former lives. Each person carried many bundles, and children and livestock

What does it mean to be "highly exalted"? The rabbis say that four creatures on earth are exalted. Among birds, the eagle is exalted; among cattle it is the ox that takes the honor; among wild creatures it is the lion. But among all living things, it is the human being that is exalted. (*Exodus Rabbah* 23.13)

stirred among the people and bundles and carts. They were weary from many years of slavery, from the last tense days in Egypt, from their hasty flight. And they were weary from the terror of the angry army that had pursued them. "When can we rest?" some were wondering. "We have only begun our journey," some replied.

And then, out of the quiet, the people heard a voice singing clearly, "Praised be You, O God of Israel, who has brought us out of bondage and delivered us from the hand of our captors."

Others joined the call, "Praised be the Lord who has given us freedom." The crowd began to stir as one after the other realized that at last they were free.

"Blessed be the God of Israel."

"Blessed be God's servants, Moses, Aaron, Miriam!"

And the people began to draw together, the men on one side and the women on the other. Miriam took a tambourine and led the women in a dance. "Yie die die die die die die die!" Thump, then jingle, went the tambourine. The women sang and swayed. "Yie die die die die die die die!" Around and around, the tambourine led the rhythm of their feet. "Thump, thump, thump, thump, thump, thump, thump, thump. Yie die die die die die die die die!"

Moses and Aaron stood in the middle of the men. Their faces uplifted, they called out to the Lord:

> "I will sing to the LORD, for he
>   has triumphed gloriously;
>   horse and rider he has thrown
>   into the sea.
> The LORD is my strength and my might,
>   and he has become my salvation;
>   this is my God, and I will praise him." (Exod. 15:1-2)

The people swayed and moved as they felt the rhythm of the song. "Yie die die die die die die!"

"Blessed is the One who saved us from our bondage," a clear voice floated above the crowd.

The voices rose and fell like the waves and sang:

> "Who is like you, O LORD,
>   among the gods?
>   Who is like you, majestic in holiness,
>   awesome in splendor, doing wonders? . . .

"In your steadfast love you led
the people whom you redeemed;
you guided them by your
strength to your holy abode."
(Exod. 15:11, 13)

"Yie die die die die! Yie die die die die! Yie die die die die die die!" The people danced and swayed and sang. "The Lord has triumphed gloriously. Blessed be the Lord's name."

They were one people saved by the Lord. One people brought out of slavery. One people guided by the Lord to the edge of the wilderness. "Thump, thump, thump, thump. Yie die die die!"

When the heavenly host saw that the children of Israel passed safely through the waters, a great shout of celebration went up. Then another shout arose when the angels saw the Egyptians drowned. God asked about the celebration. "Your children, the Israelites, passed safely through the waters," the angels said. "But the second shout of celebration?" asked God. "That was when your enemies, the Egyptians, were drowned." "No!" was God's response, "I will not allow you to celebrate while my children the Egyptians drown!" (*Exodus Rabbah* 23.7)

Food in the Wilderness

The people complain to Moses, and God provides quail and "bread" for them.

The Story

The Israelites all complained to Moses and Aaron in the wilderness. They said, 'If only we had died at the LORD's hand in Egypt, where we sat by the fleshpots and had plenty of bread! But you have brought us out into this wilderness to let this whole asesmbly starve to death.' The LORD said to Moses, 'I shall rain down bread from heaven for you. Each day the people are to go out and gather a day's supply, so that I can put them to the test and see whether they follow my instructions or not. But on the sixth day, when they prepare what they bring in, it should be twice as much as they gather on other days.' Moses and Aaron said to all the Israelites, 'In the evening you will know that it was the LORD who brought you out of Egypt, and in the morning you will see the glory of the LORD, because he has listened to your complaints against him. Who are we that you should bring complaints against us?' 'You will know this', Moses said, 'when in answer to your complaints the LORD gives you flesh to eat in the evening, and in the morning bread in plenty. What are we? It is against the LORD that you bring your complaints, not against us.'

Moses told Aaron to say to the whole community of Israel, 'Come into the presence of the LORD, for he has listened to your complaints.' While Aaron was addressing the whole Israelite community, they looked towards the wilderness, and there was the glory of he LORD appearing in the cloud. The LORD spoke to Moses: 'I have heard the complaints of the Israelites. Say to them: Between dusk and dark you will have flesh to eat and in the morning bread in plenty. You will know that I the LORD am your God.'

That evening a flock of quails flew in and settled over the whole camp; in the morning a fall of dew lay all around it. When the dew was gone, there over the surface of the wilderness fine flakes appeared, fine as hoar-frost on the ground. When the Israelites saw it, they said one to another, 'What is that?' because they did not know what it was. Moses said to them, "That is the bread which the LORD has given you to eat. Here is the command the LORD has given: Each of you is to gather as much as he can eat: let every man take an omer apiece for every person in his tent.' The Israelites did this, and they gathered, some more, some less, but when they measured it by the omer, those who had gathered more had not too much, and those who had gathered less had not too little. Each had just as much as he could eat. Moses said, 'No one is to keep any of it till morning.' Some, however, did not listen to him; they kept part of it till morning, and it became full of maggots and stank, and Moses was angry with them.

Each morning every man gathered as much as he needed; it melted away when the sun grew hot. On the sixth day they gathered twice as much food, two omers each, and when the chiefs of the community all came and told Moses, 'This', he answered, 'is what the LORD has said: Tomorrow is a day of sacred rest, a sabbath holy to the LORD. So bake what you want to bake now, and boil what you want to boil; what remains over put aside to be kept till morning.' So they put it aside till morning as Moses had commanded, and it neither stank nor became infested with maggots. 'Eat it today,' said Moses, 'because today is a sabbath of the LORD. Today you will find none outside.'

Comments on the Story

Once you are set free, staying free is no easy matter. "Can God spread a table in the wilderness?" (Ps. 78:19). At least in Egypt there was food.

The wilderness of Sin was somewhere in the western half of the Sinai peninsula. From photos, the storyteller can get the "feel" of the region: sandy, rocky, spotty vegetation. Out there for a whole month, the Israelites begin to wonder: Are we being "led"? Or are we merely wandering? Cartographers wander a bit. Most good maps plot alternate routes for the trek. Whichever way Israel went, God chose not to topple Egyptian garrisons along the direct route. Israel is bound for the promised land, but not without a detour by a certain mountain.

Much ballyhooed is the "natural" explanation for the manna. At least since Josephus (*Antiquities* 3.25.31), the honey-like deposits of the tamarisk (nowadays packaged and sold as "bread of heaven" souvenirs) have anchored the biblical story in reality. Insects suck off the shrub's sap and deposit the surplus on the branches; the residue crystallizes and falls, if not from heaven (like the dew, Deut. 33:28; Hag. 1:10), then at least to the ground. This sweet, whitish manna succumbs to the ants not long into the day. Someone figured that over five hundred pounds of this manna is deposited on the peninsula each year. While loaded with carbohydrates and sugars, manna is not made appetizing for daily fare even by boiling and baking it. The rabbis insisted that it miraculously assumed the eater's favorite flavor, but the repetitious menu wrought boredom (Num. 11:4-8).

Insects and tamarisks, though, aren't exactly the makings of a good miracle. The fancy footwork in "natural theology" may satisfy some. Who, after all, made the tamarisk, not to mention the insects who do the work? How did Israel experience God's power in this food? The "natural" production of manna lasts less than two months. The story as is must be onto something beyond this natural manna, for Exodus reports that a double portion fell on Friday but none fell

67

on Saturday. Certainly general despoliation of the environment into modern times has impeded natural manna production to some degree, but even five thousand pounds would not feed Moses' horde for even a day. This story does not pretend to be a primitive biology textbook; rather, it tells of something both humbler and greater.

Our narrative is fascinating theologically; it tiptoes along the delicate and complex interfaces between human crying and human griping, between human need and divine generosity, between human griping and divine grace, between divine grace and divine law. What is with these people? Their stomachs growl on empty, but their souls are exposed as being emptier, especially when we recall that the manna story comes right on the heels of the Marah episode. Of course, some time has elapsed, although their divine teacher seems to be into a lecture on taking the long view. What are these folks really craving?

Manna is an archaic Semitic contraction meaning: "What is it?" It's hardly a wrathful showering of brimstone. The food is heavenly, pure grace, certainly unmerited. And yet there are conditions, much as with the fruits in Eden (Gen. 2:16-17).

> Behold, God's wondrous gift is given—with strings.
> All glory be to thee, uncertain Giver,
> who wants to have his gift and give it too.
> (B. Davie Napier, *Come Sweet Death*
> [Philadelphia: United Church Press, 1967], p. 19)

In Exodus 17:1-7, the people will "test" (*nsh,* "seek proof of") the Lord, but 16:4 clarifies who is being put to the "test" (*nsh,* "proved"). These proving grounds may remind us of the wilderness fasts of Elijah, Jesus, and even Moses himself. True freedom has its disciplines. The disciplines to follow cannot be subtracted without loss to the remainder. How provocatively verses 16-20 undress the old-fashioned venial sins that doggedly snap at our heels even today: greed, gluttony, miserliness. How deftly the manna's idiosyncrasies indict! You couldn't gather too much—or too little. Thrifty squirrels couldn't even save for a rainy day, or "just in case"—or for the more insidious or mercenary purposes of stockpilers. Is their frustration, their rebellion, rooted in their inability to be in control? The purpose of the manna was not merely to satisfy physical hunger, but to teach a lesson about the reality and power of God (16:12, "You will know that I the Lord am your God"; compare Elisha's miracle in II Kings 4:42-44). Why, after all, was it so essential for these people to be kept alive? God still plans for them to be a blessing to the whole world (Gen. 12:3).

Anachronistically, the Sabbath law hasn't even been given just yet. But the biblical storyteller must lay out the cruciality of Sabbath rest for the very identity of biblical people, ancient and modern. After all, when in Israel did anybody have time to tell their stories?

The New Testament approves of Moses, but keeps him at arm's distance. John 6, while giving Moses some credit for spreading the wilderness table, does view the feeding as superficially inadequate. Jesus talks about more than just "food"; he's talking about the bread of life that keeps us from ever getting hungry again (see Deut. 8:3; compare I Cor. 10:1-13). The story in Exodus 16 bears within itself this same dynamic of "mere food" and "real food." Jesus gave the people both kinds, and so did Moses. Even in the Old Testament, the "wilderness" has already become a metaphor for the malaise of life; hearers today will make this association and may even know of devotional materials entitled "daily bread."

Philo spiritualized the story: God rains wisdom and virtue on our souls. The early church leaned toward a eucharistic understanding of the manna. In verse 32, provision is made for an omer (about a half gallon) to be preserved as a holy relic, a reminder for later generations. "Before the testimony" (v. 34) is obscure; tradition put the omer of manna in the ark. Of course, ever since Rashi, readers have recognized that there was as yet no ark to put the omer in! "Indeed, the sign of divine grace preceded the giving of the law of Sinai" (Childs, 292). On the way to Mt. Sinai, the people show themselves to be "unruly," sorely in need of the rules to come. In later messianic visions of the end times, one hoped-for sign was the return of the manna from heaven.

But first another miracle. With Exodus 15:22-27, Exodus 17:1-7 forms a watery envelope around the manna story, a triad of human need brimming over into rebellion, all met not with wrath but with grace.

Retelling the Story

Sometimes I wonder whether God is a mother hen who really knows what she's doing. Then I say, "Oh, God. Listen up a minute. I've got some major problems down here, and I need you to pay attention. We've got to have a serious chat."

We talk a lot, God and I. I say, "We haven't got a place to sleep tonight." And God says, "I love you and provide for you." I say, "The kids are crying, and we need a place to rest." And God says, "I will give you what you need. You are a precious child of mine." I say, "Listen up, God." And God says, "I am listening. I am faithful to you."

My kids and I have been homeless for two years. Ruth is five and Sonny is three. They're real good kids, but it's hard on them. It's hard on all of us.

I had a house and a husband and a car two years ago. But my husband got into drinking and started beating on us. He drank up the mortgage payment and the car payment. One night, he got so mad that I thought he was going to kill me or the kids. I gathered them up that night, and we left. I spent my last money on bus tickets to my parents' city for three of us. But they wouldn't take me back in because they didn't want me to marry him in the first place. So we were stuck on the streets.

It was terrifying. Me and two babies. We spent the first nights in a park huddled up together like a bunch of puppies. The kids cried themselves to sleep because they were hungry. We got a meal in the middle of the day from one of the churches. But the days were really long, and the kids were scared and confused. They couldn't understand why they couldn't bring all their toys to play with.

That was when I first started talking to God. I mean, I had prayed before and gone to church and all that, but there we were with no place to go and no money, no food. I said to God, "I thought you're supposed to take care of your believers. I've done the best I could. I've lived honest and tried not to do wrong. And here I am. I should have just let him kill the three of us. That would be better than having to live like this. What I am I supposed to do now?"

I didn't really expect to get an answer, but I listened anyway. And I heard a voice inside of me say, "You are not alone in this wilderness. I am with you. I will be faithful to you. I will provide as much as you need for each day. Your wanderings may be difficult, but you will have the strength you need to meet every challenge. You are my precious daughter."

> The manna that God provided the children of Israel did not have a flavor peculiar to itself. It took on the taste of whatever the one dining most hungered for. If you wanted chicken, it tasted like a fine, fat hen. If you wanted dessert, manna could taste like honey or fig jam. Perhaps this "bread of heaven" was the first, best, all-around food. (*Exodus Rabbah* 25.3)

It took my breath away, and I started to cry. It woke the kids up, and we were all crying. But I said to the kids, "It's okay, precious ones. I talked to God, and it's going to be okay. We'll have everything we need to get through this. God and I are going to take care of you. I love you, Ruth and Sonny." And they quieted down and went back to sleep.

There's no happy ending to this story. It has been really hard living in this wilderness. One night I stayed awake all night because I was afraid that this man was going to steal my kids. It's hard to find space in the shelter where I can bring my kids. They get really exhausted living on the street.

I get frustrated a lot. And God and I have a serious talk about what's going on. I still don't understand why all of this happened to us. I guess there is no sense to why things happen the way they do. I get pretty angry, and I tell God about it. God can handle it.

God has taken care of us one day at a time. It's kinda like manna from heaven. Each day there is enough food for the kids and for me. Each day we have a place to sleep that is dry and warm enough. Each day we have contact with others of God's children. Each day we get just enough food and drink and shelter and hope to make it until the next day.

That's the best part: the hope. I know that God's watching out for us and God will live up to the promises God made that first night when we talked—that God is faithful and will provide what we need for today.

It's about time for me to get the kids some lunch. Don't you forget that God is a mother hen who promises to give us what we need for today. And you can hold God to that promise.

God's ways are clearly different from human ways. If we find a bill someone owes us, we collect payment as soon as possible, but if we are the one owing we hide the bill and hope our creditor will forget. But with God if we are found wanting the fact is hidden, but if God finds something in our favor it is made public immediately. Also it was customary for students to walk ahead of their teacher holding a lamp so that the teacher could see to walk at night. But in this case it is God who goes ahead of Israel, lighting the way. (*Exodus Rabbah* 25.6)

Josephus says that the Israelites first thought manna was snow. Philo says that the giving of manna is the way all God's gifts are given. They are always fresh. In addition, certain rabbis say that only those who have eaten manna, that is those who have eaten their fill, can truly study Torah. (Plaut, p. 504)

Water from the Rock

The people complain to Moses, and God provides water for them.

The Story

The whole community of Israel set out from the wilderness of Sin and travelled by stages as the LORD directed. They encamped at Rephidim, but there was no water for the people to drink, and a dispute arose between them and Moses. When they said, 'Give us water to drink,' Moses said, 'Why do you dispute with me? Why do you challenge the LORD?' The people became so thirsty there that they raised an outcry against Moses: 'Why have you brought us out of Egypt with our children and our herds to let us die of thirst?' Moses appealed to the LORD, 'What shall I do with these people? In a moment they will be stoning me.' The LORD answered, 'Go forward ahead of the people; take with you some of the elders of Israel and bring along the staff with which you struck the Nile. Go, you will find me waiting for you there, by a rock in Horeb. Strike the rock; water will pour out of it for the people to drink.' Moses did this in the sight of the elders of Israel. He named the place Massah and Meribah, because the Israelites had disputed with him and put the LORD to the test with their question, 'Is the LORD in our midst or not?'

Comments on the Story

The itinerary fixes specific place names, lending the journey a concrete, tangibly physical setting. But where are Sin, Rephidim, and the paired Massah/Meribah? Theories abound; some maps even pretend to know. But beyond question God was in no hurry to get Israel out of the wilderness; they made no beeline for the milk and honey. The *wadi Refayid* is a candidate for Rephidim; happily it is in the vicinity of *jebel musa* (itself only a candidate for the original Mt. Sinai). The doubled name Massah and Meribah is as mysterious and fraught with poignancy as the doubled trees in Genesis 2. Massah, meaning "test" (or perhaps better, "proof"), and Meribah, meaning "dispute" (from a root linked to legal wrangling) are used separately (Num. 20:13; Deut. 6:16; 9:22; 32:51; Pss. 81:8; 106:32) or as a pair (Deut. 33:8; Ps. 95:8). Perhaps an etymology lurks in the hazy past; it would not be hard to envision a nomadic sage, having gathered a few families around the campfire, pointing to a rocky crag gurgling with fresh water, explaining to his compatriots that "we

72

call this spring Meribah, for it was here that your ancestors meribah-ed (disputed) with the Lord; but the Holy One, blessed be He, brought forth this water" (or similarly, "Massah, for here your grandparents demanded massah [proof] from the Lord"). A unique etiology it would be, though, because water is not verbally tied to the place name. What sort of rock, after all, would the Lord stand "on" or "by"?

Exodus 17 and its sister text, Numbers 20, bracket the long Sinai encounter with stories of water from a rock. We surmise that the places in question must be in the Kadesh region (Deut. 1:46; 2:14). Because *kadesh* means "holy place," we wonder: Is this where Israel had wanted to go for their weekend sacrifice in the first place (Exod. 5:1)? But Kadesh (dictionaries provide photos of today's oasis) has more water than the rest of the peninsula; of course, the pious might say that prior to Moses there was no water there at all.

Rephidim was surely the "last stop before Sinai/Horeb." In fact, the text seems to indicate that the Lord will stand "on" the rock "at Horeb." Is the Lord in the distance? Is Horeb a mountainous region, with the word *Sinai* indicating a single peak?

We do not know exactly where the Israelites were. Of course, they didn't know where they were either. A storyteller might capitalize on this uncertainty. In a visceral sense, modern hearers know exactly where Rephidim is; the people are doing their best to follow the Lord's leading, but they wind up in a desolate place, parched with thirst. Like the Samaritan woman at the well (John 4), they are thirsty at two levels. That deeper thirst is imaged often in the Bible, perhaps most profoundly in the deer sniffing the air for the scent of a flowing stream in Psalm 42 (compare also Pss. 63; 84; Isa. 43; Ezek. 47; Rev. 21).

Two patterns may be distinguished in the "murmuring" stories.

> Pattern I—need /// complaint /// intercession /// miracle
> Pattern II—complaint /// punishment /// intercession /// reprieve

Indeed, fire, plague, and serpents are unleashed to punish Pattern II murmurers (Num. 11:1-3; 16:41-50; 21:4-10). But here the cautious narrator will eschew reading into Moses' frustrations with these Pattern I murmurers any hostile rebuke from God; the water in this instance is pure mercy. You can't fault them for being thirsty, can you? The drama in Exodus 17 is riveted on the people's displacing their exasperation on Moses (much as in the case of Cain, whose quarrels with God are placed on innocent Abel). Curiously, it is only the elders who witness the actual miracle, wrought once more through the unmagical rod of, not Moses, but the Lord.

The original storyteller was not careful about grammatical consistency. The pronouns in verse 3 (polished up by the REB) unveil a trajectory of self-regard: "Why have you brought US out of Egypt with MY children and MY herds to let ME die of thirst?" In the pericope's closing verse, the question "Is the Lord in our midst or not?" undergirds the whole. The people had to be wondering. People today are troubled by the same question. Often it lurks secretly behind a facade of piety and churchmanship. But the finest rhetorical feature of this vignette is the way the writer of Exodus masterfully lifts up their excruciating dilemma. The question never actually passes their lips. But it is the very heart of all that they do and say. Why do they test? Why do they dispute? Their deepest thirst is to get this issue resolved. Is the Lord among us—or not?

A modern exposé of sorts may cast an even longer shadow on this question. Journalist Ian Wilson (*Exodus: The True Story*, p. 149) regales us with a story of the Sinai Camel Corps stumbling into a seemingly long dried-out wadi bed in the 1930s. A bedouin attached to the unit wielded a spade, shattering the weathered, crusted-over limestone. The aperture he dug spewed forth a small geyser, to the astonishment of the British. Bystanders cried out, "Look at him! The prophet Moses!"

The confrontation at Meribah/Massah figures prominently in two liturgical pieces in the Psalter. Psalms 81 and 95 mirror a festival gathering in the Jerusalem Temple. God's mercy is remembered and celebrated, albeit with dire warnings. A Levitical prophet would rise, almost in an ecstatic trance, daring to speak God's very words: "O that you would listen to me, Israel" (81:8). Do not be stubborn as you were at Meribah (95:8; cf. 106:32). As Spurgeon restated it, "Let the example of that unhappy generation serve as a beacon to you; do not repeat the offenses which have already more than enough provoked the Lord" (*Treasury of David,* vol. 2 [New York: Baker Book House, 1983], p. 167).

The assembly at which these psalms were featured was the Feast of Tabernacles (or "booths," *sukkoth*), when the gift of water in the wilderness was commemorated, culminating in a vast worship extravaganza at the new moon. A modern storyteller could profitably adopt the point of view of a Jewish worshiper, awed by the splendor of the Temple, pushed along in the throng of pilgrims, thrilled by the trumpets, lyres, and choirs, moved even to pulsate to the drum beat, to swirl with the other dancers, hearing again the story of the gift of water in the dry wilderness (Ps. 105:41).

This story must also be the background to the marvelous saying of Jesus in John 7:37-39. The festival's climax was reached when the people gathered around the waters of Gihon and Siloam at the foot of Mt. Zion. The priest would dip a golden pitcher into the water and carry it at the head of a frenzied procession of singers and the waving of the lulab to the Temple precincts. After marching around the Temple seven times, the priest would pour the water out on the ground. We may well imagine Jesus, waving to get the attention of those so zealous in their worship: "If anyone is thirsty, let him come to me and drink. You're thirsty for God? I am what you are thirsty for." Teasingly our story may send us scurrying to John 4 or back to Isaiah 55 or most profoundly to John 19:34. In all these parallel texts, the source of grace is in God alone (Exod. 33:19).

Retelling the Story

"Grandfather, I'm thirsty. No one has ever been as thirsty as I am now." Benjamin ran to where his grandfather was cutting a piece of wood to repair a broken tool.

Benjamin's grandfather picked him up and said, "Not thirstier than we were in the wilderness when I was a little boy. We were the thirstiest people who ever lived. Let's get some water for you, Benjamin."

They walked to the well, drew some water, and sat down to drink it. Benjamin drank quickly and then asked,

> The rabbis compare the Israelites to a child riding on its parent's shoulders. When they meet someone in the street, the child asks, "Have you seen my parents?" The parent responds, "I'm right here, carrying you. Didn't you know that it was I who carried you all this time?" Just so, it was God who had led, cared for, and provided for the Israelites all the time they were wandering. (*Exodus Rabbah* 26.2)

"Grandfather, will you tell me about when you were a little boy and you were the thirstiest people who ever lived?" Benjamin looked at his grandfather with anticipation.

"Yes, I'll tell you," answered Grandfather. "It was a long, long time ago. The people were following Moses on the way to the Promised Land."

Benjamin spoke up, "That's where we live now, isn't it?"

"Yes, that's right. I say that the people were following Moses, but God was leading Moses. I don't know whether anyone but God knew where we were. My grandfather said we were lost, that we had wasted years wandering around in the wilderness. Maybe there wasn't really a Promised Land, that Moses was leading us around in circles. My grandmother said that maybe we were lost, but as long as the Lord was with us, we were right where we were supposed to be.

"Anyway, the people followed Moses for many years. And sometimes things just got to be too much and everybody got upset—like that time when we were thirsty. Everybody went to Moses and complained to him. They wanted to know why he brought them out of Egypt to die of thirst in the wilderness. They could remember the life back in Egypt. Me, I was born in the desert, and all I ever heard about Egypt were the stories of oppression."

"But what about being the thirstiest people who ever lived?" Benjamin asked.

"Oh, yes. Well, we had been traveling for quite some time. Everybody was tired. It takes a long time to get very far when you travel as we did, with bundles and children and livestock. We finally set up camp at a place called Rephidim. Don't ask me where that was, because we didn't know where we were. We were tired and ready for a rest, but there was no water to replenish our water supply.

"We stayed where we were, too weary to go on. We assumed that we would be able to send scouts to find water somewhere close by. But the days went by, and our supply of water dwindled, and the scouts brought no news of water. First our water was rationed, and then it ran out. Everyone was dismayed and angry. How could this have happened? That was when the people went to Moses to complain. They were really loud! My father feared that people and animals would soon begin to die of thirst."

"Did anyone die of thirst?" Benjamin's eyes were big.

"We lost several head of livestock, but all the people were okay. But we were the thirstiest people that ever lived. I chewed on a piece of leather just to moisten my mouth."

Benjamin reached for the water and took another big drink. Then he asked, "How did you get water, Grandfather?"

The rabbis say that the same rod God used as an instrument to bring the plagues on Egypt was also used to strike the rock that would yield water for the wanderers. The reason the same rod was used is that while people cut with a knife and heal with a bandage, God punishes and heals with the same instrument. (*Exodus Rabbah* 26.2)

"Well," he said, "Moses called on the Lord. He was afraid the people were going to stone him. The Lord told him to take some of the elders out into the countryside to a particular place. My grandfather was one of those who went with Moses. Moses led the elders to a rock where the Lord was standing, and Moses struck the rock with his rod. And out of the rock came water. It was, Grandfather said, a beautiful sight. He guessed, after that, maybe Moses *did* know what he was doing.

"We all got plenty of water to drink. It was the best-tasting water I've ever had. I can still remember the cool wetness on my tongue. Moses called the place Massah and Meribah because the people quarreled and tested the Lord."

Benjamin said, "I think God should have called it 'The Best-tasting Water for the Thirstiest People Who Ever Lived.' "

Grandfather reached over and hugged Benjamin. "That's a good idea, Grandson. Let's go tell your grandmother."

Israel and Amalek

The Israelites battle the Amalekites inspired by the staff of God, held aloft by Moses.

The Story

The Amalekites came and attacked Israel at Rephidim. Moses said to Joshua, 'Pick men for us, and march out tomorrow to fight against Amalek; and I shall stand on the hilltop with the staff of God in my hand.' Joshua did as Moses commanded and fought against Amalek, while Moses, Aaron, and Hur climbed to the top of the hill. Whenever Moses raised his hands Israel had the advantage, and when he lowered his hands the advantage passed to Amalek. When his arms grew heavy they took a stone and put it under him and, as he sat, Aaron and Hur held up his hands, one on each side, so that his hands remained steady till sunset. Thus Joshua defeated Amalek and put its people to the sword.

The LORD said to Moses, 'Record this in writing, and tell it to Joshua in these words: I am resolved to blot out all memory of Amalek from under heaven.' Moses built an altar, and named it 'The LORD is my Banner' and said, 'My oath upon it: the LORD is at war with Amalek generation after generation.'

Comments on the Story

Israel's sense of security and aloneness in the wilderness is shattered by the noxious Amalekites. No tablet or inscription has surfaced to share independent information about these nomadic marauders. Amalek is listed as Esau's grandson (Gen. 36:12); unique among Esau's progeny, Amalek's mother is a concubine. This branch of suspect cousins not surprisingly became ruffians, jealously guarding their turf in the vicinity of Rephidim. We still aren't sure exactly where Rephidim was, but this vignette would indicate that it was near an oasis and some pasture. If you were an Amalekite chieftain, what would your response be to the scouting report that a vast horde was coming your way?

Strike first! The Amalekite tactics are described in the parallel version of Deuteronomy 25:17-19: The guerrillas surprised the Israelites, who were exhausted and hungry, with a rear-guard sortie against the "stragglers." Who would straggle? The frail and elderly? We may want to give the Amalekites the benefit of the doubt; they did not know Israel's intentions, and they probably were so outnumbered that a guerrilla assault was their only hope of success.

Mortal enmity was sown that day. Deuteronomy 25 is instructive. Insistently Moses urges Israel to "remember" that day, to be relentless in avenging the dastardly deed. The Amalekites formed a coalition with some Canaanites to repulse Israel's futile foray into the Promised Land (Num. 14:45). These miscreants struck often after Israel infiltrated the land (Judg. 3; 6; 7). Despite the gruesome butchery of Saul (finished off by Samuel, I Sam. 15), the Amalekites lived on to annoy the Hebrews (I Sam. 27:8; 30:1-20; II Sam. 2:1; I Chron. 18:11), as did other foes. Self-defense would be a persistent issue for Israel.

What sort of self-defense would be appropriate for Yahweh's people? Swords, daggers, chariots? Or "mere words" (Isa. 36:5)? Hastily drafted, "some men" are chosen to fight. But in this brief story, victory is contingent not on the bravery and might of the militia, but on where Moses holds his hands. When his hands are raised, the troops surge ahead; when dropped, the troops begin to be routed. Is he lifting his hands in prayer? If so, why would his praying cease when his arms faltered? Are the uplifted hands an inspiration or a pre-scientific mediation of divine power? Was he holding something? The "rod of God"? Normally the rod was not deployed to sway the battle (as was the ark). Did he need both hands to hold it? Or (as many scholars suppose) was he hoisting a banner? After the skirmish, Moses named the altar "Yahweh is my banner." Verse 16 is nearly untranslatable, but a banner seems to figure into the explanation of the altar. Ancient armies toted banners with religious symbolism onto the battlefield for inspiration and even a semi-magical infusion of power. We might recall Constantine's chi-rho or the stars and stripes on Iwo Jima.

Plainly, though, the narrator's purpose is to glorify God, to clarify Israel's utter dependence on God through this mysterious gesture. At the same time, the human element in the story is unmistakable. Aaron and Hur (was he, as Josephus tells us, Miriam's husband?) had the fortitude to keep Moses' hands elevated. Joshua and his conscripts risked life and limb, hitting, stabbing, hurling, ducking, even bleeding. The Puritan Joseph Hall wrote: "In vain shall Moses be upon the hill, if Joshua be not in the valley. Prayer without means is a mockery of God" (Childs, 317).

Our story may be enriched if we use such traditional materials with caution and a touch of humor. Because the name Jesus is Joshua in Hebrew, Origen could see in the raised hands the cross, in triumph over evil. Augustine built a "just war" theory on stories such as this. In terms of "spiritual" warfare, Luther deduced that the vast array of Hebrew men would have dispatched a band of nomads with ease, had not their vigor been sapped through disobedience (see Childs, 316-17).

Retelling the Story

It was late in the evening when our lookouts brought word that the Amalekites were taking position to attack some of our slower travelers. I ran to tell Moses, and he said to me, "Joshua, take some men with you and go fight the Amalekites. I will go to the top of the hill tomorrow with the staff of God in my hand."

Why did Moses choose Joshua? Some say that it was preparation for his leading the people into the Promised Land. Others say that it was because he was a descendant of Joseph (the original Hebrew in Egypt) and thus in the family line of the one who followed God. (*Exodus Rabbah* 26.3)

I did not understand the logic of this servant of God, but I followed his instructions. I went to my strongest men and asked who would be willing to go with me to defend the people. Those men spent the night preparing themselves and saying good-bye to their kin. At dawn we went out to the battlefield to meet Amalek.

I had never seen such fierce fighting as I did that day. Our opponents were strong and brave. My men matched their courage and their strength. For some time, our forces were equal, neither gaining the advantage. Then we began to push them back. I glanced up to the top of the hill and saw Moses and Aaron and Hur standing there. Moses had his arms in the air, holding the staff of God. As I watched, his hand lowered, and soon the tide of battle began to turn against us.

And it went that way, back and forth between us. First my line of men folded under the strength of our enemy. And then their forces fell backwards under our hand.

It went thus for many hours. I saw many brave men injured. Some fell under the blow of a sword. Many fought bravely in hand-to-hand combat.

But I discovered that when I looked to the top of the hill for inspiration for leaders, I knew whether Moses' arms would be raised or lowered by the progress of the battle. It seemed that when his arms were raised in glory to the Lord, our warriors received God's favor and were able to push back the Amalekites. But when his arms tired and he lowered them, we folded before the strength of our foes.

We were all beginning to tire from the length of battle. I feared that we may all lose our lives before it was over. I prayed to the Lord to protect our fragile children and elders from slaughter should we be defeated in battle.

And then I looked to the hill and saw Moses, our leader, seated on a rock with Aaron and Hur on either side holding his arms in the air. At that point, the battle turned to our advantage, and we were able to drive away our enemies.

Why does Moses call his staff the staff of God in this story, whereas in other stories it is called "Moses' staff"? Because when Moses used it he called it his, but when God was at work through it Moses called it God's staff. Apparently Moses wanted the people to know that he was not to be given credit for what God was doing. (*Exodus Rabbah* 26.3)

The battle over, we were weary. We returned to the camp and received food and nurture from our kin. The injured received help for their wounds. The dead were taken to be prepared for burial.

At sunset, we all gathered in front of Moses and Aaron and Hur. Victory was bittersweet, for we wished to live in harmony with our neighbors. Moses looked weary, as if he had been in battle himself. He spoke these words, "I have built an altar and called it, 'The Lord Is My Banner,' for the Lord has protected us from Amalek. If we should have to fight again, we will be safe under the banner of the Lord. The Lord is everything. Just as you brave men fought to protect our people, so also I raised my arms in supplication to the Lord. And when my arms were too weary to stay raised, Aaron and Hur held them up in glory to God. Praised be the Lord, the God of Israel, who has brought us out of the land of Egypt and delivered us from the hand of the Amalekites."

Then Moses offered a prayer to the Lord, thanking the Lord for freedom and safety. And, gratefully, we all returned to our kin.

God's Offer to Israel

God tells Moses that Israel is to be a whole people if they will keep the divine covenant, and the people agree.

The Story

In the third month after Israel had left Egypt, they came to the wilderness of Sinai. They set out from Rephidim and, entering the wilderness of Sinai, they encamped there, pitching their tents in front of the mountain. Moses went up to God, and the LORD called to him from the mountain and said, "This is what you are to say to the house of Jacob and tell the sons of Israel: You yourselves have seen what I did to Egypt, and how I have carried you on eagles' wings and brought you here to me. If only you will now listen to me and keep my covenant, then out of all peoples you will become my special possession; for the whole earth is mine. You will be to me a kingdom of priests, my holy nation. Those are the words you are to speak to the Israelites.'

Moses went down, and summoning the elders of the people he set before them all these commands which the LORD had laid on him. As one the people answered, 'Whatever the LORD has said we shall do.' When Moses brought this answer back to the LORD, the LORD said to him, 'I am coming to you in a thick cloud, so that I may speak to you in the hearing of the people, and so their faith in you may never fail.'

When Moses reported to the LORD the pledge given by the people, the LORD said to him, 'Go to the people and hallow them today and tomorrow and have them wash their clothes. They must be ready by the third day, because on that day the LORD will descend on Mount Sinai in the sight of all the people. You must set bounds for the people, saying, "Take care not to go up the mountain or even to touch its base." Anyone who touches the mountain shall be put to death. No hand may touch him; he is to be stoned to death or shot: neither man nor beast may live. But when the ram's horn sounds, they may go up the mountain.' Moses came down from the mountain to the people. He hallowed them and they washed their clothes. He said, 'Be ready by the third day; do not go near a woman.' At dawn on the third day there were peals of thunder and flashes of lightning, dense cloud on the mountain, and a loud trumpet-blast; all the people in the camp trembled.

Moses brought the people out from the camp to meet God, and they took their stand at the foot of the mountain. Mount Sinai was enveloped in smoke because the LORD had come down on it in fire; the smoke rose like the smoke from a kiln; all the people trembled violently, and the sound of the trumpet grew ever louder. Whenever Moses spoke, God answered him in a peal of thunder.

Comments on the Story

At last, the congregation reaches its destination. Yes, Canaan is the ultimate goal, but in retrospect we understand that the stopover at Sinai is properly the zenith of the story. It all happens here: the fulfillment of God's assurance from the burning bush (3:12); the granting of Moses' initial request of Pharaoh (5:1); and the apogee of Israel's religion, the cementing of the eternal covenant between the Lord and the people (the narration of which stretches to Num. 10!).

The identification and character of the mountain and Rephidim were discussed earlier. To articulate what transpires on and around the mountain will test the storyteller's mettle. The movements are confounding. In a display of shuttle diplomacy, Moses thrice ascends and descends; the Lord too descends and ascends. One moment, Moses the mediator seems to lead the people in their meeting with God; another moment, Moses is called up privately to fashion a covenant for them (compare Deut. 5:4-5). The good news between the lines is that there is traffic between heaven and earth; Sinai is the meeting point between heaven and earth.

The story comes to us in a form refined in the cauldron of Israel's worship life. Rituals of purification are prescribed (see Pss. 24:4; 26:6). Boundaries of holiness are delineated. As with the ark of the covenant, the slightest contact with even the edge of the numinous zone is fatal. Trumpets blow. Is it not easy to transfer the whole scene to the Temple of Solomon in all its splendor? Gradations of holiness marked the holy place on Zion. Only the priests, the plenipotentiaries of Moses, could trespass the inner sanctum.

"On the third new moon" after the Exodus is ambiguous to date. But on the nation's liturgical calendar, the giving of the Torah was celebrated at Pentecost (the Feast of Weeks), seven weeks after Passover. Israel must have renewed its covenant with the Lord regularly (see below on Josh. 24); how timely at Pentecost! Just as Easter and Pentecost are theologically one in Christianity, so also the deliverance from bondage and the giving of the Torah are one in Judaism. The covenant invitation is issued not by immutable decree of a lawmaker, but by the compassionate Lord who acted to deliver those who cried out. Emancipation is no end in itself; a new society must be birthed. This society is to live its life in the web of worship and fidelity, in a most profound freedom (see Walzer, 52).

Pregnant phrases adorn our story. The picturesque phrase "borne on eagles' wings" captured the imagination of later poets (see Deut. 32:11; Ps. 103:5; Isa. 40:31; Rev. 12:14). The people are granted a threefold honorific: (a) "a treasured possession" (*segullah* has been found on clay tablets in which mighty kings claim vassals as their "treasured possessions"), (b) "a kingdom of priests" (just as priests are set apart within a nation, consecrated for special service, so also Israel would be set apart to "bless" other nations [see Gen. 12:3; I Pet. 2:9]), and (c) "a holy nation," set apart in this case for a distinct lifestyle (Lev. 19).

Most remarkably, the people resoundingly commit themselves (v. 8) before they have even heard the stipulations (forthcoming in chaps. 20–23)! God has rescued them; any and every response will gladly be given. Like an enamored couple blushing at the altar, at this moment Israel has what Maggie Ross calls the "willingness for whatever" (*Fountain & the Furnace* [New York: Paulist, 1987] p. 80). Likewise, the disciples, who indeed "put down their nets" and followed, only later learned the cost. In the *Mekilta's* midrash on verse 19, God spoke only after Moses had said, "Speak, for thy children have already accepted" (Childs, 379). Would they have so unreservedly taken the plunge had they known what they were getting into? Joseph Heller imagines them in need of a decent lawyer: "Uh, as your attorney I must advise you to wait until we can pore over the fine print" (*God Knows*).

All hangs on what the people have "seen." But henceforth, the organ of faith will not be the eye but the ear. The show is over; now freedom hinges on Israel's hearing (see John 20:29). Our inclination is to want more show and less hearing. But faith's sensor is the ear. Luther reminds us that "the eyes are hard of hearing."

The text's ability to discern God's presence in meteorological phenomena, obviously crucial to our story, is hard to fathom (see Ps. 68:7-9). Geologists find no trace of volcanic activity on the peninsula within that time frame. The storm continued to be a powerful element in Israel's worship. Primal dependence on rain and fear of lightning lurk in the background. While many of the psalms (29; 97; 114) fix on the manifestation of God in peals of thunder (we may compare Zeus and the Norse gods who tossed thunderbolts around) and torrential downpour (the provenance of the Canaanite god Baal), we may appeal to the fascinating parallel to Exodus 19 in I Kings 19 for help. Elijah is awed by the furor of nature. But God is not actually in the pyrotechnics; these phenomena are the witness to God's might, the "background music, the orchestral harbinger" (Sarna, 134). Even in our story, the negotiations between God and Moses (and the people) are in full gear before even the first thick cloud peeks over the mountain's crest (v. 9). Mercifully, God allows preparation time before unleashing a seismic tumult (see Matt. 27:51; Luke 23:44); the quake is at dawn on the third day (see Matt. 28:2). The Bible never underestimates God's power (as put so eloquently by Elizabeth Achtemeier in her sermon on this text, "Our Ordinary Worship" in *Preaching as Theology and Art* [Nashville: Abingdon Press, 1984], pp. 93-101).

We are infuriated to think that God could have ordered the males, "Do not go near a woman." Did Moses and his successors hear God correctly? Judith Plaskow has unmasked the most discomfiting detail in our narrative:

The specific issue at stake is ritual impurity: an emission of semen renders both a man and his female partner temporarily unfit to approach the sacred (Lev 15:16-18). But Moses does not say, "Men and women do not go near each other." At the central moment of Jewish history, women are invisible (*Standing Again at Sinai* [San Francisco: Harper & Row, 1990], p. 26).

Many of the purification laws, sexist or not, imply that nearness to God requires a time of separation from things normally permitted and good in themselves.

Many Christians view the Sinai episode through suspicious spectacles, perhaps overly emphasizing the negative bias about the law in Paul's epistles. Stephen positively labels the Torah as "living oracles" (Acts 7:38). Hebrews 12 locates angels on the mountain (following haggadic tradition). Christians can relearn the significance of Sinai, for our freedom is lost if we refuse to don the yoke of worship and obedience.

Retelling the Story

They had wandered far in the wilderness, following Moses and this God who liberated them from slavery. Surely there was such a God, the leaders argued, or they would have perished in the desert. But they were provided bread and meat and water. They had not been overcome by starvation or by thirst or by warring people.

They were moving again, from Rephidim into the wilderness of Sinai. And now they have arrived at Mt. Sinai, the mountain of God. At last they have arrived somewhere.

The rabbis say that "the house of Jacob" refers to women, while "the children of Israel" refers to men. In that case, women are mentioned first as God prepared to give the law to Moses. Why is that the case? The rabbis say that God knew that women were quick to observe the commandments and that they would be the ones teaching them to the children. Thus women are mentioned first when God presents the law to Moses. (*Exodus Rabbah* 28.2)

Excitement was in the air. People were talking and whispering, straining to see. All they could see was a mountain. It did not look like the mountain of God, but what would God's mountain look like anyway?

They set up their tents at the foot of the mountain. The livestock was moved to the edges of the camp. Women and men went about their familiar tasks—setting up tents, gathering fuel for the fires, unrolling bed rolls, looking after children—but there was a feeling of expectation, of curiosity, of something important about to happen.

Word spread among the people that Moses was seen walking toward the mountain. "He looked as though he had a thousand things on his mind. He seemed to be talking to himself," the witness shared.

Then later, youth came running to say that Moses had returned to camp and was calling a meeting of all the elders of the people.

Moses came before the elders and said to them, "The Lord has spoken these words to me in order that I might speak them to you. The Lord says 'You have seen what I did to the Egyptians, and how I bore you on eagles' wings and brought you to myself. Now therefore, if you obey my voice and keep my covenant, you shall be my treasured possession out of all the peoples. Indeed, the whole earth is mine, but you shall be for me a priestly kingdom and a holy nation' (Exod. 19:4-6)."

And the people answered immediately, "Everything that the Lord has spoken we will do" (Exod. 19:8).

> It is said that other nations were offered the Torah, but before they would accept it they wanted to hear the restrictions it would place on them. When they heard that it would go against some of their national practices and customs, they refused it. The Israelites, however, accepted before even hearing the restrictions it would place on them, saying, "We will do everything the Lord has said." (Plaut, p. 529; Ginzberg, VI, p. 31)

The eyes of all the people watched as Moses went again to the mountain of God and returned from the mountain of God. Then Moses said to the people, "Everyone must prepare to meet with the Lord. The Lord will come before you in a dense cloud so that you may hear the Lord as the Lord speaks to me. Follow the preparations closely, because it is a fearful and awesome thing to come before the Lord."

Moses instructed them not to go near the mountain or touch any part of the mountain. Any people or livestock who touched the mountain would be put to death. The people trembled at such a thought. Mothers watched their children closely and scolded them to stay near their tents. The livestock were moved farther away from the mountain.

And so the people made preparations to come before the Lord. Like young people getting ready to meet their beloved, the people prepared with care. They consecrated themselves—their hearts, their bodies, and their clothes.

On the morning of the third day, the people awoke to thunder and lightning on the mountain. Surrounding the mountain was a thick cloud. And then a trumpet sounded. It was loud enough to cause the people to tremble.

Moses said, "It is time. Gather the people to go and meet the Lord." The youth ran through the camp, alerting the people. And all of them came out of their tents. They wore fear on their faces, but they stood tall. Men and women, old and young, boys and girls—they were the Lord's treasured possession. They were a holy nation going to meet their God. Moses led the people to their place at the foot of the mountain. The mountain was no longer visible. Instead, the people saw billows of smoke covering the mountain and felt the ground shaking below them. The trumpet blast grew louder and was answered by claps of thunder. In the thunder, God spoke to Moses. And the people waited with awe and fear and trust for the words of the Lord their God.

The Ten Commandments

God speaks the commandments, and the people are filled with fear by the divine voice.

The Story

God spoke all these words:
I am the LORD your God who brought you out of Egypt, out of the land of slavery.

You must have no other god besides me.

You must not make a carved image for yourself, nor the likeness of anything in the heavens above, or on the earth below, or in the waters under the earth.

You must not bow down to them in worship; for I, the LORD your God, am a jealous God, punishing the children for the sins of the parents to the third and fourth generation of those who reject me. But I keep faith with thousands, those who love me and keep my commandments.

You must not make wrong use of the name of the LORD your God; the LORD will not leave unpunished anyone who misuses his name.

Remember to keep the sabbath day holy. You have six days to labour and do all your work; but the seventh day is a sabbath of the LORD your God; that day you must not do any work, neither you, nor your son or your daughter, your slave or your slave-girl, your cattle, or the alien residing among you; for in six days the LORD made the heavens and the earth, the sea, and all that is in them, and on the seventh day he rested. Therefore the LORD blessed the sabbath day and declared it holy.

Honour your father and your mother, so that you may enjoy long life in the land which the LORD your God is giving you.

Do not commit murder.

Do not commit adultery.

Do not steal.

Do not give false evidence against your neighbour.

Do not covet your neighbour's household: you must not covet your neighbour's wife, his slave, his slave-girl, his ox, his donkey, or anything that belongs to him.

When all the people saw how it thundered and the lightning flashed, when they heard the trumpet sound and saw the mountain in smoke, they were afraid and trembled. They stood at a distance and said to Moses, 'Speak to us yourself and we will listen; but do not let God speak to us or we shall die.' Moses answered, 'Do not be afraid. God has come only to test you, so that the fear of him may remain with you and preserve you from sinning.' So the people kept their distance, while Moses approached the dark cloud where God was.

The LORD said to Moses, Say this to the Israelites: You know now that I have spoken from heaven to you. You must not make gods of silver to be worshipped besides me, nor may you make yourselves gods of gold. The altar you make for me is to be of earth, and you are to sacrifice on it both your whole-offerings and your shared-offerings, your sheep and goats and your cattle. Wherever I cause my name to be invoked, I will come to you and bless you. If you make an altar of stones for me, you must not build it of hewn stones, for if you use a tool on them, you profane them. You must not mount up to my altar by steps, in case your private parts are exposed over against it.

Comments on the Story

It seems that the more firmly a particular text is anchored in the popular consciousness, the greater the tendency for it to be cut adrift from its moorings in history and in its literary context. In the case of the Ten Commandments, the Bible itself is to blame. In both the Old and New Testaments, references and allusions to the decalogue are numerous, showing us how those ten basic commands carried astonishing weight in the life of the Jewish and Christian communities. The prophets set Israel's sin in bold relief under the glare of the commandments (Hos. 4; Jer. 7). In the liturgy, the ten were rehearsed as a warm-up for prophetic denunciation (Pss. 50; 81). Jesus himself is at once liberal (Mark 2:23) and severe (Matt. 5:21) in his interpretation of these self-evidently pivotal commandments (see Matt. 19:18). And Paul, the champion of salvation apart from the law, urges their adherence upon the Christians in Rome (Rom. 13:8).

The commandments play pivotal roles in countless later contexts. In many biblical narratives, a commandment, its interpretation, and obedience (or lack thereof) to it figure as the catalyst. In the following explanations of the Ten Words, the storyteller will be linked to dozens of episodes and anecdotes. These narratives will show how Israel's law is lived out within its stories. The decalogue (as intended by God) is played out in the real life of the community of the faithful.

1. In the bout between Yahweh and the Canaanite deities on the ridge of Mt. Carmel (I Kings 18), Elijah poses the question: "How long will you limp between two opinions?" The first commandment is a window, not into intellectual monotheism, but into the jealous heart of God, who brooks no rival. Yahweh insists on exclusive loyalty, no matter what the cost or travail (Ps. 73:25). The non-existence of competitor gods is only the corollary to this primal expectation of single-minded fidelity (Isa. 45:6-21).

2. The classic violation of the commandment against "graven images" occurs even as the tablets are coming down the mountain, when the people of God build a golden calf (see Exod. 32). The issue again is posed most sharply

(and humorously) in the incident of the theft of the ark (I Sam. 5), when the toppled idol of Dagon ominously bows during the night in submission to the ark. Later, Daniel, Shadrach, Meshach, and Abednego are rewarded for their fidelity (Dan. 2–3). And idolaters are nowhere more soundly lampooned than in Isaiah 44:9-20.

How unique was Israel to abhor such images, the very stuff of all other religions. The expositor might be cautious to refrain from deriding religions that employed images, though. No religion (in Israel's day or since) thought that the graven image was really divine. Each religion requires something tangible to embody the meeting point between God and believers. For Israel, that "point" is the ark and later the Temple, and even later the Torah itself. Yahweh wishes that the faculty of faith be not the eye but the ear. But the distinction between a graven image or idol and a mere symbol is a tricky one. Little wonder controversy continually erupted over what was and was not such an image. The iconography of Solomon's Temple was deemed acceptable, whereas Jeroboam's bulls (I Kings 12:25-33) were not. And food sacrificed to idols (I Cor. 8) was all right for Christians to eat—or was it? Iconoclastic controversies, (e.g. whether to have a cross represented with Jesus on it), have simmered throughout church history.

The only image positively appraised in the Bible is the human creature, made "in God's image." The sixth "station of the cross" pictures a woman emerging from the crowd to wipe Jesus' face after he falls under the weight of the cross. Her name, Veronica, means "true image." In her simple act of love and charity is revealed the only image of God (and of humanity) forthcoming (see Matt. 25:31-46).

3. The misuse of the divine name may originally have referred to magical incantation. Even when it "works" as Saul deals with the Witch of Endor (I Sam. 28), it is sternly renounced. In the long run, any effort to manipulate God to one's own advantage is doomed. Jeremiah castigates those false prophets who pretend to speak in Yahweh's name, saying, "Peace, peace" when there is no peace (Jer. 6:14; see Ezek. 13). "Cussing," tacky and crude as it may be, is not as power-packed as unleashing the divine name (see the comments for Num. 22–24 below on the Balaam adventure).

4. The Sabbath injunction is framed positively ("Remember, the Sabbath"), and it is greatly elaborated. The rationale given refers to creation itself (Exod. 31:12-17). By resting himself, God wove this day of rest into the very fabric of creation. Ecologically sensitive hearers will delight in God's care for the earth. Fields get a vacation centuries before agricultural science discovered why land gets scorched from overuse (Exod. 23:10-14; Lev. 25:2-7).

Verse 10 demonstrates that the Sabbath is the great day of equality, a weekly festival of freedom and justice. In Deuteronomy 5:12-15 (compare Exod. 23:12), Israel is reminded of what unrelenting labor was like back in Egypt.

Indeed, in Israel slaves and debtors were granted the ultimate break—freedom itself in the "Jubilee" (Lev. 25; Luke 4:16-20).

So grievous was any violation that Exodus 31:14 prescribes capital punishment; John Wesley merely withheld Holy Communion tickets! The manna episode captures the intent beautifully (see comments on Exod. 16:2-15). The Sabbath indeed is a day of faith: In order to rest, you must believe, you must trust God, and you must acknowledge that not everything depends on your own feverish activity.

But the Sabbath, cherished symbol of Israelite identity, fell into the hands of those ever-present religious wardens who would erect walls, deny freedom, and quash faith. Jesus courted condemnation in a marvelous pair of stories (Mark 2:23–3:6). He urges the disciples to pluck grain on the Sabbath—and what sort of mentality would be appalled by a Sabbath healing?

5. The other command framed positively would honor parents. In ancient times, the elderly were more revered than today. But aged parents could also be a liability. With no social security, some persons, no doubt, were throwing them out on their ears. In Israel, decrepit, non-contributing parents could not be driven out from their only hope of succor. To strike or to curse one's parent was to incur a penalty of death (Exod. 21:15).

Honor means more than *obey*. Parents are to be esteemed highly, cared for, and respected (see Prov. 1:8; 4:8; 15:5; Eph. 6:2). So complex could be the web of obligations, though, that parental ties were not always the ultimate. Ruth touchingly clings to Naomi. Michal and Jonathan, never dispensing with their obligation to care for Saul, are loyal to his foe, David. Joseph's brothers wound not only Joseph but also Jacob, who nonetheless has "favorites." Lot (disgustingly) offers his own daughters to the men of Sodom and Gomorrah. Absalom revolts against David, who is scolded by Joab when he weeps over his recalcitrant son's demise. Jacob and Rebekah hardly honor Isaac by their chicanery. Even Jesus keeps his own mother at arm's distance: "Who is my mother, my brother? Whoever does the will of God" (Mark 3:31; see Matt. 8:21).

6. With what must have been the brevity of the original tablets, a salvo of hyphenated word pairs (in Hebrew) opens with "no killing." But does *rṣh* mean illegal killing? Killing out of hatred? Killing that mandates blood vengeance? Taking the law into your own hands? There is no shortage of killing (much of it divinely sanctioned) in the Bible: Cain's treachery, Lamech's bloodletting, Moses' stab at justice, the fury of the Levites in the wake of the golden calf, the whole conquest of Canaan, Jephthah's daughter, the messenger bearing Saul's death notice, Jehu's purge, Ahab and Naboth, Haman's gallows, John the Baptist's beheading, Stephen's martyrdom. Jesus extends the principle to the internal attitude of hatred (Matt. 5:21-26), which was anticipated already at Sinai (Lev. 19:17-18).

7. The staccato pace continues: no adultery. Contrast Potiphar's wife and Uriah's wife (I Sam. 11 also portrays killing). The penalty for adultery was death (Deut. 22:22), tempered, however, by Hosea (with Gomer) and Jesus (with the self-righteous stoners in John 7:53–8:11). Adultery indeed is inimical to the peace of any community. Jesus again strikes at the root issue of "lust" (Matt. 5:27-28). In our day, lust is regarded as normal, healthy, even to be encouraged in the form of fantasy.

8. Stealing referred in the distant past to kidnapping (Rashi had noticed this). Illegal seizure and pressing an unwilling person into slavery were practiced openly by the pharaoh (Exod. 1), and no less inimically by the wealthy in Israel (Amos 4). Simple theft is self-evidently intolerable in community life.

9. We must set the legal scenario to grasp what "false witness" is all about. Village elders would gather to hear a case. The Psalms (4; 5; 7; 10; 27) prove that there was no shortage of false accusations—and unprincipled sorts who would level the accusations, no doubt for seedy gain. The incident of Naboth's vineyard illustrates the situation perfectly (I Kings 21; this travesty of justice in fact portrays the breaking of the ninth, tenth, eighth, sixth, third, and perhaps even the seventh commandments!). Not surprisingly, this command was widened in later interpretation to cover generalized lying.

10. Uniquely, the last commandment seems to prohibit not a deed but an inner feeling. Some have distinguished the word used here (*ḥmd*) as denoting an action, whereas another word (*hitawweh*) denotes the mental attitude. In fact, *ḥmd* is a comprehensive term; it describes the inner state that often does lead to action. Jesus' interpretation of the parable of the sower (Mark 4:19) clarifies how deadly it is to harbor such cravings in the heart (see also Matt. 6:24-34).

Taken as a whole, the Ten Commandments offer comprehensive guidelines for the safeguarding of community life under the aegis of Yahweh. In form, the laws are "apodictic"; unlike case law, no stipulations are included detailing punishments. With solemn simplicity, these ten set the minimal borders around community life. To violate any of the ten is to step outside the covenant community, out of relationship with people and God. The juxtaposition of vertical and horizontal relationships, theological and social, unveils how following God will issue in responsibility toward the neighbor, how community relationships are the very stuff of obedience to God. Notably, all ten are written in the second person—not "one must not . . ." or "man shall not . . ." but "you shall not. . . ." Nothing could be more intensely personal than this style of speech, direct from God. It is little wonder these ten, while etched in stone and stored in the ark, have played a vital role as embodying the living will of God for the shaping of community life.

The tablets become the crucible in which Israel's identity is forged. Indeed, God's very own character is nowhere more fully revealed. Augustine and Luther grasped the depth of the decalogue; for Augustine, these commandments are the charter of freedom for the believing community; for Luther they offer instruction on the new life of freedom (Childs, 432). Our text is something of a "constitution" for Israel, or even a "bill of rights"—although the "rights" are all God's, the privileged relationship Israel's. Sibley Towner employs another image: "In function, the Ten Commandments can be compared to ten posts supporting the fence separating the viable community of Israel from the marauding beasts of disorder, confusion, and bloodshed howling outside the pale" (Paul J. Achtemeier et al., eds., *Harper's Bible Dictionary* [New York: Harper & Row, 1985], p. 1033).

Scholarly debate has been riveted on the linkages between Israelite law and ancient Near Eastern treaty making. Beyond question, though, both have the "historical prologue" as the basis of the relationship. Just as Mursilis, son of the great Shuppiluliumas the Hittite, protected Duppi-Tessub and the Amurru from alien invaders and so demands allegiance (in a treaty one century before the exodus), so also Yahweh has the right to issue orders to these people who have been so recently rescued from the jaws of Egypt. The commands are not thundered from heaven by an immortal, immutable deity, but by the one who heard the people cry, who came down, who lovingly gave life where there was no life. The storyteller will need to anchor the commandments in this context of unmerited salvation. God doesn't save them because they are perfect in obedience; rather, God mercifully saves them, and the commandments stretch out before them as the more long-lasting gift of life with God and with one another.

Similarly, clogged-up Christian ears need to hear the genuinely faithful attitude in Israel toward the law and its giver, nowhere more eloquently expressed than in Psalm 19.

The style, number, and rhythmic feel of the commandments indicate that they were intended for memorization and for common recital when the congregation gathered for worship. Certainly the tablets figured prominently in covenant renewal ceremonies (see comments on Josh. 24); perhaps a preacher offered up a contemporary exposition (Hos. 4). The commandments can speak powerfully in worship even today. Luther wanted them to be read as a preparation for the confession of sin. Calvin wanted them to be read after the declaration of pardon, as liberating directives for the newfound life of freedom in Christ. The Ten Commandments truly can come alive in the human story of every generation in manifold ways.

Retelling the Story

The children squirmed and whispered on their pallets near the fire. The moon was bright enough to cast shadows around the camp, and the black fabric of sky was covered with needle pricks of starlight. The old woman moved as silently as a breeze among the tossing, restless bodies of children. Finally she spoke.

"No one can sleep tonight," she said almost to herself. Faces reflecting the firelight appeared from under the blankets. "Would anyone like to hear a story?"

As soon as she said the word *story,* a great rustling of blankets could be heard as the children gathered closer to the fire. "What story would you like to hear?" she asked as she added several more sticks to the fire. A cloud of sparks rose from the embers.

"Tell us about the mountain of fire and smoke," a voice said from the darkness.

"Very well." The woman settled on an outcropping of stone near the fire. "It was after we had been brought out of slavery in Egypt, and we were afraid of everything. We were afraid to step into the corridor that crossed between the walls of water through the Sea of Reeds. After we arrived safely on the other side, we were afraid that we would starve to death. Never did we have to find our own food in Egypt. Though we had only slave rations to eat, still they came like the sunrise and sunset every day.

"And this Moses—we were afraid of him. Was he a trickster who had lured us into the wilderness to die? We had seen the plagues brought on the Egyptians, and some said that Moses was a very powerful magician. He claimed to be able to hear God speak and to understand the words, but who could know for sure?

"And we were afraid of the God of whom Moses spoke. This God's invisible presence attracted us as none of the statues in Egypt ever had; yet, at the same time it frightened us. How could you predict what a God you couldn't see might do? How could you influence such a God with your prayers or offerings? How could you know for sure if you were pleasing or displeasing such a God? We had no answers, but daily we fed upon the bread from heaven, which we found upon the ground.

"Finally, after three months we came to the mountain of God, and Moses told us that we would finally get to see the God whose hand had brought us out of slavery. We were to prepare ourselves by washing our clothes and preparing our racing hearts to see God on the mountain. Our husbands would not so much as kiss us, saying Moses warned against it. This continued for three days. We were ordered to go nowhere near the mountain, for if we touched it we would be put to death.

"Then we gathered to wait. A haze, like smoke, wrapped itself around the mountain like a cloak. Then the mountain began to tremble, but no more than we shook in our sandals at the sight. Then it seemed the entire mountain was ablaze, flames reaching out to us through the smoke. Moses' voice battered the wall of smoke and flame as he spoke to God. God's answer shook the very earth like rumbling thunder. It was all we could do not to scatter like startled birds.

As Moses came near the people, he thought, "How can I give them these commandments? If they break them, they will be condemning themselves to death." He turned and began to return to the mountain, but the elders grabbed the tablets and started to wrestle with Moses for them. Moses pulled them away from the elders but saw that the writing had disappeared from the tablets. "How can I give them this . . . this . . . nothing?" So he broke the tablets. (Judah Goldin, trans., *The Fathers According to Rabbi Nathan* [New Haven: Yale University Press, 1955], p. 20)

Someone asked a rabbi, "If God is so opposed to idols, why not destroy them instead of just telling people not to worship them?" "Have you seen how many things in the world people choose to worship?" replied the rabbi. "They worship the sun and moon, their houses and money, their nation and culture—even other human beings. If God destroyed all that we might worship, nothing would be left." (Plaut, p. 545)

The Sabbath is a gift to Israel, not a master that the people should be slaves to. For example, it is permitted to break the

" 'You tell us what God says, for if this is the way God speaks, the power of the divine voice will consume us.'

"These are the words that came like burning coals from our God of fire and smoke:

'I am the God who brought you out of Egypt, out of slavery, nothing else in all creation shall be God to you but me.

'You shall make no image of anything in all creation to worship as a God.

'You shall not use my name to do harm, for that is to misuse my name.

'You shall save the Sabbath as a holy time. You shall rest and allow everyone else in your household and communities to rest as well.

'You shall act in ways that honor your father and mother, for if your days are long upon the earth you will be parents as well.

'You shall not kill.

'You shall not be unfaithful to your wife or husband.

'You shall not steal.

'You shall not lie about your neighbor to the courts or to anyone else.

'You shall not desire to have anything that belongs to your neighbor.'

"Now, looking into the coals of our fire here, I remember those words and the night of fascination and terror we spent with our God. Each command is like a coal glowing in my heart's memory. I take them out so that they might set all your little hearts alight with that same fire we felt that night.

"Now off to bed with you all!"

Sabbath commandment to save a life so that the one saved may celebrate many more Sabbaths. (Plaut, p. 551)

The honor due parents is like the honor due God, because it takes three to give us birth: a mother, a father, and God. (Plaut, p. 559)

The commandment against stealing includes lying, according to the Talmud. Lying is simply stealing another's mind. Thus lying to either a Jew or a non-Jew is forbidden. (Plaut, p. 560)

The giving of the Torah can be compared to a child whose parents say, "Watch where you step. Don't trip and hurt yourself. Take care that you do not allow harm to come to yourself, because you are so precious to me." God gave the commandments to Israel because its people are more precious in the divine sight than are even the angels. (*Exodus Rabbah* 30.6)

Blood and the Covenant

A second time, the prologue to God's covenant.

The Story

The LORD said to Moses, 'Come up to the LORD, you and Aaron, Nadab and Abihu, and seventy of the Israelite elders. While you are still at a distance, you are to bow down; then Moses is to approach the LORD by himself, but not the others. The people must not go up with him.'

Moses went and repeated to the people all the words of the LORD, all his laws. With one voice the whole people answered, 'We will do everything the LORD has told us.' Moses wrote down all the words of the LORD. Early in the morning he built an altar at the foot of the mountain, and erected twelve sacred pillars for the twelve tribes of Israel. He sent the young men of Israel and they sacrificed bulls to the LORD as whole-offerings and shared-offerings. Moses took half the blood and put it in basins,and the other half he flung against the altar. Then he took the Book of the Covenant and read it aloud for the people to hear. They said, 'We shall obey, and do all that the LORD has said.' Moses then took the blood and flung it over the people, saying, 'This is the blood of the covenant which the LORD has made with you in the terms of this book.'

Moses went up with Aaron, Nadab, and Abihu, and seventy of the elders of Israel, and they saw the God of Israel. Under his feet there was, as it were, a pavement of sapphire, clear blue as the very heavens; but the LORD did not stretch out his hand against the leaders of Israel. They saw God; they ate and they drank. The LORD said to Moses, 'Come up to me on the mountain, stay there, and let me give you the stone tablets with the law and commandment I have written down for their instruction.' Moses with Joshua his assistant set off up the mountain of God; he said to the elders, 'Wait for us here until we come back to you. You have Aaron and Hur; if anyone has a dispute, let him go to them.'

So Moses went up the mountain and a cloud covered it. The glory of the LORD rested on Mount Sinai, and the cloud covered the mountain for six days; on the seventh day he called to Moses out of the cloud. To the Israelites the glory of the LORD looked like a devouring fire on the mountain-top. Moses entered the cloud and went up the mountain; there he stayed forty days and forty nights.

Comments on the Story

Since Moses was summoned by a thunderbolt into the dark cloud hovering over Sinai (20:18-21), God has spoken over one hundred verses, ranging from how to sell your daughter into slavery to capital punishment for striking your mother, from keeping your ox from goring people to who keeps the loose donkey that falls into an uncovered cistern, from eschewing gossip and the charging of interest to leaving the land fallow; and by all means, never boil a kid in its mother's milk! But all this is only the warm-up to the plethora of laws that stretch from Exodus 25 onward, through all of Leviticus, and dominating much of Numbers. While scholars can ascertain a gradual accumulation of legal casuistry in these chapters, the canonical storyline envisions Moses receiving it all in just a few weeks. How did Moses remember it all? Rabbi Yohanan claims that Moses memorized large blocks of ordinances each night. Being already advanced in years, though, Moses suffered from a spotty memory—until God miraculously granted him photographic recall (Silver, *Images of Moses,* p. 185). In Jewish tradition, all this covenant making took place fifty days after the exodus. Hence, the feast of Pentecost became the preeminent celebration of the gift of the Torah.

Our text is sandwiched between the first legal section (chaps. 20–23, often dubbed the "Covenant Code") and the lengthy blueprint for the tabernacle (chaps. 25–31). At the same time, the first legal section (20–23) finds itself sandwiched between our last "story" (the thunder and lightning of chap. 19) and our present passage (Exod. 24). In chapter 19, with temerity and trembling the people humbly approached God, with the startling commitment, "Whatever the Lord has said we will do" (19:8). The Lord hadn't said anything yet! But after the first one hundred verses of the Lord's speaking, the people in a sense have an opportunity to stick with it or to say, "No thanks. we'll go back to Egypt."

Moses repeats what the Lord has said. In unison they affirm once more, "We will do everything the Lord has told us" (24:3, reiterated in 24:7). An altar of a dozen symbolic pillars is erected. Bulls are butchered, and blood is flung upon the altar and upon the people, all climaxed by a sacred feast. The solemnity of these doings indicates that we have a glimpse of what was an ongoing ceremony. On perhaps a yearly schedule, the people would gather to hear the reading of the law. Blood was applied. Oaths were sworn. A sacred meal was shared. Blood was the agency of deliverance during the tenth plague, and blood will be the paradoxical "life" of Israel's worship. Hidden in the sacrificial blood is the very forgiving and healing life of God (see Heb. 9:18-22).

The seventy elders "ate and drank." How boldly our story claims in the same breath that "they saw God"! In chapter 33, even Moses sees only God's "backside," for "no mortal may see God and live" (33:20). The verb used in

24:11 for "see" is not the usual *r'h* (which connotes normal "looking at" with the eyes), but *ḥzh,* used throughout the Hebrew Bible to describe "prophetic" seeing. The "seer" sees not with eyes but with a sixth sense, granted by special dispensation. These elders are the forebears of later prophets, whose leadership is defined by what they "see" of God, which is never by the naked eye. Christians will grasp the links between Exodus 24 and that portentous moment when the two disciples find their hearts on fire over supper as Jesus explains the scriptures (Luke 24).

The Israelite Temple (as with its predecessor, the tabernacle) was designed to be a "paradise on earth," a meeting point between earth and heaven. Mount Sinai fills this same function, nowhere more mysteriously than in our text. On Sinai, earth touches heaven. An elusive, intimate togetherness with God happens here. In the meal, we get just a taste of paradise lost, of paradise regained (see Isa. 25:6-9). God is seen, and the language founders in its inadequacy to describe the glory of the divine presence. The REB captures the sense of the sapphire (stunning, translucent lapis lazuli) pavement with the phrase "as it were" ("There was something like a pavement of sapphire stone, like the very heaven for clearness" [Exod. 24:10 NRSV]). No archaeologist will ever find a sapphire pavement on any mountain in the Sinai peninsula. This mystical happening defies description. C. S. Lewis said that our human attempts to describe heaven are "guesses, of course, only guesses. If they are not true, something better will be" (*Letters to Malcolm* [New York: Harcourt Brace & World, 1964], p. 124). Somehow, by standing in a temple adorned with the likes of lapis lazuli, in hearing stories from those who have "seen," through sharing a meal, we get the best glimpse possible for mere mortals of what fellowship with God is like.

Strangely, the whole crowd is not privy to this encounter; yet, it is not vouchsafed to Moses alone. These men, Aaron, Nadab, Abihu, and the seventy elders creep into the story as the priesthood will later creep in between worshipers and their God. In Exodus 24, the elders and some select "young men" stand in for the as yet nonexistent priesthood. (God has not published the book of Leviticus yet). A gradation of closeness to God is prevalent in later Temple worship. Gentiles are relegated to the perimeter. Women encroach only a bit further. The men cannot get all the way in. A hierarchy within the priesthood progressively thins the crowd until finally only the highest of the high priests actually gets in to the holy of holies. We may cringe at the sexism; we may revel in the torn curtain of Good Friday. But in this story, the separateness was deemed crucial by the original narrator. We need neither disparage nor dismiss, but only tell the story.

The storyteller may profitably pull together threads from other analogous moments of covenant renewal. In Joshua 24, the people solemnly commit themselves to serve the Lord. Josiah hears the reading of the law book we call

Deuteronomy and launches sweeping reforms. Ezra's recitation of the law stands as the highest moment in post-exilic Judea.

Retelling the Story

Korah figured that he was known to Moses and the inner circle. Aaron had told him that soon he would be an elder and a ruler. Abihu and Nadab had been courting his favor now for weeks. He knew that he could not wait much longer.

He had paid his dues! All those years in Egypt lifting straw and making bricks, doing whatever he was told by one incompetent and brutal guard after another. He never did make foreman, and he resented it. Aaron warned him to keep his mouth shut and not make any waves, if Korah wanted to join their government and be in charge of people and goods some day.

Now this neverending marching and waiting. Now this God-awful diet of manna. Now this neverending thirst. Who is in charge around here anyway? What is Moses doing up there on the mountain? Praying? What happened to our revolution? We trounced the Egyptians. Where's the plan?

Aaron came near to Korah and waved him over to a boulder where they could talk in whispers. "This is very hard for me to explain. Moses has come down from his perch on the mountain, and he wants me to pick out seventy men who will be escorted up the mountain to hear how we are to run this community."

> When the people answered "in one voice," say the rabbis, at that moment those of low estate and those who were wealthy and powerful became one before God. (Plaut, p. 595)

"Moses specifically asked that you organize a building crew to start erecting twelve monuments near the mountain, one for each tribe of Israel."

Korah started to complain: "Not again! I am sick of building useless pillars. First for the pharaoh and now for Moses! Why are we building things here? Don't tell me that this is the Promised Land!"

Aaron responded sharply: "You'll get your chance. Prove yourself with this building task. Show how patient you must be to become an elder, and we'll discuss your future at another time."

Korah sputtered a few curses but was silenced as Aaron slapped him on the back and turned to go. "By the way," Aaron added, "make some basins for blood sacrifice too, and round up some young men to corner a dozen bulls."

Korah formed a work crew and built the pillars. While he was carving out a stone basin, he looked up toward Sinai and saw an incredible bluish glow, as bright as the sun on a slab of polished sapphire. "I should be up there," he mumbled to himself. "I don't know how much more of this grunt work I can take."

The people say they will do what God says before they say they will listen to the divine voice. The rabbis say that this indicated Israel's intent to follow the Torah even before they heard what would be required of them. The rabbis add that people whose good deeds exceed their understanding are wise, indeed. (Plaut, p. 595)

After a few hours the glow of the mountain faded, and the seventy elders glided down from Sinai with Moses, Aaron, Nadab, and Abihu. The bulls were sacrificed in the basins that Korah carved, and Moses read the Book of the Covenant to all the tribes of Israel.

As Moses launched one half of the blood of the sacrifice against the altar, he shared the meat of the bulls with the people to ratify the covenant God had made with the elders. He flung the rest of the blood over the worshipers nearby. A warm red spot soaked Korah to the skin near his heart as he heard the words of Moses, who said, "This is the blood of the covenant, which was shed for you."

The Golden Calf

The people become impatient when Moses fails to return from the mountain, and Aaron fashions a bull-calf of gold for them to worship.

The Story

When the people saw that Moses was so long in coming down from the mountain, they congregated before Aaron and said, 'Come, make us gods to go before us. As for this Moses, who brought us up from Egypt, we do not know what has become of him.' Aaron answered, 'Take the gold rings from the ears of your wives and daughters, and bring them to me.' So all the people stripped themselves of their gold earrings and brought them to Aaron. He received them from their hands, cast the metal in a mould, and made it into the image of a bull-calf; then they said, 'Israel, these are your gods that brought you up from Egypt.' Seeing this, Aaron built an altar in front of it and announced, 'Tomorrow there is to be a feast to the LORD.' Next day the people rose early, offered whole-offerings, and brought shared-offerings. After this they sat down to eat and drink and then gave themselves up to revelry.

The LORD said to Moses, 'Go down at once, for your people, the people you brought up from Egypt, have committed a monstrous act. They have lost no time in turning aside from the way which I commanded them to follow, and cast for themselves a metal image of a bull-calf; they have prostrated themselves before it, sacrificed to it, and said, "Israel, these are your gods that brought you up from Egypt.' " The LORD said to Moses, 'I have considered this people, and I see their stubbornness. Now, let me alone to pour out my anger on them, so that I may put an end to them and make a great nation spring from you.'

Moses set himself to placate the LORD his God: 'LORD,' he said, 'why pour out your anger on your people, whom you brought out of Egypt with great power and a strong hand? Why let the Egyptians say, "He meant evil when he took them out, to kill them in the mountains and wipe them off the face of the earth"? Turn from your anger, and think better of the evil you intend against your people. Remember Abraham, Isaac, and Israel, your servants, to whom you swore by your own self: "I shall make your descendants countless as the stars in the heavens, and all this land, of which I have spoken, I shall give to them, and they will possess it for ever." ' So the LORD thought better of the evil with which he had threatened his people.

Comments on the Story

This fascinating upstairs/downstairs story juxtaposes two simultaneous happenings. Up on the mountain, in the silent calm, hidden in the clouds, Moses listens to God. Down in the valley, in the frenzied cacophony of the worst kind of religiosity, the people rebel against what is going on up on the mountain. Deftly the writer exposes the enormity of human sinfulness, exemplifying the long history of humanity, stretching even into the late twentieth century.

For seven long chapters, the Lord has been doing quite a lot of "spaking" (to recall the KJV's dignified way of describing divine speech). The people's yawning silence, broken so pathetically in 32:1, began in 24:7. When they last spoke, their tune was "We shall obey and do all that the Lord has said." Their about-face in 32:1 proves that they are indeed "prone to wander." Are they resistant to all the "spaking"? or are they anxious over whether there will indeed be "any word from the Lord"? Wiesel is on target: "Despite the divine manifestations, the crossing of the Red Sea and the other miracles, something of this stiff-necked people had stayed behind in bondage in Egypt" (*Messengers of God,* p. 196).

The clever editor of Exodus sandwiches the boxed set of stories in chapters 32–34 between the detailed blueprints for the tabernacle (chaps. 25–31) and its actual construction (chaps. 35–40). But at the foot of Mt. Sinai, the people have received no memos about what is forthcoming. And, while we may criticize them for their forgetfulness, it has been forty days (v. 1: "so long") with no sign of Moses. Was he ever coming back? Had he been (as would be expected) devoured by the fiery divine presence? They half-feared he wouldn't come back; they half-feared he would! Skillfully the text portrays an emotional distance between the people and Moses to match the physical and temporal with a tiny Hebrew demonstrative, *zeh*: "As for *this* Moses. . . ." Heretofore he has not been the most celebrated of leaders; part of the function for this segment will be to establish most firmly Moses' (previously ambiguous) role as leader.

The pronouns in the dialogue are emphatic. The Lord's subtle reaction to the noxious revelry is a disclaimer, deeding the people over to the hapless Moses: They are "your" (not "my") people; "you" (not "I") delivered them. With temerity Moses deeds them right back in verse 11 ("your people whom you brought out"). The Lord even contemplates a new deluge to wipe out the people, preserving Moses as a new Abraham, the new progenitor of the promise (v. 10 matches Gen. 12:2). Indeed, the shock of the story is not that the Lord might destroy such people, but that Moses is actually able to stand in the breach and deter God's wrath! The Lord says, "Let me alone," but that is precisely what Moses will not do. How reminiscent of Jacob's "I will not let you go until you bless me" (Gen 32:26); Moses did have some of his great-great-grandfather's blood!

The upstairs/downstairs contrast is stunning: Aaron is too weak to restrain the people, but Moses is strong enough even to restrain God! Moses mounts a four-pronged defense of the accused before God, who is plaintiff, prosecutor, judge, and jury. Reminding God of earlier promises, of the earlier stories, Moses caps his argument by appealing to God's own sense of pride and honor: What will the Egyptians think? Won't God look foolish to have saved these people only to lose them so quickly (see Ezek. 20:14)? Pharaoh only enslaved them; will the Lord slay them?

The biblical God—not the omniscient, ineffable, infinite, absolute of philosophical theology—is unabashedly said to have changed the divine mind. God seems to "obey" Moses—a miracle that rivals the parting of any sea (see J. Clinton McCann's comments in "Exodus 32:1-14," *Interpretation* 44 [1990]: 278-81). The storyteller may with integrity play on the notion that God leaves the door slightly ajar for Moses, with a pregnant pause: "I'll destroy them. . . . Well, do you have anything to say?" God lets God's own self be persuaded. The story enfleshes grace most profoundly. The people know nothing of the mountaintop verdict. At the very moment God is relenting, they are indulging in a religious "orgy" (the root sense of *zhq,* "revelry," in v. 6). They are not getting their due! They are saved even before they know they have been indicted and condemned.

Aaron's self-defense is not as successful. In words reminiscent of the fall of Adam and Eve, Aaron faults the people: "You know how wicked *they* are" (v. 22). The Hebrew of verse 1 is ambiguous. Do they congregate "before" Aaron? "Around" him? "Against" him? Aaron himself probably wasn't sure. While in verse 4 Aaron "cast the metal in a mould and made it," his own revisionist history shrugs and wonders, placing the onus on some evidently higher power: "They gave the gold to me. I *threw* it in the fire, and *out came* this bull-calf." Out came? Aaron's job was to be a spokesman, not an innovator.

What were they really up to? Bull and calf images were extremely common in contemporary religion; the Apis bull of Memphis and the Mnevis bull of Heliopolis were renowned (see the photo in *Harper's Bible Dictionary* [1985], p. 145). Surely Aaron and the people weren't thinking that an Egyptian god delivered them from Egypt, although some have argued that Israel's yearning was to go back and worship the old Egyptian gods. In fact, the bull image was employed in many cultures. The bull or calf symbolized virility, vitality, and fertility.

Were the Israelites building a genuine idol in the sense of another God? Or were they merely trying to develop some symbol, so necessary for mortals in their religious practice? In a crucial sense, Israel downstairs got in trouble because they did not yet know what was going on upstairs. The tabernacle would fulfill what they sought through the bull. The cherubim, after all, were animal-like images fully endorsed by God. Of course, cherubim were mysterious, not exactly seen walking about in secular life, and they were basically hidden from view in the inner sanctum of the tabernacle. The bull, a well-known and often-used animal, was here publicly displayed. However vigorously the intentions of the Israelites might be defended (Aaron does proclaim a feast to the Lord in v. 5), the violation of the second commandment should have been clear; similarly the warnings of 23:32 were ignored.

The real purpose of the acquired gold (lifted humorously from Egypt) was to adorn the tabernacle. How risky to hoist the very image used by various foes. Even the Baal nemesis was imaged as a bull. Throughout Israel's history, the temptation was to take seemingly innocent elements from neighboring religions and make them "fit in" to Israel's worship. But a thread runs from Elijah through Hosea to Isaiah: no images, no syncretism, no accommodation. Even subtle compromise is intolerable in Israelite religion. A storyteller may profitably play upon the seeming innocence of the people. Indeed, religion itself often becomes the most pernicious vehicle of sinfulness in the human story.

So vividly etched in Israel's memory is the lapse of memory that this story became paradigmatic of all human rebellion. Repeatedly within Scripture, this image is reintroduced as the very epitome of sin. Psalm 106, well-paired in the lectionary with our text, singles out this moment when "they exchanged their God for the image of a bull; they forgot God their deliverer who had done great things." This travesty punctuates the great confession in Nehemiah 9 (vv. 16-19), Stephen's peroration (Acts 7:39-41), and Paul's warning to Corinth (I Cor. 10:7-8); indeed, Romans 1:25 may well mirror this incident. Like Stephen and Paul, Moses is even prepared to give up his own life (Exod. 32:32).

Indeed, the church fathers were zealous in parading this story as being indicative of Jewish intransigence. This kind of blatant anti-Semitism unmasks a nagging peril: Like Aaron, we are quick to point the finger rather than confess our own tendency toward idol making. Dare the storyteller actually name some modern-day bulls and calves we fashion in the very name of being religious? In our "therapeutic" society, are we not lured into doing whatever it takes to help people "feel good," enabling and indulging the idolatry of "religious needs"?

While the story could viably be retold from Nehemiah's or Stephen's or Paul's perspective, its fascinating links to I Kings 12 may offer an enriching point of view. Scholars have long noticed the odd plural in Exodus 32: gods. There was but one bull. But Jeroboam, the first king of the newly seceded northern kingdom of Israel, did commission a pair for the new sanctuaries of Bethel and Dan, with words identical to Aaron's in Exodus 32:4: "Here are your gods, Israel, that brought you up from Egypt" (I Kings 12:28). Jeroboam's intentions were probably honorable as well (in a sense, a bull would rally popular support), but he had crossed a theological threshold that earned him the highest censure (see I Kings 13).

The story has an even closer analogue in the fate of Saul. The people demand a physical, tangible substitute, a "king, like all the nations." Saul, too, grew anxious while waiting for Samuel (who almost seems to have been hiding behind a rock!). His own sacrifice, however religious and well-intended, was out of sync with God's mandate (I Sam. 8–15).

Moses, so calm in negotiating the verdict of grace upstairs, comes downstairs and flies into a rage. The staging is brilliant. First, Moses hears a noise that grows into a din. Then he sees with his eyes the sorry source of the racket. The suspense is shattered when the wrath of Moses (not God) "burns hot." Swiftly he reacts, as did Jesus in clearing the Temple. Throughout the world, smashing tablets was a well-known symbol for dissolving a contractual relationship. The sequence, burn/grind/sprinkle, is attested in texts from other cultures that want to dramatize the utter annihilation of a god/idol. The forced drinking of the mixture, perhaps reflective of the "ordeal" administered to ascertain adultery or lack thereof (see Num. 5:11-31), provides a poignant image of what the book of Isaiah calls "drinking the cup of the Lord's wrath to the dregs" (see Isa. 51:17, 22; Ps. 75:8).

The culminating stroke is at once the delight of militant revolutionaries and the nightmare of every pacifist. While the question, "Who is on the Lord's side?" may, out of context, be provocative, the draconian measures of the slaughter (were there three thousand or, as Paul has it, twenty-three thousand?) sound more like how the pharaoh would handle such misbehavior. Moses mobilizes his comrades (foreshadowing the Maccabean summons to arms in I Macc. 2:27). The text does not explicitly say that God ordered the bloodletting, but it's there, rather unique among these stories. Church leaders have justified capital punishment for heretics; many groups even today would justify "purges" in the name of revolution. The rabbis rationalized the vendetta: God must have ordered it. Such an "emergency measure" was not to be repeated; it was the "mixed multitude" that caused the problem. God orchestrated the whole affair precisely to unmask the idolaters in the crowd. The storyteller's luxury is not having to offer a rational explanation for what transpires. In this case, while the lectionary may wish to amputate the killing (as did Josephus), the biblical writer did think it worth passing along.

The story pairs the demanding severity of the Lord with the gracious loyalty of the Lord. The narrative is coming to grips with the very character of this Yahweh. The message is clear: The lukewarm may well be spat out. The drama forces a decision with unambiguous clarity: Who is on the Lord's side?

Retelling the Story

Moses was gone a very long time—forty days and forty nights. The people had no idea that Moses was in God's presence and was receiving further instructions from God. However, they feared that something had happened to God's spokesman and covenant mediator—the man who had led them out of Egypt. The people felt very vulnerable without him, and they began to say that he had disappeared.

Moses had left Aaron and the elders in charge while he was on the mountain with God. Aaron had no real authority of his own. Yet, he was very flattered when the people came to him and asked him to be their leader. He also saw an opportunity to seize power from his brother, Moses. The people wanted the gods to lead them. They rejected Moses' leadership for false gods. They did not really want Aaron to take Moses' place. Rather, they wanted a God over whom they had control, and they saw Aaron as one who could help them accomplish their rebellious goal.

The people of Israel had entered into a covenantal relationship with God. However, they wanted to renegotiate the covenant once they discovered that it was too demanding. They wanted God's help, but felt that God's demands were no longer in their best interest. Therefore, they decided to break the covenant.

> Earthly rulers hold the best interests of their citizens at heart, as long as those citizens are loyal. Earthly kings bestow gifts on their subjects as long as the subjects do not rebel against them. But with God things are different. While the children of Israel were rebelling and making a golden calf to worship, God was preparing the gift of the Torah to give to them. (*Exodus Rabbah* 41.4)

Aaron cooperated fully with the people. He showed them how they could produce a god. He told them to take off their rings of gold and bring them to him, and they obeyed. Aaron melted all their rings and from the molten gold fabricated a golden calf, explaining that it was a symbol of fertility. The people exclaimed, "These are your gods, O Israel, which brought you up out of the land of Egypt." When Aaron saw this, he built an altar and prepared to ratify a new covenant with this new god.

God observed everything that the people of Israel were doing. God went to Moses and said that Moses had been away from the people of Israel long enough and that it was time he returned to them. God warned Moses to go back to the people because they had become corrupt and had broken their covenant with God. "I told them that they should not have any gods before me. Now they have made themselves a golden calf. They have worshiped it, and they have sanctified it. They were even making fun of me! They say that this golden calf is the one who brought them out of the land of Egypt. I can't tolerate having these people attribute my acts to something else. This is beyond insult! They have made me angry, and now something must be done to punish them. They have spoiled my plans. I had chosen them to make for me a great nation, but now they have let me down."

Moses began to talk to God. He told God to calm down—with great respect, of course. He then began to intercede with God on behalf of the people of Israel. Moses asked, "Why get so angry?" After all, it was God who had brought the people out of Egypt. Moses reminded God that perhaps even the Egyptians would question why God had brought the people out of their land. Was it only for some evil intent? Then Moses, in a bold move, told God to turn from wrath and repent of this evil feeling against the people of Israel. Moses called to God's mind the promises made to Abraham, Isaac, and Israel—that they would inherit a land and become a great nation. The Lord actually listened to Moses and repented of the wrath that was intended for the children of Israel.

Some say that God paved the way for Moses' pleading for the people by the very way the divine words of rebuke were spoken. It was like a friend who has something difficult to say to another but does not want to be alienated from that friend. God's gentle words provide the pathway of mercy that Moses walked for the people. (*Exodus Rabbah* 42.2)

The rabbis say that Moses acted as the defense attorney for the children of Israel. When he saw that God was about to destroy the people for worshiping the golden calf, Moses knew that if no one took their side they would vanish from the face of the earth. So he quickly began to remind God of all the stories of the people's faithfulness. After hearing these stories, God decided to give these wayward children another chance. (*Exodus Rabbah* 42.1)

Moses Glimpses God

Moses asks to view God's glory and is allowed a brief glimpse of God's back.

The Story

Moses said to the LORD, 'You tell me to lead up this people without letting me know whom you will send with me, even though you have said to me, "I know you by name, and, what is more, you have found favour with me." If I have indeed won your favour, then teach me to know your ways, so that I can know you and continue in favour with you, for this nation is your own people.' The LORD answered, 'I shall go myself and set your mind at rest.' Moses said to him, 'Indeed if you do not go yourself, do not send us up from here; for how can it ever be known that I and your people have found favour with you, except by your going with us? So we shall be distinct, I and your people, from all the peoples on earth.' The LORD said to Moses, 'I shall do what you have asked, because you have found favour with me, and I know you by name.'

But Moses prayed, 'Show me your glory.' The LORD answered, 'I shall make all my goodness pass before you, and I shall pronounce in your hearing the name "LORD". I shall be gracious to whom I shall be gracious, and I shall have compassion on whom I shall have compassion.' But he added, 'My face you cannot see, for no mortal may see me and live.' The LORD said, 'Here is a place beside me. Take your stand on the rock and, when my glory passes by, I shall put you in a crevice of the rock and cover you with my hand until I have passed by. Then I shall take away my hand, and you will see my back, but my face must not be seen.'

Comments on the Story

God graciously changes the divine mind in Genesis 32:14, but chapter 33 opens with the people in grave danger of being burnt to a crisp. On the edge of our seats, we await God's next step, for it is upon God alone that the future depends. The whole section (chaps. 32–34) seems riddled with inconsistencies—a problem that has vexed dozens of commentaries that divide the text into literary strands. But even if there were unanimity regarding how such division should be made (and there is none), the resulting clean and sensible storyline would rob the canonical text of its vital tension, which seems to be an exploration along the exceedingly tenuous line between protection in the shadow of God's presence and extinction in the fire of that same presence. In the text as it stands, the consequences of sin are still being felt. "Ornaments" are removed in mourning and repentance. Not quickly will Israel take the holiness of God for granted again. According to the Talmud, Israel refused the Torah until God threatened to drop a mountain down on top of them. They accepted the Torah in lieu of death (Wiesel, *Messenger of God,* p. 195).

Scholars have unraveled the various bits of ancient lore to find two traditions about a portable holy place. Was there a full-blown tabernacle, complete with appurtenances, in the center of the camp (Num. 2:17), attended by Levites (Num. 3:5ff.)? Or was there the smaller "tent of meeting" just outside the camp (Num. 11:26), attended by Joshua, a private oracle of sorts for Moses? Or both? The smaller "tent of meeting" is somehow more primitive, more original. And the tabernacle is made to sound like the later Jerusalem Temple in its dimensions and appointments. Since the space "outside the camp" is usually a place of impurity, has the spatial element been inverted, the people "in camp" having proven themselves unworthy of the divine presence? The sinister rebellion in Exodus 32 has brought on a delay. The tabernacle will not be constructed just yet. But in the meantime, there will be a focal "meeting point"—namely, the tent of meeting—for interactions between God and the people, with Moses as intermediary.

The *Common Lectionary* rivets our attention on the remarkable tête-à-tête between Moses and the Lord in 33:12-23. Moses, perhaps teasingly, expresses his need for a guide as they move out into the uncharted wilderness. Perhaps he wants Hobab (Num. 10:31), or perhaps more subtly he is hoping for the restoration of the Lord's guidance. Ultimately, it is this divine guidance that is sorely needed on the journey. Any ancient would understand this issue: Will the Lord stay here on this mountain or come with us? The people indeed want the Lord to go with them. At the same time a certain ambivalence is unveiled, for in Israel there is a persistent tendency to try to contain this Lord, to corner him, to localize the presence. (Consider the Lord's resistance to the building of a temple in II Sam. 7.) Of greater importance is the identity of this God—and the evolving identity of Moses. All the repartee about "knowing you by name" ought to conjure up the memory of that much earlier meeting on this same mountain. At the burning bush, names were exchanged; only now are the identities being fleshed out.

How tantalizingly the conversation ends! Moses wants to see God's "glory"; whatever that may be in itself, the human perception of it as blinding luminosity makes it simply too threatening for mere mortals. Responsive, yet with a merciful divine reserve, the Lord substitutes "goodness" for "glory" and promises to utter his actual name (how was it pronounced?). The sense of the verbal name is probably nowhere better encapsulated than in verse 19. While our ears may strain to hear double predestination in this couplet, the sense of it

109

is all mercy, all compassion, a grace not at all dependent on human merit, deserts, or calculation.

The mystery of the Lord passing by, the putting of Moses safely into a crevice in the rock, the "hand" shielding Moses' view, the notion of God's "back" as opposed to God's "face"—all are stunningly graphic anthropomorphisms that simply cannot be explained or even translated into some other language, terminology, or metaphorical scheme. In the "tent" Moses speaks "face-to-face," but here he cannot see the "face" of God. In vain the reader will look for some internal logic to the dialogue and its terminology of the divine presence. Childs would chalk it up to "an emotional tone of the highest intensity" (Childs, 594). Beyond doubt, language can never stretch itself into enough extravagance to describe the transcendent adequately or sensibly; it is little wonder that visionary talk in the Bible is so fantastic. The storyteller had best shrink before the mystery. Perhaps after removing one's sandals, the literally stark-naked data of the encounter may be related to listeners who in humble incomprehension can only say "Wow!"

The only mortal who may have been vouchsafed some glimmer of what this was all about was Elijah; the equally elusive story in I Kings 19 (which shares this same mountain setting) may be told for comparison. We need look no further for reasons why the transfigured Jesus is situated with Moses and Elijah. What is beyond questioning in the text is the stirring sense of the mercy of God and the desire of God to grant fellowship. God could just have said "No, it's impossible." But God works around human frailty, mercifully condescending to give the greatest possible access to at least this one mortal. And this one mortal wrests a sorely needed concession from the Lord: God will journey with the people.

A dramatic movement from the ruptured covenant (chap. 32) to the restored covenant (chap. 34) is mysteriously taking place. This God cannot tolerate sin; yet, God would not destroy the sinners. Any telling of the story "must preserve the tension which lies at the heart of a God who is both fiercely demanding and unfailingly forgiving" (McCann, "Exodus 32:1-14"). For Christians, that tension is embodied in the cross of Christ. Indeed, when Martin Luther was asked about this "backside" of God in Exodus 33, he proclaimed that, in the crucifixion, God mercifully shows us all we mortals can bear: the hidden "backside" of God.

Retelling the Story

Moses sought assurance from God that God would support the people of Israel in spite of their sins of idolatry when they had worshiped the golden calf. God told Moses to tell the people to continue their journey toward the land that had been promised to Abraham, Isaac, and Jacob. God promised that an angel would go with them and that obstacles would be removed from their path. However, God said to Moses: "I will not go among you lest I consume you on the way, for you are a rebellious people."

Moses had the habit of speaking very frankly with God. He didn't worry about being charged with insubordination or about suffering retaliation from God. Furthermore, he had some questions he wanted God to answer.

Moses indicated to God that he understood God's instructions. Moses knew that he was to lead the people to the Promised Land. He wanted to know whom God would send if God did not plan to accompany him. God assured Moses that God's presence would definitely be with him. Moses did not hear God clearly, so he questioned God again: "If your presence will not accompany me, leave us here, and we shall go no further." Moses was having difficulty understanding God's purpose. He was wondering whether God was planning to forsake the people of Israel.

> In what voice did God speak to Moses? Knowing that humans were not used to divine utterance, God debated whether to speak in a loud or a soft voice. The loud voice might frighten Moses unnecessarily, while the soft voice might lead Moses to take God's words too lightly. So God spoke in the voice of Moses' father, and at first Moses asked, "What is my father doing here?" God replied, "I am not your father, but your father's God." (*Exodus Rabbah* 45.5)

Moses insisted that he needed assurances of God's intent. He wanted God's presence, God's protection, and God's continued leadership of the people of Israel. God responded to Moses' concern very favorably, saying: "The very thing that I have spoken to you I will do; do not worry. You and the people of Israel have again found favor with me."

Moses was delighted with God's reassurance. Then Moses said that he wanted to see the character of God revealed in its fullness. Moses wanted full disclosure from God. God was very patient with Moses and granted his request. God decided to let Moses see God's goodness as an additional way of reassuring him. God had forgiven Israel because of Moses' intercession, and God decided to affirm this through self-revelation. This self-revelation was given as a sign of God's grace and mercy. God wanted to confirm to Moses and the people of Israel that God was merciful as well as judgmental.

God warned Moses, "My presence is too much for you to see. No one can see God's face and live." However, God told Moses where he could stand so he would not be harmed as God passed by. God explained to Moses that God's hand would cover him as added protection as God passed by. Further, God told Moses, "I will take away my hand, and you will see my back, but my face will not be seen." Thus God reassured Moses that God was compassionate and mer-

Rabbi Hillel said, "When I sit at the feet of scholars is the time I stand tallest. But when I am praised and flattered by others, that is the time I am about to fall. Whenever I exalt myself, I am humbled. But when I humble myself, then I am exalted." Moses exalted himself by asking to see the divine presence, but he was humbled by seeing God from behind. (*Exodus Rabbah* 14.5)

ciful and could forgive the sins of the people of Israel.

· Moses' Shining Face

When Moses came down the mountain from being with God, his face shone so that he had to wear a veil.

The Story

At length Moses came down from Mount Sinai with the two stone tablets of the Testimony in his hands, and when he came down, he did not know that the skin of his face shone because he had been talking with the LORD. When Aaron and the Israelites saw how the skin of Moses' face shone, they were afraid to approach him. He called out to them, and Aaron and all the chiefs in the community turned towards him. Moses spoke to them, and after that all the Israelites drew near. He gave them all the commands with which the LORD had charged him on Mount Sinai.

When Moses finished what he had to say, he put a veil over his face. But whenever he went in before the LORD to speak with him, he left the veil off until he came out. Then he would go out and tell the Israelites all the commands he had received. The Israelites would see how the skin of Moses' face shone, and he would put the veil back over his face until he went in again to speak with the LORD.

Comments on the Story

Chapter 34 recounts the climactic restoration of the covenant that was broken in chapter 32; symbolically God rewrites the tablets. A parallel narrative is that of Noah. God is grieved over human rebellion, but in the end makes a compact within God's own heart and with humanity, symbolized in the rainbow. Here God makes the same resolution with the chosen people, ratified by the tablets. The covenant is renewed. Perhaps Israel savored this happy resolution to the calf-making incident with special gratitude at later "covenant renewal" ceremonies.

As Plaut put it so well, "The newly liberated people struggle to understand their God and, as it were, God struggles to understand His people" (Plaut, 643). The gradual unveiling of the divine identity takes another step forward in verses 5-7, in which the Lord utters the holy name once more, adding qualifiers—hardly timeless attributes, but those hard lessons from the calf episode. The nature of the Lord is further elaborated in verses 10-28; miracles are to be granted, but the greater miracle seems to be the Lord's expectation that com-

113

mandments will be obeyed. How ominously they resound in the ears of those familiar with Israel's subsequent history (the commandments repeat specific directives in chaps. 13 and 23). Alliances indeed proved to be a snare (see Isa. 28–32); syncretistic altars poisoned Israel's life. Bordering on satire, the Lord makes the "no images" commandment pointedly specific: "Do not (again) make yourselves gods of cast metal."

The lectionary for Transfiguration Sunday neatly carves for us the glorious but baffling verses 29-35. Yet, it is crucial for readers to remember that the experience of Moses is set in the context of law-giving on Mt. Sinai and in his role as intermediary for the people of Israel. This is no private beatific vision for Moses' own edification and enjoyment. The writer's purpose, beyond sharing what is a truly stunning encounter between the Lord and a mere mortal, is to illustrate the shoring up of Moses' authority (compare Num. 12, where Miriam and Aaron challenge his privilege). The radical shift from the people's cynical readiness to dispense with Moses in chapter 32 ("that fellow Moses . . .") to their recognition of his indispensability comes to a climax in these verses.

The vignette is surprising and almost out of character. Elsewhere, the storyteller seems at pains to deemphasize Moses as being heroic in any sense. Usually he is basically a cipher, a pure instrument in the Lord's hands. Perhaps it is the blessing of such an emptiness, of such a will to be an "earthen vessel," to come to radiate God's very own glory (in the attempted coup in Num. 12, Moses is called "a man of great humility, the most humble man on earth"). Personal features would shroud the divine glory. As they recede, the glory shines more brightly.

Moses uses a "veil" (*masveh*), apparently out of mercy for those not as "enlightened" as he. Scholars have been quick to point to a variety of masks worn by priests and shamans in ancient cultures, even in Egypt and Mesopotamia, as being somehow parallel to Moses' veil. Strangely enough, though, Moses' veil is worn, unlike those of other primitive priests, when he is functioning as a normal person and is removed when he performs his cultic duties. Yet, does the text really mean to say that Moses wore the mask during all of his civilian hours? Or just for a "cooling off" period after a meeting with God? If he wore the mask all the time, we might imagine that his social life would suffer! If he wore it only for short periods, though, the mask would be comparable to Egyptian and Mesopotamian holy masks. The next time Moses is summoned, it is into the tabernacle, not onto the mountain. In our broader storyline, then, the Sinai experience was unique. Even Moses was not granted a second audience of such splendor; similarly, the Transfiguration occurs but once.

Of course, in other passages God's own face is figuratively spoken of as "shining" (Num. 6:25). With awe Israel must have recounted this literal shining that left even a residual "afterglow" of sorts on Moses' own face. We are not looking at some generalized facial expression (we might, for instance, speak of the parents of a newborn baby "glowing" or "beaming"). What happens with Moses is unique, never again observed, even among the likes of Samuel, David, Elijah, or Ezra.

Paul picks up on this glory in II Corinthians 3:7-18. The storyteller observes Paul's reinterpretation of the original story. Emphatically the apostle assumes that the reader understands his enigmatic addition, which describes the glory as "fading." Exodus does not say that it fades, but Exodus also never mentions the glowing after chapter 34. A hermeneutical tradition must be lurking in the background; perhaps early Jewish interpreters read Exodus 40:35 (according to which Moses cannot enter the tent because of the divine glory) and extrapolated a loss of the radiance. Paul exploits this mercilessly.

While the storyteller could tell the story from Paul's perspective, an even more fascinating approach might be taken from the history of Christian art. San Pietro in Vincoli, one of Rome's many sumptuous churches, is adorned on its right hand nave by Michelangelo's duly famous sculpture of Moses. Brimming with vitality, power, and resolve, this Moses certainly does appear as if about to rise from his seat. Michelangelo, though, was hardly the originator of the statue's most curious feature: the horns. In painting, fresco, and iconography of various sorts, Moses is pictured as having horns. The reason? When verse 29 reports that his face was radiant, the Hebrew verb used is *qaran*. Because *qeren* was originally linked etymologically to the Hebrew word for "horn," error was bound to creep in. The Latin Vulgate took the *qrn* root and rendered it *cornuta esset*, "was horned." Again, in the ancient world, horns were a sign of power and authority. However, by the Middle Ages, practically demonic associations cast a pall over popular (mis)understandings of Moses.

Retelling the Story

God had forgiven the people of Israel, had renewed the covenant they had broken, and had rewritten the commandments on two tablets of stone. Moses received these new tablets of stone while on Mt. Sinai in the presence of God. Moses was with God forty days and forty nights without food or drink.

Moses came down out of the mountain with the two tablets of commandments in his hand. He had no way of

The rabbis say that part of the law given to Moses was written and part was preserved orally. When Moses asked why he was not to write the Talmud, Mishna, and Haggadah as well as the Torah, God replied, "There will come a time when idol worshipers will overtake my people and take the written words away, but the words that are written on their hearts can never be taken away." So the Torah was given in writing, but the Talmud, Mishna, and Haggadah were all passed on by word of mouth. (*Exodus Rabbah 47.1*) knowing that the skin on his face shone brightly because of what he had seen. When Aaron and the others saw Moses and that his skin shone brightly, they were afraid to go near him.

They began to wonder what had gone on while Moses was gone. They began talking among themselves. One person said, "Surely it must be God's presence shining through Moses." "Can't you remember we reacted with the same fear when God spoke to us directly?" said another. Another spoke up, "Yes, I remember. It was quite a time. It was dangerous and wonderful at the same time." Another spoke up, "I was afraid for God to see me. I felt so inadequate and unworthy in God's presence. I would have done anything to get away from God that day. I really didn't like myself on that day."

Moses' shining face may have been a reflection of God's light. Discussing why God created light before creating the world, the rabbis suggest that God is like a king who wants to build a palace in a dark grove and lights torches so the workers can see to work. How did God light the world? The Holy One put on a robe of light, and the whole world was illuminated by its shining. Perhaps this is what Moses glimpsed in the cleft of the rock and why his face shone afterward. (*Exodus Rabbah* 50.1)

Those seeing Moses began to look at themselves again. One person spoke up, "Seeing Moses come down the mountain reminds me of the fact that we broke the covenant. I surely don't want to face Moses at all. I am sure that he has some very negative words to bring from God about our behavior. I just can't bear to hear God speaking through Moses."

Moses had no idea that the people of Israel saw God's presence in him. He saw them shrinking back from him with fear, but he called out to them. In spite of their fears and uneasiness, Aaron and the rest of the people of Israel returned to Moses. He began to talk to them and to recount the words that had come to him from God.

Moses told them about everything that had taken place. He told them how God was angry and wanted to disown them. They asked Moses why God had not let the wrath and anger be God's last word. Moses explained that God was not only a judge, but that God was also merciful and gracious. He told them that God still had the promise in mind and that the people of Israel were still central to those plans. Furthermore, he said that God had reconsidered and decided to renew the covenant in spite of their sins.

Manna and Meat

God provides manna, meat, and seventy leaders for the people.

The Story

The people began complaining loudly to the LORD about their hardships, and when he heard he became angry. Fire from the LORD broke out among them, and raged on the outskirts of the camp. Moses, when appealed to by the people, interceded with the LORD, and the fire died down. They named that place Taberah, because fire from the LORD had burned among them.

A mixed company of strangers had joined the Israelites, and these people began to be greedy for better things. Even the Israelites themselves with renewed weeping cried out, 'If only we had meat! Remember how in Egypt we had fish for the asking, cucumbers and watermelons, leeks and onions and garlic. Now our appetite is gone; wherever we look there is nothing except this manna. (The manna looked like coriander seed, the colour of bdellium. The people went about collecting it to grind in handmills or pound in mortars; they cooked it in a pot and made it into cakes, which tasted like butter-cakes. When dew fell on the camp at night, the manna would fall with it.) Moses heard all the people lamenting in their families at the opening of their tents. The LORD became very angry, and Moses was troubled, and said to the LORD, 'Why

have you brought trouble on your servant? How have I displeased the LORD that I am burdened with all this people? Am I their mother? Have I brought them into the world, and am I called on to carry them in my arms, like a nurse with a baby, to the land promised by you on oath to their fathers? Where am I to find meat to give them all? They pester me with their wailing and their "Give us meat to eat." This whole people is a burden too heavy for me; I cannot carry it alone. If that is your purpose for me, then kill me outright: if I have found favour with you, spare me this trouble afflicting me.'

The LORD answered Moses, 'Assemble for me seventy of Israel's elders, men known to you as elders and officers in the community; bring them to the Tent of Meeting, and there let them take their place with you. I shall come down and speak with you there. I shall withdraw part of the spirit which is conferred on you and bestow it on them, and they will share with you the burden of the people; then you will not have to bear it alone. And say to the people: Sanctify yourselves in readiness for tomorrow; you will have meat to eat. You wailed in the LORD's hearing; you said, "If only we had meat! In Egypt we lived well." The

LORD will give you meat and you will eat it. Not for one day only, nor for two days, nor five, nor ten, nor twenty, but for a whole month you will eat it until it comes out at your nostrils and makes you sick; because you have rejected the LORD who is in your midst, wailing in his presence and saying, "Why did we ever come out of Egypt?" '

Moses said, 'Here am I with six hundred thousand men on the march around me, and you promise them meat to eat for a whole month! How can the sheep and oxen be slaughtered that would be enough for them? If all the fish in the sea could be caught, would they be enough?' The LORD replied, 'Is there a limit to the power of the LORD? You will now see whether or not my words come true.'

Moses went out and told the people what the LORD had said. He assembled seventy men from the elders of the people and stationed them round the Tent. Then the LORD descended in the cloud and spoke to him. He withdrew part of the spirit which had been conferred on Moses and bestowed it on the seventy elders; as the spirit alighted on them, they were seized by a prophetic ecstasy, for the first and only time.

Two men, one named Eldad and theother Medad, who had been enrolled with the seventy, were left behind in the camp. Though they had not gone out to the Tent, the spirit alighted on them none the less, and they were seized by prophetic ecstasy there in the camp. A young man ran and told Moses that Eldad and Medad were in an ecstasy in the camp, whereupon Joshua son of Nun, who had served since boyhood with Moses, broke in, 'Moses my lord, stop them!' But Moses said to him, 'Are you jealous on my account? I wish that all the LORD'S people were prophets and that the LORD would bestow his spirit on them all!' Moses then rejoined the camp with the elders of Israel.

There sprang up a wind from the LORD, which drove quails in from the west, and they were flying all round the camp for the distance of a day's journey, three feet above the ground. The people were busy gathering quails all that day and night, and all next day, and even those who got least gathered ten homers of them. They spread them out to dry all about the camp. But the meat was scarcely between their teeth, and they had not so much as bitten it, when the LORD'S anger flared up against the people and he struck them with a severe plague. That place came to be called Kibrothhattaavah, because there they buried the people who had been greedy for meat.

Comments on the Story

In the Hebrew Bible, the book of Numbers is titled "In the Wilderness." Indeed, after the throng is numbered (the census in chap. 1 explains the title "Numbers"), and after extensive orders for marching and holiness are issued, the people are herded into the wilderness for an unexpectedly long, tortuous journey. The march, which should have taken days, was protracted into forty years of loitering about. Having at long last broken camp at Sinai, the Israelites are a mere three days into their trek toward the Promised Land. Why are we

not really surprised to learn that they begin complaining? With growing inso-
lence they complain "loudly" ("bitterly," Jewish Publication Society's [JPS]
translation of the Torah), not just to Moses but directly to the Lord (literally "in
the ears of the Lord"). Perhaps scarcity of water was the issue (as in Exod.
15:22). Like Esau, stupidly swapping his birthright for some grub, Israel suf-
fers from shortsightedness. The Lord answers their astigmatism with fire (perhaps a bolt of lightning)—an unwanted display of God's miraculous power.
Their pace slows to a dawdle and finally to a grinding halt.

The previously unnamed site of God's fiery reminder is called "Taberah,"
meaning "burning," a reminder no less haunting than the next stop on the
itinerary: Kibroth-hattaavah, translated "the graves of those who craved." Not
exactly the stuff of pilgrimage, places with names and memories like this pair
are better forgotten. Their exact location is uncertain, but probably the mob
was inching along the coast of the Gulf of Eilat (or perhaps even the Gulf of
Suez), an arid flatland not totally bereft of vegetation. To this day, mass movements of quail swarm across the Sinai, from the south in the spring, from the
north in autumn, wafted aloft by strong winds off the Mediterranean or the Red
Sea (see Ps. 78:26). Flopping on the turf in exhaustion, the quail are easily
trapped. This familiar occurrence was perceived as divine intervention, so
swift was their arrival after the prayer of Moses.

Like most biblical narratives, this story proceeds principally by dialogue.
Notice the parallel sequence of events right after Israel left Egypt. After three
days, they complain (Exod. 15:22-27), but this time God's reply is not water but
fire. Next, they specifically grumble for food, heaping on top the curious longing to return to Egypt (Exod. 16). At least there was food in Egypt. But surely
extended exposure to the Sinai sun has improved Israel's memory of conditions
in Egypt, which was known as the breadbasket of the world, even as the world's
"vegetable garden" (see Deut. 11:10). Fish were available (and inexpensive) in
Egypt. But what was really being boiled in the "fleshpots" of Egypt? Not
gourmet delicacies for the Hebrew palate, but literal Hebrew flesh for the
pharaoh's pleasure! The diet of manna, not as substantive as fish or melons, was
at least partaken in freedom. Surely, to later generations this yearning for Egypt
looked like materialism, the same urge that leads the prodigal son into a far-
away country, only to learn he has chosen a pig sty over his father's mansion.

Admittedly, the manna was repetitive, eaten at each meal, every day. Verses
7-9 defend the heavenly cuisine: The manna was easy to spot, easy to pick,
clean, rich and creamy in taste, and free (see Milgrom, p. 84). If you grew tired
of grinding it between millstones, you could pound it with a pestle. With a discerning eye, the narrator sees an exotic color in the blasé manna—and it was
not even all that monotonous, being edible raw or boiled, and kneadable into
tasty cakes. The rabbis even argued that it amazingly took on a unique flavor
agreeable to each person.

Moses' response is not easy to interpret. He cannot feed them; he cannot lead them; death seems the most pleasant option. But the Hebrew of verse 10 (REB: "Moses was troubled") means literally "It was evil in the eyes of Moses." But what was evil? Their belly-aching? The Lord's getting them into such a quandary? Verse 11 straddles the fence; Moses seems to be as uncomfortable as the mob, but with the additional burden of his role as leader. Echoing God's impersonal pronoun from the golden calf travesty (Exod. 32:9), Moses calls them "this" (not "my" or "your") people. As sarcastic as Cain ("Am I my brother's keeper?"), Moses takes a maternal approach, distressed over the more unpleasant tasks of motherhood (birth pains, nursing, aching back, lost sleep, even diapering—all are appropriate here). The storyteller might exploit the question "Am I their mother?"

Foreshadowing another disastrous pronoun selection in Numbers 20 (see below), Moses, strangely out of character but in unmistakable frustration, wonders aloud, "Where am I to find meat? They are too heavy for me; I cannot carry them." The storyteller may delve into this outburst from the one not divinely charged with meat-finding or carrying.

God answers Moses' "burnout" with the provision of seventy elders, who will share leadership responsibilities. Are these the same seventy from Mt. Sinai (Exod. 24:1)? The number may be symbolic: Jacob's original entourage in Egypt was seventy; the worldwide genealogy after the flood charts seventy nations; neighboring countries instituted councils of seventy; and the Sanhedrin of New Testament times was composed of seventy men.

But clearly the principle of delegated leadership would find its legitimation in this story. The seventy are gifted with the "Spirit" of God. The Hebrew word *ruah* means at once "Spirit" and "wind." God restrains the primordial waters in creation with this *ruah* (Gen. 1:2); the flood waters (Gen. 8:1) and the "sea of reeds" (Exod. 14:21) are dried up by the *ruah*; the *ruah* stirs "bones" (Ezek. 37) to shake, rattle, and rise—so forcefully does the Lord grab hold of individuals (see the early stories of prophets in I Sam. 10:10; 19:20). But is this praiseworthy gift of God's Spirit really largess for Moses? Or is it a punishment of sorts? As verse 25 intimates, the full measure of the *ruah* is drained from him! Punishment wouldn't be out of order; Moses has had some cross words for the Lord. Joshua feels compelled to shore up Moses' authority, but Moses wishes for a dosage of prophecy upon them all (see Joel 3:1; Acts 2), a genuine priesthood of all believers (Exod. 19:6; I Pet. 2:5-9).

Does the story try to absolve pure-bred descendants of Jacob? Verse 4 singles out the "mixed company of strangers" (the assonance of *asafsuf* is brilliantly captured by the JPS: "riffraff") as the instigators of the grumbling. Furthermore, in the Hebrew of verse 33, "the people" is preceded by a little *b,* which probably means "some of." Did God's wrath truly rage against only "some of" them—presumably the "riffraff"? Certainly non-Israelites had jumped on the liberation bandwagon (see Exod. 12:38). Isn't it likely that, out in the wilderness, the newcomers—the outsiders—provided handy scapegoats? Isn't this the same trait that made Adam point the finger at Eve? By the end of verse 4, the entire crowd, as wholeheartedly as Adam, plunges into whining.

The Lord doles out an ironic thrashing: "You asked for it." They ask for meat and gorge themselves on the "gift" of quail. A "homer" is somewhere between six and fourteen bushels; even those who got least gathered ten homers—a minimum of sixty bushels (almost five hundred gallons)! What a contrast to the single "omer" (not "homer") of daily manna—about one-half gallon, a sufficient amount of food. It is little wonder that they were sickened by their own greed! As Mays discerned so well, "Israel had the fixation, common to all religions, which associated God with success. She wanted her religion to 'work' " (*Leviticus, Numbers,* p. 87).

Retelling the Story

The people of Israel found life in the wilderness very difficult. There were no assurances that the variety of food they ate in Egypt would be provided. Rather, the diet they ate in the wilderness was very boring and tiresome. They consumed the same thing every day—water and manna. They grew very weary of this predictable diet. There were very few pleasures they could enjoy in the wilderness, and they felt that eating at least should be one of those pleasures.

Manna, a gummy substance found on the ground in the morning dew, was what God had provided in the desert for food for the people of Israel. Manna was sweet and sticky, the size of popcorn, and yellowish in color. Many called the substance "the bread which the Lord had given." It satisfied the people's hunger.

The people of Israel would prepare the manna in several ways. They boiled it, baked it, flaked it, and shook it. They wanted something more. They wanted more variety.

One of the Israelites who was most bored with this diet spoke up. He began to find others who were as unhappy with the food as he was. Then he began to complain about the food publicly. His complaints struck a responsive cord in others.

Their complaints went something like this: "Moses, through the inspiration of God, has brought us here into the desert to have us die of danger and bad food. At least in bondage in Egypt the food was plentiful and rich in variety. We did not have to eat the same thing day in and day out. Do you remember what we used to eat in Egypt? Think about it. The food in Egypt was great. There were not only the choicest meats, but also there were fruits, vegetables, spices, and herbs. There were cucumbers, melons, leeks, onions, and garlic. This manna can be prepared in only a few ways, but in Egypt there were many different flavorings to add taste to the food. Here we have nothing."

Moses heard the complaints of the people. He knew that they were blaming him for their unhappiness with the food, and he was very upset with the people. He couldn't understand why they complained so much and craved the food that they could get only in slavery. Moses thought, "Not long ago these same people were complaining that the Egyptian taskmasters were cruel and harsh. They have very short memories. They must be suffering from amnesia. Would these people want to exchange their freedom for better tasting food? Isn't the food that God provides enough for them? Isn't the food nourishing and low in fat and high in fiber?"

Moses realized that leadership of the people of Israel was not glamorous. Even with God's help and guidance, the people's expectations and demands on him were overwhelming. Moses did not have a messianic complex. He would gladly have given up his leadership to find peace of mind. He would say to himself, "Being elevated to leadership over an entire community is a responsibility that I can live without."

Moses was the kind of leader who took his concerns to God, and God was not indifferent to Moses' feelings. God heard Moses and was able to empathize with him. God offered Moses a solution to the dilemma he was facing with the people of Israel that he could quickly embrace.

God told Moses to share his leadership responsibilities with seventy other people. God said, "Moses, I am going to do two things. First, I am going to give the people of Israel all the food they want. They will have so much food that they will tire of it quickly. Second, I will take some of the Spirit from you and give it to seventy people. In this way, these seventy people will have to bear some of the burden of leadership with you. You will not have to bear it alone and shoulder all of the complaints of the people."

Moses felt relieved. He was glad that God saw his predicament and acted immediately. He looked forward to sharing his leadership.

Some of the rabbis tell that the seventy chosen to help Moses lead were teachers, and thus predecessors of the rabbis. The custom of standing in the presence of one's teacher to show respect traces back to Moses' day. One of the rabbis said that he avoided crowds of disciples so they would not have to put themselves out by standing for him. But another objected that it was a rabbi's duty to allow disciples to stand, since if they could respect their rabbi they could thereby learn to respect God. (*Numbers Rabbah* 15.17)

The rabbis compared God to an orchard owner who hired a keeper. One day the keeper came to the owner and said that he could not watch over the orchard by himself and asked to employ some helpers.

The owner replied that the care of the orchard was given to the keeper and that he could do whatever he wanted so long as he looked after it. But the money to pay the helpers would come from the keeper, not from the owner, because the owner had paid all he was willing to pay for the care of the orchard. Even so, Moses lost nothing of what God had planned for him, though he called on the seventy to help him care for God's orchard, Israel. (*Numbers Rabbah* 15.25)

Moses Retells the Story

Moses rehearses all that God has done during the time in Egypt until the present time.

The Story

The LORD said to Moses, 'Send men out to explore Canaan, the land which I am going to give to the Israelites; from each ancestral tribe send one man, a man of high rank.' . . .

When Moses sent them to explore Canaan, he said, 'Make your way up by the Negeb, up into the hill-country, and see what the land is like, and whether the people who live there are strong or weak, few or many. See whether the country in which they live is easy or difficult, and whether their towns are open or fortified. Is the land fertile or barren, and is it wooded or not? Go boldly in and bring some of its fruit.' It was the season when the first grapes were ripe. . . .

They came to the wadi Eshcol, and there they cut a branch with a single bunch of grapes, which they carried on a pole between two of them; they also picked pomegranates and figs. That place was named the wadi Eshcol from the bunch of grapes the Israelites cut there.

After forty days they returned from exploring the country and, coming back to Moses and Aaron and the whole community of Israelites at Kadesh in the wilderness of Paran, they made their report, and showed them the fruit of the country. They gave Moses this account: 'We made our way into the land to which you sent us. It is flowing with milk and honey, and here is the fruit it grows; but its inhabitants are formidable, and the towns are fortified and very large; indeed, we saw there the descendants of Anak. We also saw the Amalekites who live in the Negeb, Hittites, Jebusites, and Amorites who live in the hill-country, and the Canaanites who live by the sea and along the Jordan.'

Caleb silenced the people for Moses. 'Let us go up at once and occupy the country,' he said; 'we are well able to conquer it.' But the men who had gone with him said, 'No, we cannot attack these people; they are too strong for us.' Their report to the Israelites about the land which they had explored was discouraging: 'The country we explored', they said, 'will swallow up any who go to live in it. All the people we saw there are men of gigantic stature. When we set eyes on the Nephilim (the sons of Anak belong to the Nephilim) we felt no bigger than grasshoppers; and that is how we must have been in their eyes.'

At this the whole Israelite community cried out in dismay and the people wept all night long. Everyone complained against Moses and Aaron: 'If only we had died in Egypt or in the wilderness!' they said. 'Why should the

LORD bring us to this land, to die in battle and leave our wives and our dependants to become the spoils of war? It would be better for us to go back to Egypt.' And they spoke of choosing someone to lead them back there.

Then Moses and Aaron flung themselves on the ground before the assembled community of the Israelites, and two of those who had explored the land, Joshua son of Nun and Caleb son of Jephunneh, tore their clothes, and encouraged the whole community: 'The country we travelled through and explored', they said, 'is a very good land indeed. If the LORD is pleased with us, he will bring us into this land, a land flowing with milk and honey, and give it to us. But you must not act in defiance of the LORD. You need not fear the people of the country, for we shall devour them. They have lost the protection that they had: the LORD is with us. You have nothing to fear from them.' As the whole assembly threatened to stone them, the glory of the LORD appeared in the Tent of Meeting to all the Israelites.

The LORD said to Moses, 'How much longer will this people set me at naught? How much longer will they refuse to trust me in spite of all the signs I have shown among them? I shall strike them with pestilence. I shall deny them their heritage, and you and your descendants I shall make into a nation greater and more numerous than they.' But Moses answered the LORD, 'What if the Egyptians hear of it? You brought this people out of Egypt by your might. What if they tell the inhabitants of this land? They too have heard of you, LORD, that you are with this people and are seen face to face, that your cloud stays over them, and that you go before them in a pillar

of cloud by day and in a pillar of fire by night. If then you do put them all to death at one blow, the nations who have heard these reports about you will say, "The LORD could not bring this people into the land which he promised them by oath; and so he destroyed them in the wilderness."

'Now let the LORD'S might be shown in its greatness, true to your proclamation of yourself—"The LORD, long-suffering, ever faithful, who forgives iniquity and rebellion, and punishes children to the third and fourth generation for the iniquity of their fathers, though he does not sweep them clean away." You have borne with this people from Egypt all the way here; forgive their iniquity, I beseech you, as befits your great and constant love.'

The LORD said, 'Your prayer is answered, and I pardon them. But as I live, and as the glory of the LORD fills the whole earth, not one of all those who have seen my glory and the signs which I wrought in Egypt and in the wilderness shall see the country which I promised on oath to their fathers. Ten times they have challenged me and not obeyed my voice. None of those who have set me at naught shall see this land. But my servant Caleb showed a different spirit and remained loyal to me. Because of this, I shall bring him into the land in which he has already set foot, the territory of the Amalekites and the Canaanites who dwell in the Vale, and I shall put his descendants in possession of it. Tomorrow you must turn back and set out for the wilderness by way of the Red Sea.'

The LORD said to Moses and Aaron, 'How long must I tolerate the complaints of this wicked community? I have heard the Israelites making complaints against me. Tell them that this is the word of the LORD: As I live, I shall do to you the very things I have heard you say. Here in this wilderness your bones will lie, every one of you on the register aged twenty or more, because you have made these complaints against me. Not one of you will enter the land which I swore with uplifted hand should be your home, except only Caleb son of Jephunneh and Joshua son of Nun. Your dependants, who, you said, would become the spoils of war, those dependants I shall bring into the land you have rejected, and they will enjoy it. But as for the rest of you, your bones will lie in this wilderness; your children will be wanderers in the wilderness forty years, paying the penalty of your wanton faithlessness till the last one of you dies there. Forty days you spent exploring the country, and forty years, a year for each day, you will spend paying the penalty of your iniquities. You will know what it means to have me against you. I, the LORD, have spoken. This I swear to do to all this wicked community who have combined against me. There will be an end of them here in this wilderness; here they will die.'

Comments on the Story

In Deuteronomy, Moses' retelling of the wilderness sojourn is bracketed by the people's two most atrocious apostasies: the golden calf and the debacle of the scouts (Deut. 1:20-46; 9:11-26). In both instances, finding themselves on the threshold of glory, the people take matters into their own hands, with disastrous results.

The journey to the Promised Land was not uninterrupted travel. A lengthy stay at Sinai was followed by a semi-permanent stopover in the wilderness of Zin (not Sin), at the southern edge of Palestine. The region's attraction was the oasis at Kadesh-Barnea, to this day gushing with fresh water. It is little wonder that Israel was molested by marauders like the Amalekites and the Midianites. In a desert region, a good watering hole would be hotly contested.

But the oasis of Kadesh-Barnea was not their ultimate destination. The land is about to be granted. Momentously (Mann labels this "D-day"), Numbers 13 opens with God's directive to send "scouts" (the root *twr* is to be distinguished from *rgl,* "spy." "Spies" has the connotation of stealth or subterfuge, while these twelve make no effort to cloak their activities.) The twelve are not identical to the tribal leaders listed in Numbers 1:1–2:7. Younger, more vigorous men are chosen to climb over hill and vale. How dutifully they are named. One after the other, they are guilty of little faith.

Numbers 13:22-24 believably fixes the surveillance at the southern edges of Canaan, through the Negeb (literally "arid land," Palestine's southern portal) to near Hebron. A storied history lay before Hebron, the most sacred site in the southern hills. The patriarchs and their families lived there and were buried there. In this vicinity, Abraham had been promised the land—an ignominious spot to repudiate that same promise! The city's prestige is magnified by the notice that it is seven years older than Egypt's capital, Zoan (called Tanis). From Hebron David would rule for seven years; his coronation in this region took place in part because of his marriage to Abigail, widow of Nabal, a Calebite.

In these same sections in which the scouting is limited to Hebron and its environs, Caleb (meaning "dog") is depicted as the lone faithful explorer (see Num. 13:30; 14:24; see also Num. 32:9; Deut. 1:24; and Josh. 14:7-9). Indeed, Caleb and his descendants eventually settled in precisely that area—apparently as a reward for his fidelity.

But Numbers 13:2 and 21 extend the maneuver over one hundred miles, almost to Antioch. Rehob and Lebo-hamath (Libweh, a well-known city at the sources of the Orontes) are in the far north, marking the northern limits of Israel under King Solomon (I Kings 8:65). Did they really go so far, or is the entirety of the later nation included by extension in the report of an originally more restricted investigation? The fact that they traverse so far as the subsequent borders indicates a symbolic claiming of the promise more than genuine surveying. In this panoramic version, Joshua is paired with Caleb, who is no longer alone (14:6, 38). Was Joshua, as architect of the full-scale invasion, later remembered as a faithful scout, while the original story focused on Caleb's fidelity and his corresponding reward?

The nearby valley was appropriately dubbed "Eshcol" (meaning "cluster of grapes"), to this day dotted with vineyards; the "eshcol" specimen was so stupendous that not one but two men were required to hoist it. This motif crops up in many legendary tales; an old Norse saga tells of a man and woman who ventured into the bush along the coast of America, returning with a sheaf of grain and a clump of grapes (see Northrop Frye, *The Great Code: The Bible and Literature* [New York: Harcourt Brace Jovanovich, 1981], p. 43).

The surveillance filled forty (the usual number) days, most likely in late July or early August ("when the first grapes were ripe"). Aptly the scouts respond with glowing answers to the very questions Moses had given. The truth of the traditional epithet, "flowing with milk and honey" (in ancient mythology the fare of the gods), is confirmed. The "honey" (*devash*) was not bee-honey but the juice of dates. The Hebrew text gets carried away, doubling the adverb *very* (*me'od me'od!*); this land is very, very good.

By Numbers 13:33 the inhabitants are not just "Anakites," but "Nephilim"— the semi-divine beings feared ever since Genesis 6:1-4. Notice the progression: There are people; they are big, very big; they are practically gods! Before these men, the ten scouts feel like "grasshoppers" (the smallest edible animal). We might say "shrimp" (or Milgrom's perfect adjective, "lilliputian," p. 107). Hadn't the census counted a gargantuan fighting force of 603,550 (Num. 1:46)? Even the land's largess begins to fade. The idiom "the land will swallow us up" connotes infertility, barrenness, an assessment contradicted by the very rack of grapes paraded through the camp!

Actually, the majority and minority reports agree; there's no disputing what was seen. The crisis hangs on what to do about the unanimous report. The drama of the people's choice is heightened by the minority report. Caleb "silenced" the people (the Hebrew word sounds very much like "Hush!"); he shows a "different spirit" (4:24). Somewhat surprisingly he speaks of military clout, not divine intervention ("We are well able to conquer it"). Joshua, being the next closest thing to God after Moses, should have been heeded.

But from a theological perspective, it would not matter if Goliath had taller cousins occupying bigger and more imposing fortresses. The issue is one of trust, not in surprise or guerrilla tactics, but in the Lord. Mann summarizes the situation: "Israel's greatest enemy was not the Canaanite force, not even the giants among them; Israel's greatest enemy was the enemy within—Israel's lack of trust" (Mann, 131).

Who, after all, decided the land needed scouting? In Numbers 13:1, it is the Lord who says, "Send men out to explore." But in Deuteronomy 1:22, the initiative rests with the people, not God. The Hebrew idiom in Numbers 13:1, *shelah-leka,* literally means "send for yourself." Ramban points out that lots were not cast to select the men. Did God simply acquiesce, allowing the foolishness to play itself out? Indeed, on their return, the scouts leave God out of the picture entirely, referring to "the land to which you (not the Lord) sent us" (Num. 13:27).

The popular response is, by now, predictable: blaming, murmuring, longing for Egypt; in Deuteronomy 1:27 they even conclude that the Lord "hates" them. They want to replace Moses with another leader, just as God would replace them with Moses (Num. 14:12*b*; compare Exod. 32:10*b*). Indeed, this obstinate crowd would even stone Joshua and Caleb (see Acts 7:57-60). Moses is left persuading God not to destroy them—again (as in Exod. 32) not for their own sakes, but to preserve God's own good reputation (compare Ezek. 36:16ff). Pathetically the people regroup, perceiving their own folly, and they belatedly plunge into the land. The death knell is sounded in 14:42: "The Lord is not with you." As in the story of Cain, a note of mercy rings through (see Hos. 11). Their lives are extended, albeit in the wilds. Having expected little but misery and death, the mob is granted their expectations. They preferred retreat into the wilderness, and God grants their desire. They feared God couldn't finish the job; now God refuses to finish it. Only the meek (the young, innocent generation) will inherit this earth (see Matt. 5:5).

In a more positive appraisal of the people's failure, some writers have noted how oppressed groups become dispirited, even internalizing a "crushed identity," over time coming to believe what the pharaohs have been telling them (see Walzer, 46; J. Severino Croatto, *Exodus: Hermeneutics of Freedom* [Orbis: 1983]). Surely the storyteller will in humility be as gracious as God is with our failures.

Retelling the Story*

Julie came to counseling with her pastor because she had a chronic disease of the pancreas. She was not able to find an answer for her pain through consultation with many doctors and experimentation with different medicines and surgeries. Nothing seemed to work to decrease her pain and cure the actual disease. The overwhelming pain she suffered persisted in spite of all the medical people did.

Julie slowly came to the conclusion that there might be a spiritual basis for her pain. She thought about seeking help from a counselor who had a spiritual background to help her work through some of the problems she felt might be contributing to her pain.

After several sessions of counseling, Julie made a discovery. She said: "I find Bible stories helpful when I am trying to figure things out. Often, I can gain some insight into my problems from reading Bible stories. Recently, I have been studying Joshua and Caleb and the people of Israel as they journeyed through the wilderness toward the Promised Land. I will tell you what I learned about myself from the spy story that is told in the book of Numbers, chapters 13 and 14.

"You know that Moses sent out spies to do research in the Promised Land. These spies were leaders from each tribe of the people of Israel. He gave them instructions for gathering data, telling them to find out if the people who dwell in the Promised Land were few or many, whether the land was good or bad, whether the cities were

God can be compared to a king who promised a gift to a friend. Some time later the friend died, but the king went to the friend's son and said that the gift promised to his father would not be withheld but would be given to the son. Thus the promise made to God's friend, Abraham, was finally fulfilled among Abraham's descendants. (*Numbers Rabbah* 16.3)

"A rich man possessed a vineyard. Whenever he saw that the wine was good he would say to his men: 'Bring the wine into *my* house,' but when he saw that the wine had turned to vinegar, he would say: 'Bring the wine into *your* houses.' It was the same with the Holy One, Blessed Be He. When he saw the elders and how worthy their deeds were, He called them His own; as it says, 'Gather for *Me* seventy of Israel's elders' (Num. 11:16). But when He saw the scouts and how they would later sin, He ascribed them to Moses, saying *shelah-leka,* 'Send men for *yourself.*' " (Milgrom, p. 100).

The rabbis tell that Moses did not know that he was choosing foolish or cowardly people to serve as spies. In fact, he asked God about each and every person chosen, and God approved them all. The spies were righteous when they were chosen, but something happened to them between that time and their return to report to Moses. The rabbis do not speculate as to what happened to change them, just that they were changed. (*Numbers Rabbah* 16.5)

When the people cried out that it would have been better if they had died in the wilderness, they passed judgment on themselves. They were like someone appearing before a judge and who not only unwittingly confesses his or her crime, but also in the process suggests a punishment for the guilty party. The judge allows the judgment and the sentence to stand. Just so the people who said, "It would have been better if we had died in the wilderness," died in the wilderness without seeing the Promised Land. (*Numbers Rabbah* 16.21)

well fortified or not, and whether the land was rich or poor."

She continued: "After the spies received their instructions, they left on their mission. They traveled into several areas and entered several cities. They gathered not only the necessary information but also fruit the land produced.

"At the end of forty days the spies returned from their mission. They showed Moses, Aaron, and the people of Israel the fruit they had gathered from the land. They gave their report: 'We came to the land to which you sent us; it flows with milk and honey, and this is its fruit. The cities are well fortified and large, however.'

"The people were excited. Moses said, 'Let us go now and take the land.' However, the majority of the spies countered that this was not possible. They insisted that the people of this land were stronger than the people of Israel. They said that the people of Israel would be destroyed and would perish if they tried to seize the land.

"The people began to get upset. They said: 'Why has the Lord brought us here to die in the wilderness? Let us choose captains who can take us back to Egypt.'

"Joshua and Caleb were among the spies who brought back reports. They were in the minority, however. They said: 'Don't rebel against God, and don't fear the people in the land. God will make a way for us to go into the land and take it.' "

After Julie finished the story, she turned to her spiritual counselor and said: "All my life I have always identified with the majority of the spies. God had made a new future possible for them in the Promised Land. However, they were fearful of allowing God to lead them to their future. I am the same way. God has called me to a glorious future. Now, all that I need to do is to take on the courage of Joshua and Caleb. I need to accept God's future for me seriously and embrace it. I am in pain now, but I can see a new future eventually emerging for me."

* This retelling is based on a story told by Edward P. Wimberly in *Prayer in Pastoral Counseling* (Louisville: Westminster/John Knox Press, 1990), pp. 46-49.

The Revolt of Korah

Korah revolts against God and Moses, then he and his followers suffer the consequences.

The Story

Korah son of Izhar, son of Kohath, son of Levi, along with the Reubenites Dathan and Abiram sons of Eliab and On son of Peleth, challenged the authority of Moses. Siding with them in their revolt were two hundred and fifty Israelites, all chiefs of the community, conveners of assembly and men of good standing. They confronted Moses and Aaron and said, 'You take too much on yourselves. Each and every member of the community is holy and the LORD is among them. Why do you set yourselves up above the assembly of the LORD?' When Moses heard this, he prostrated himself, and he said to Korah and all his company, 'Tomorrow morning the LORD will declare who is his, who is holy and who may present offerings to him. The man whom the LORD chooses may present them. This is what you must do, you, Korah, and all your company: you must take censers, and put fire in them and place incense on them before the LORD tomorrow. The man whom the LORD then chooses is the man who is holy. You take too much on yourselves, you Levites.'

Moses said to Korah, 'Listen, you Levites. Is it not enough for you that the God of Israel has set you apart from the community of Israel, bringing you near him to maintain the service of the Tabernacle of the LORD and to stand before the community as their ministers? He has had you come near him, and all your brother Levites with you; now do you seek the priesthood as well? That is why you and all your company have combined together against the LORD. What is Aaron that you should make these complaints against him?'

Moses sent to fetch Dathan and Abiram sons of Eliab, but they answered, 'We will not come. Is it not enough that you have brought us away from a land flowing with milk and honey to let us die in the wilderness? Must you also set yourself up as prince over us? What is more, you have not brought us into a land flowing with milk and honey, nor have you given us fields and vineyards to inherit. Do you think you can hoodwink men like us? We are not coming.' Moses became very angry, and said to the LORD, 'Take no notice of their murmuring. I have not taken from them so much as a single donkey; I have not wronged any of them.'

Moses said to Korah, 'Present yourselves before the LORD tomorrow, you and all your company, you and they and Aaron. Each man of you is to take his censer and put incense on it. Then you shall present them before the LORD with their two hundred and fifty censers, and you and Aaron shall also bring your censers.' So each man took his censer, put fire in it, and placed incense on it. Moses and Aaron took their stand at the entrance to the Tent of Meeting, and Korah gathered his whole company together and faced them at the entrance to the Tent of Meeting.

Then the glory of the LORD appeared to the whole community, and the LORD said to Moses and Aaron, 'Stand apart from them, so that I may make an end of them in a single moment.' But Moses and Aaron prostrated themselves and said, 'God, you God of the spirits of all mankind, if one man sins, will you be angry with the whole community?' But the LORD said to Moses, 'Tell them all to stand back from the dwellings of Korah, Dathan, and Abiram.'

Moses rose and went to Dathan and Abiram, and the elders of Israel followed him. He said to the whole community, 'Stand well away from the tents of these wicked men; touch nothing of theirs, or you will be swept away because of all their sins.' So they moved away from the dwellings of Korah, Dathan, and Abiram. Dathan and Abiram had come out and were standing at the entrance of their tents with their wives, their children, and their dependants. Moses said, 'By this you shall know that it is the LORD who sent me to do all I have done, and it was not my own heart that prompted me. If these men die a natural death, merely sharing the common fate of man, then the LORD has not sent me; but if the LORD works a miracle, and the ground opens its mouth and swallows them and all that is theirs, and

they go down alive to Sheol, then you will know that these men have set the LORD at naught.'

Hardly had Moses spoken when the ground beneath them split apart; the earth opened its mouth and swallowed them and their homes—all the followers of Korah and all their property. They went down alive into Sheol with all that they had; the earth closed over them, and they vanished from the assembly. At their cries all the Israelites around them fled. 'Look out!' they shouted. 'The earth might swallow us.' Fire came out from the LORD and consumed the two hundred and fifty men presenting the incense.

Then the LORD said to Moses, 'Order Eleazar son of Aaron the priest to set aside the censers from the burnt remains, and scatter the fire from them a long way off, because they are holy. The censers of these men who sinned at the cost of their lives you shall make into beaten plates to overlay the altar; they are holy, because they have been presented before the LORD. Let them be a sign to the Israelites.' Eleazar the priest took the bronze censers which the victims of the fire had presented, and they were beaten into plates to cover the altar, to be a reminder to the Israelites that no lay person, no one not descended from Aaron, should come forward to burn incense before the LORD, or his fate would be that of Korah and his company. All this was done as the LORD commanded Eleazar through Moses.

Next day the whole Israelite community raised complaints against Moses and Aaron and taxed them with causing the death of some of the LORD's people. As they gathered against Moses and Aaron, they turned towards the Tent of Meeting and saw that the cloud covered it, and the glory of the LORD appeared. When Moses and Aaron came to the front of the Tent of Meeting, the LORD said to them, 'Stand well clear of this community, so that in a single moment I may make an end of them.' They prostrated themselves, and then Moses said to Aaron, 'Take your censer, put fire from the altar in it, set incense on it, and go with it quickly to the assembled community to make expiation for them. Wrath has gone forth already from the presence of the LORD; the plague has begun.' As Moses had directed him, Aaron took his censer, ran into the midst of the assembly, and found that the plague had indeed begun among the people. He put incense on the censer and made expiation for the people, standing between the dead and the living, and the plague was stopped. Fourteen thousand seven hundred died of it, in addition to those who had died for Korah's offence. When Aaron came back to Moses at the entrance to the Tent of Meeting, the plague had stopped.

Comments on the Story

Numbers 14 ended on a sour note, the belated occupation attempt in shambles, the people staring at a forty-year wilderness sentence for their stupidity. The "dump Moses" movement could only gain momentum now. If he had any usefulness at all, it was to get them into the land. Failing that, his habit of speaking for God almighty, and that not in the most soothing of tones, fanned the flames of insurrection. Numbers 15, a bunch of stipulations unanticipated in this context, was one more negative off the lips of Moses; he even had a man stoned to death for gathering sticks on the Sabbath (15:32-36). Milgrom rightly characterizes the rabble as "psychologically receptive to demagogic appeals" (p. 129).

It is no surprise then when a challenge to Moses' authority erupts. In fact, it erupts all over. As many as four separate rebellions are confusingly woven together in the tapestry of Numbers 16. Critics have unscrambled four story lines: (1) Dathan and Abiram against Moses, (2) the Levites against Aaron, (3) the tribal chieftains against Aaron, and (4) the community against Moses and Aaron. But the text itself holds these together, and we dare not alleviate the confusion. As is the case with civil strife in our own age, there is a disorderliness about the internecine hostility. Moses and Aaron sensed barbs flying from every direction. The storyteller needs to capture the sense of madness, the wildfire crackling in a dry forest.

The common complaint is voiced in verse 3. The REB, "You take too much on yourselves," bears a hint of compassion. The NRSV, "You have gone too far," is closer to the sense of the Hebrew, which says literally, "You have too much"—too much power, too much prestige. How is authority to be exercised among equals, among siblings? The case made by the 250 has strong theological grounding; at Sinai, the Lord did establish all of Israel as a "kingdom of priests" (Exod. 19:6). The laity, not without foundation, revolt against the clergy! Verse 13 echoes the sarcastic question of Exodus 2:14 (not to mention the outcry of Joseph's brothers in Gen. 37:8). The seeds of unrest have been sown, and we need not be shocked when trouble arises.

The single common thread in all of the trouble seems to be Korah, who is fomenting rebellion wherever he can. Korah was the ancestor of a great clan of Levites who centuries later would become a major guild of bakers (see I Chron. 9:19, 31). The Korahites are singled out in the headings of eleven psalms (42; 44–49; 84–85; 87–88). Cast in the genealogy of Exodus 6 as Moses' first cousin, Korah may be imagined to have succumbed to petty family jealousy.

Dathan and Abiram, however, are plainly stated to be descended from Reuben, Jacob's oldest son, the original titular head of the tribes. Could not their uprising represent the earliest stage of the story, in which the Reubenites fought (albeit unsuccessfully against God's logic) for their firstborn rights against the thirdborn Levites?

The consequences of the rebellion are ghastly. The storyline clarifies that the mutiny ultimately is not against Moses or Aaron but against the Lord. And this Lord will not be trifled with. If picking up sticks on the Sabbath was serious, then encroachment on divinely instituted liturgical boundaries is even more grievous. Paralleling the unauthorized entry into Canaan (Num. 14), the 250 take up the familiar flat pans, designed to remove ashes or burning embers from the altar, determined to be priestly, with or without Moses' (but therefore God's) blessing. It is biting irony that sin here takes the form of holy, religious action—biting irony, too, that the ashes and embers to be handled at the story's close are the charred remains of the 250! Moses turns their complaint against them: "It is *you* who have gone too far/taken too much on yourselves" (v. 7). The fundamental issue is clear: Are the wilderness happenings of God? Or merely the bungled effort of Moses to wield some clout?

We may disentangle the various punishments meted out:

> Dathan and Abiram—swallowed by the earth
> The Levites—sentence not mentioned explicitly
> The tribal chieftains—consumed by divine fire
> The community—spared by the intercession of Moses and Aaron

Moses shores up his authority by insisting that something unheard of must occur. Fires were not unusual; sudden death was not unprecedented. But a sudden chasm in the earth? The fate of Korah himself is shrouded in ambiguity. Was he incinerated with the chieftains (as Num. 17:5, the Samaritan Pentateuch, Josephus, and the context might intimate)? Or was he engulfed by the earth with Dathan and Abiram (as Num. 26:10; Deut. 11:6; and the Mishnah indicate; compare Ps. 106:16-18)? Where, after all, are the people? At the tent of meeting outside the camp (v. 19)? Or at the dwellings of the conspirators (v. 25)? An uneven seam for the storyteller to manage!

An ominous warning for future would-be encroachers, the fire pans of the rebels are hammered into a shiny bronze plating to cover the altar (Num. 17:3). Does the story mask a later struggle for priestly prerogatives? Scholars discern a long history of unrest in the priesthood. The Zadokites of Jerusalem are resented by the old Shilohite priests. The Levites are caught in the squeeze when worship is centralized in Judea. After the exile, claimants to priestly power brandished their pedigrees. This story's intent, though, is to demonstrate that priestly prerogative is not a matter of arrogance, however arrogant particular priests may have turned out to be. God inscrutably wills a delineation of who does what in worship. Mercifully God provides for mediators to bridge the tragic gap between God's holiness and human trifling. To violate or even question that holy ordering is tantamount to refusal to obey God, a denial of the very means graciously given by God to grant redemption.

The Levites, after all, are given crucial tasks, indeed privileges: to disassemble, carry, and reassemble the tabernacle and its furnishings, as well as various attending and musical functions. Perhaps they needed to hear the apostle Paul's words about the eye, hand, and the foot, all coordinated in the smoothly functioning body (I Cor. 12).

Retelling the Story

Dear Family and Friends:

I am sorry it has taken me so long to write you. As you might imagine, I have been so busy I have hardly taken time to sleep. The state of the world being what it is, this may be the only chance I get for a while to let you know that I am well.

And I am fine—physically, that is—but emotionally this work takes its toll. I never even guessed when I was in medical school that I would ever arrive in a place like this. There are no beds (a cot would be a luxury). There is no such thing as sterile instruments, because there isn't even basic sanitation. Here we are attempting to save lives while working up to our elbows and knees in mud and muck (believe me you don't want to ask what you are walking through).

On my bad days I ask why I even bother. If these refugees aren't killed or dead from exposure before they get to our camp, then many will starve when

> The rabbis emphasize the injustice of Korah's rebellion in its effects as well as its motives. They say that divine justice does not punish those under twenty years of age and that earthly justice refuses to penalize those who have not reached the age of thirteen. But during Korah's rebellion babies of one day suffered—a grave injustice. (*Numbers Rabbah* 18.4)

the food shipments are late, or infection will set up through the very procedures that were supposed to save them.

Or, worse yet, they kill each other. Old women have their blankets ripped off their bodies, and children's bowls are grabbed from them by grown men. Perhaps, if I were desperate, I would do the same. You never know.

If starvation or disease don't wipe them out, then their own power struggles will. Let me give you an example: A rather large group of refugees came through here some time back. They seemed remarkably well nourished, considering the journey they had made. The problem was that they had recently passed through a part of the country prone to earthquakes. During their encampment, a fissure opened up and swallowed about 250 of them. Then, of course, this catastrophe was accompanied by the usual post-quake diseases.

Now listen to the explanation I got from their chief on why this all happened. It seems this larger group is composed of a number of smaller tribes. Well, some intertribal squabbling arose when the leader of one of these tribes challenged the leadership of the chief and his clan. In the midst of this quarrel, the quake came along, and—wouldn't you know—it gulped down the encampment of the troublesome tribe! So now the chief is telling everybody that this was the judgment of their god on anyone who questions the chief's family's leadership.

And get this, the chief was raised in an upper-class family back in the country they escaped from, educated there in the universities and then turned revolutionary. And a religious revolutionary at that; he thinks their god is leading them to a land of "milk and honey," as he puts it. This guy is no savage, not by a longshot.

If all this sounds more like politics than theology to you, then join the club.

> Moses attempted to persuade Korah against violence with a voice of reason, but Korah would not respond with even so much as a word. He thought that, if he responded, the brilliance of Moses' arguments would overcome his resistance and that he would be persuaded to make peace. So Korah kept silent and held to his violent ways. (*Numbers Rabbah* 18.9)

> The rabbis describe Korah sneaking around among the tribes of Israel, saying that Moses wanted honor only for his own family. He claimed that Moses wanted to be king and to install his brother, Aaron, as the high priest. Such honor should not be kept to one family, Korah told the others, but should be spread around among all the tribes. In this way he gained support for his rebellion. (*Numbers Rabbah* 18.10)

But that's the way it is out here on the edge of the world. Things are different here. It's like you stepped back in time several thousand years. It may sound strange, but you could almost come to believe some of the stories they tell. Maybe their god was involved in all this. Who knows?

Believe me, stranger things have happened. But those will have to wait for my next letter. I have to get some sleep.

Stay well and think of me from time to time. Write when you can. Your letters mean more than I can say.

Love,

Doc

Moses Is Excluded from the Promised Land

Moses gains water for the people but loses his chance to enter the Promised Land.

The Story

In the first month the whole community of Israel arrived in the wilderness of Zin and stayed some time at Kadesh. Miriam died and was buried there.

As the community was without water, the people gathered against Moses and Aaron. They disputed with Moses. 'If only we had perished when our brothers perished before the LORD!' they said. 'Why have you brought the LORD's assembly into this wilderness for us and our livestock to die here? Why did you make us come up from Egypt to land us in this terrible place, where nothing will grow, neither grain nor figs nor vines nor pomegranates? There is not even water to drink.'

Moses and Aaron went from the assembly to the entrance of the Tent of Meeting, where they prostrated themselves, and the glory of the LORD appeared to them. The LORD said to Moses, 'Take your staff, and then with Aaron your brother assemble the community, and in front of them all command the rock to yield its waters. Thus you will produce water for the community out of the rock, for them and their livestock to drink.' Moses took his staff from before the LORD, as he had been ordered. He with Aaron assembled the people in front of the rock, and said to them, 'Listen, you rebels. Must we get water for you out of this rock?' Moses raised his hand and struck the rock twice with his staff. Water gushed out in abundance and they all drank, men and animals. But the LORD said to Moses and Aaron, 'You did not trust me so far as to uphold my holiness in the sight of the Israelites; therefore you will not lead this assembly into the land I am giving them.' Such were the waters of Meribah, where the people disputed with the LORD and through which his holiness was upheld.

Comments on the Story

For some thoughts on geography germane to Numbers 20, the storyteller should review our comments on Exodus 17:1-7. Numbers 20 is so like its counterpart in Exodus 17 that scholars (at least as far back as Bekhor Shor, the twelfth-century Jewish commentator from northern France) have claimed that the pair are duplicate versions of a single story. But the differences are well worth noting.

Several "doublets" tumble off either side of Mt. Sinai in a definite pattern. Before arriving at Sinai, the Israelites murmured for water, bread, quail—and God indulgently met their need. But after leaving Sinai, they murmur for water, bread, quail—and God vents rage! The feel of the broader narrative is that, before the covenant was forged, Israel didn't know any better—like a toddler. But once the covenant was sealed, Israel was without excuse, accountable for its actions. So in Numbers the food is not filling but sickening; the brunt of God's wrath is finally felt.

This post-Sinai incident at Meribah puts a halt to Moses' good fortunes. Something goes awry, and his demise is sealed: He may not enter the Promised Land. No more heartbreaking sentence could be passed down. But what exactly did he do wrong? Was it that he struck the rock rather than speaking (Rashi)? Or was it his vitriolic outburst against the people (Maimonides)? The surest solution is to focus on the "fatal pronoun" *we* in verse 10 (see Milgrom, p. 165).

Beyond question, Moses was angry. Although the text (as usual) does not describe his emotional state, we infer his feelings from the action and the dialogue. Stretched beyond human limits by this recalcitrant people (see Ps. 106:33), Moses finally explodes. Deviating from God's exact directive, he strikes with his rod—notice the delicious detail, "twice." But it is the "we" that brings down the curtain. Heretofore, Moses has not been much of a miracle-worker. His role is so obviously ancillary that no one would think of him as much of a thaumaturge. The text is at pains to give the credit to God alone.

With the simple "we" (just a single letter's difference in Hebrew: *notsi*, "must we get water," instead of *yotsi*, "must he [God] get water"), Moses and Aaron usurp God's turf in the eyes of the multitude. This slip of the tongue seems trivial. Admittedly, the "we" is uttered before one and all by the one privileged to speak with God face to face. But we are reminded of Saul, the tragic character upon whom God seemed eager to pounce. Saul's crimes were burning a sacrificial offering to God moments too soon and waiting moments too long to murder Agag. This comparison of Moses and Saul may point to a vital conclusion. Saul was practically the scapegoat for the people's sinful craving for a "king like the other nations." As the embodiment of their foolhardy desire, he had no real chance. Analogously, Moses, who dared in solidarity to represent the people before God, was dragged down with them. Deuteronomy (1:37, 3:26, 4:21) plainly attributes Moses' exclusion from the land to the sin of the whole people; as mediator he bears their infidelity in his own death.

Milgrom has deepened our understanding of the incident. Pagan magic involved a manual act paired with a verbal incantation. Today even children learn the pattern of tapping a wand while eerily chanting "abracadabra." How many heroes in folklore have produced water by striking a rock? Gaster (*Myth,*

Legend & Custom in the Old Testament [New York: Harper & Row, 1969], p. 233) lists Poseidon, Rhea, Dionysus, Atalanta, and others with "magic wand" feats in their legends.

Israelite miracle workers proved disappointing. Naaman scoffed at Elisha's unspectacular method (II Kings 5). Jesus exhibits no showmanship at all, even hushing those who try to tell about the miracles he performed. The Israelites would have been familiar with accomplished spell casters in Egypt. Moses outmaneuvers them, but even his methods are odd; he makes no sport of Pharaoh in person, but usually leaves to pray in private, reciting no incantations, no esoteric names. In Numbers 20, Moses begins to look and act like a pagan magician—a performance intolerable to the Lord before these people and their toddler covenant. Milgrom puts it well: "Israel had to be released from more than chains; it still had to be purged of its pagan background" (Milgrom, 452).

We may want to sharpen this analysis even further. The word-element was crucial in the biblical miracle stories—not as an "abracadabra" incantation, but as an advance announcement of who was about to intervene. A silent rap upon the rock that produced water could be underrated as a mere provision of water. The word from God would move the people beyond quenching of physical thirst toward satisfaction of a deeper thirst (Deut. 8:3; Ps. 42). In the church, a "sacrament" is a tangible, physical action—but with the word attached (see I Cor. 10:4). At Meribah, the people saw Moses, but they didn't hear the Word. Since the ears are the faculty of faith, we are reminded once more of Luther's dictum: "The eyes are hard of hearing."

With gripping irony, Moses' fall from grace comes right on the heels of the death of Miriam. In our story's opening act, Moses' life depended on hers, on her watchful oversight of the rush basket, on her arrangements for Jochebed's employment as his wet nurse. Now that she is dead, now that his guardian angel is gone, Moses strays from his course.

Retelling the Story

Edna is an African-American mother living in the deep South. She is about sixty years old. Her husband had died, leaving her to raise three children alone. Now, she is a grandmother and has several grandchildren. She is especially thankful to have Richard as her grandson because, she says, he is so dependable.

Edna has experienced many losses in her life in addition to the loss of her husband. Her mother died when Edna was a teenager. Although Edna's father is still living, he was aging and had serious heart problems and depended on Edna a great deal. He finally had to give up his home and go to live with Edna. After she had worked eight hours a day as a nurse in the county hospital, she would come home and care for her aging and ailing father.

Two of Edna's three children have died. One, Windy, was born retarded and lived away from home in a special school. She died suddenly when she was in her late thirties.

Edna felt Windy's death deeply. After Windy's burial, Edna got word that her son who was living in the North was dying of a liver disease. He also was only in his late thirties. Edna could not believe what was happening. She wondered why so many terrible things were happening to her children. Yet, she continued to trust in God. At the same time, she did not know how she could continue to hold on with so many adverse things happening to her. She felt life would eventually simply crush her under its own weight.

Edna finally was able to go up North to see her son before he died. When he had died, she was able to bring him back to the South to be buried in the family church's cemetery.

Two years passed uneventfully, and Edna is grateful that God had given her the resources to sustain her in the time of her deepest need. She often says: "Jesus never fails. I am so glad that I know this man called Jesus."

One night the phone rang. It was Edna's third child on the phone, her daughter Rebecca, who also lived in the North. Edna knew immediately that something was wrong. She could tell from Rebecca's voice.

"What's wrong, Rebecca?" Edna cried out. "I know that something terrible has happened."

"Calm down, Mother," said Rebecca. "Everything will be all right," she said. "But I do have something disturbing to tell you. I discovered that I have cancer. They say that it is inoperable."

Edna was stunned but quickly pulled herself together. She was able to be supportive of Rebecca while she was on the phone with her. She asked Rebecca how much time the doctor estimated she had to live. Rebecca explained that the cancer was at the last stage of development.

Edna became very depressed after she got off the phone. She cried out: "Lord, you have given me too much to bear this time. How can I bury my last child? I never thought that I would outlive my children. It is always the prerogative of the child to outlive the parent. Why is the order being reversed? Lord, I have lost two children already.

> Moses had survived all those years in the wilderness surrounded by the complaints of the people without losing his temper. But when he struck the rock, only a trickle of water came out. So the people complained again, "Do you call that a spring? There is hardly enough for one lamb, let alone all of us." At this, Moses finally lost his composure and struck the rock with a fierce blow, and the water poured forth. The people got what they wanted, but Moses was punished for his rash action. (*Numbers Rabbah* 19.9)

I have an aging, dependent father. I can't take any more days off from work without losing my job. Lord, can't you do something to change this situation? It's too much for me."

After Rebecca's funeral, Edna told her pastor about the state of her spiritual life. "You know, this time I didn't know how I was going to make it for even one more day. I felt like the children of Israel wandering around in the wilderness desert without food or water. I thought for sure God had brought me to the wilderness and left me to face the dangers of the desert with no resources. However, God did not fail me. Just as Moses struck the rock and water came forth, God provided me with the resources to face my trials and burdens. My grandson came into this world in the most difficult circumstances. Windy had been sexually assaulted by an attendant in one of the centers she lived in. She gave birth to my grandson. God must have known then that I would need some help later on. God made the best of this situation. This boy has been a blessing to me. He has been my water from the rock."

> To show the greatness of Moses, the rabbis say that an ordinary person, if betrayed by a friend, would walk away and never see that person again. But Moses, having lost his chance to enter the Promised Land on account of the people, did not walk away but continued to lead them. Moses fulfilled his duty despite the people's complaints and with no hope of reward. (*Numbers Rabbah* 19.15)

Edna continued: "I can see that God allowed him to come into the world because of the need. He is twenty now. He helps me look after my father. He drove me up North to care for my children. He even took time off from his job to come North to look in on my children when I could not get off work. Indeed, this grandson of mine is God's gift of water."

The Plague of Serpents

The people complain against God and Moses, and snakes infest the camp as the people's punishment.

The Story

From Mount Hor they left by way of the Red Sea to march round the flank of Edom. But on the way the people grew impatient and spoke against God and Moses. 'Why have you brought us up from Egypt', they said, 'to die in the desert where there is neither food nor water? We are heartily sick of this miserable fare.' Then the LORD sent venomous snakes among them, and they bit the Israelites so that many of them died. The people came to Moses and said, 'We sinned when we spoke against the LORD and you. Plead with the LORD to rid us of the snakes.' Moses interceded for the people, and the LORD told him to make a serpent and erect it as a standard, so that anyone who had been bitten could look at it and recover. So Moses made a bronze serpent and erected it as a standard, in order that anyone bitten by a snake could look at the bronze serpent and recover.

Comments on the Story

Forced to circle around Edom (Num. 20:14ff.) near the Red Sea (this time, *yam suf* really is the Red Sea), the people murmur pointedly against not just Moses but also God! Their faith has evaporated, and the Israelites have come full circle since first dealing with God at the *yam suf* (see the comments above on Exod. 14). Edom eventually (two hundred years later) expanded southward to Elath on the Red Sea, but the Arabah was only sparsely settled at the time of Israel's wanderings.

The region was infamous for its lethal serpents. In verse 6, the Hebrew adjective *seraph* (root meaning "to burn") is attributed to the live, biting snakes. Does it mean "fiery" (RSV) or by extension "poisonous" (NRSV) or "venomous" (REB)? What a frightful penalty for murmuring!

The antidote (a hoisted metallic serpent) reeks of superstition and magic. The principle is called "homeopathic"—a person or object is controlled by its image or effigy. To look at the uplifted snake icon would cure the ill effects of the deadly snakes crawling on the ground. Such a "charmed" object would have a tenuous future in Israelite religion. Five centuries later, Isaiah was "healed" by a flying seraph (Isa. 6). But the reformer Hezekiah smashed the serpent, "for up to that time the Israelites had been in the habit of burning sacrifices to it" (II Kings 18:4). Worshipers no doubt saw it in the Temple courtyard. Seeking healing themselves, they came to misunderstand it as somehow divine— just as their neighbors, the Canaanites, had a cultic appreciation for snakes.

Indeed, serpents were widely used in Egyptian religion. Serpentine amulets were placed on the dead to fend off snakes. Cobras (in headdresses and other regalia) denoted royalty. Asclepius, god of healing, was symbolized by a snake, as were other ancient healing divinities.

In the royal palace at Nineveh, a bronze bowl engraved with a winged snake (on a rod) has been unearthed. The bowl was likely part of the loot Tiglath-Pileser III, the bloodthirsty Assyrian, took from King Ahaz. But even more remarkable, in the vicinity where the Israelites skirted Edomite hegemony, there were copper mines. An inchoate smelting industry has bequeathed many objects to us, and none is more fascinating than a five-inch-long copper snake affixed to a staff, found at Timnah, a snake fashioned between 1200 and 900 B.C.E.—our very era! This figure (pictured in Aharoni, *Archaeology of the Land of Israel* [Philadelphia: Westminster Press, 1978], photo 25) was found in a nomadic holy place, perhaps that of the Midianites. The site in turn had previously been an Egyptian temple (situated before rugged cliffs anachronistically called the "pillars of Solomon") dedicated to Hathor, the patron goddess of miners.

For Israel, copper indeed made a perfect snake. Beyond the similarity in color, a Hebrew word play clinches its appropriateness: *nehoshet* ("copper") resembles *nehash* ("snake").

The Israelites had failed miserably; they grew "impatient" (the Hebrew word used in v. 4 means "short of soul"). Whining about death, they learned a lesson about real death. The terror compels a confession on their part. In a profound sense, the story hints at a redemptive purpose in the unleashing of the serpents.

But why didn't God just heal the bites and remove the snakes? Although the antidote is provided, the serpents are still permitted to prowl around the camp. The seraph-snake is evidently yet another test, a summons to obedience— indeed, a reminder of how precarious life is without devotion to God. The cure is also the mnemonic. Not surprisingly, Jesus sees in the uplifted serpent a type of his own offer of grace (John 3:14). James L. Mays states this intra-testamental juxtaposition of danger and grace with eloquence: "Men who look in faith behold in the Cross simultaneously the reality of their sin and the means of their redemption from it" (*Leviticus, Numbers* [Atlanta: John Knox Press, 1963], p. 115).

Retelling the Story

Jane had a chronic illness that went undiagnosed for many years. However, she finally found a physician who had a hunch about the type of illness she had. The physician sent her to a specialist, and Jane found relief from her illness in a matter of weeks.

Jane had spent most of her time in those last few years preoccupied with her illness. She had very little time to do much else. She had neither the energy nor the interest to maintain her career or her friendships. All of her efforts went into seeking a medical solution to her problem.

Jane had hated her diseased body. She felt as if her body were an enemy that had turned on her and imprisoned her, so she was happy to finally find medical relief that would allow her to recover the time she had lost while ill. She was finally looking forward to being well and doing the things she liked to do.

However, Jane did not fully recover as fast as she thought she would. Medically, she was fine. Emotionally and spiritually, however, she was very depressed. While she had been in bondage to her diseased body, she did not give much attention to what she was losing as the result of her illness. When she found relief, however, many new feelings surfaced that prevented her from returning to the kind of life she had prior to her illness. Feelings of resentment surfaced because she had suffered so long, even though there was a cure for her illness. But her doctors

> Despite all that they had done to alienate him when the people came to Moses to ask him to intercede with God to take the poisonous snakes away, Moses went to God on their behalf. This not only proves the greatness and humility of Moses, but it also teaches that if someone sins against you, then asks forgiveness, you are to forgive that person. Otherwise, you sin against that person and become like the one you refuse to forgive. (*Numbers Rabbah* 19.23)

had not found that cure soon enough, and she was bitter at the medical profession because she felt most doctors were inept. She became preoccupied with feelings of revenge at those who had deprived her of their best medical expertise.

Jane was also angry with God. She felt that God could have come to her aid and healed her sooner. She felt that if God really cared for her, God would have intervened and cured her sooner. She also felt that luck or fate had saved her and not God. She had feelings of hurt that she needed to sort through with God.

Not long after Jane had been healed, she was approached by a man who had the same illness that had put her out of commission for such a long time. The man said that he was very frightened by the disease and the treatment that was required to recover from it. He wanted Jane for a friend so that he could talk about what was taking place during his treatments. The man told Jane that he felt God had led her to him, and for this he felt very grateful to God.

Jane became even more angry and resentful toward God. She said to her doctor, "I just got my own healing, no thanks to God. Why would God send someone like this man to me with the very same illness that I had? Is God playing some sort of game? There is nothing I can do for this man. Besides, God didn't send anyone to help me."

The doctor was surprised at Jane and asked her how she had found out about seeing a specialist for a possible cure for her illness. Jane said: "It was purely by accident. One of my relatives called me about you, suggesting that you could help me."

The doctor responded: "Could God have been involved in your finding me?" Jane said nothing. Then the doctor said: "Part of the cure is also using the illness you once had to help others who have the same disease. That is to say, your disease has been turned from a curse into a blessing to be used for

> Philo states that the serpent Moses lifted is a symbol of the patience that endurance requires, something the people showed little evidence of having. (Plaut, p. 1168)

the benefit of someone else. God knows that your healing will be complete only when your diseased body becomes a blessing for another who needs healing. God sent this diseased person to you not only for this person's healing, but also to complete your healing."

Jane was silent. She could not find words to reply. She thought to herself, "Maybe the doctor does make sense. Perhaps God was involved in the healing process all the time. Maybe cures are not complete until the wounds become blessings for someone else."

God Will Not Allow Balaam's Curse

Balaam's donkey refuses to pass the angel of the Lord, and the donkey speaks stubbornly when Balaam beats it.

The Story

Balak son of Zippor saw all that Israel had done to the Amorites, and Moab was in terror of the people because there were so many of them. The Moabites were overcome with fear at the sight of them; and they said to the elders of Midian, 'This horde will soon eat up everything round us as an ox eats up the new grass in the field.' Balak son of Zippor, who was at that time king of Moab, sent a deputation to summon Balaam son of Beor, who was at Pethor by the Euphrates in the land of the Amavites, with this message, 'A whole nation has just arrived from Egypt: they cover the face of the country and are settling at my very door. Come at once and lay a curse on them, because they are too many for me. I may then be able to defeat them and drive them out of the country. I know that those whom you bless are blessed, and those whom you curse are cursed.'

But God was angry because Balaam was going, and as he came riding on his donkey, accompanied by his two servants, the angel of the LORD took his stand in the road to bar his way. When the donkey saw the angel standing in the road with his sword drawn, she turned off the road into the fields, and Balaam beat her to bring her back on to the road. The angel of the LORD then stood where the road ran through a hollow, with enclosed vineyards on either side. The donkey saw the angel and, squeezing herself against the wall, she crushed Balaam's foot against it, and again he beat her. The angel of the LORD moved on farther and stood in a narrow place where there was no room to turn to either right or left. When the donkey saw the angel, she lay down under Balaam. At that Balaam lost his temper and beat the donkey with his staff.

The LORD then made the donkey speak, and she said to Balaam, 'What have I done? This is the third time you have beaten me.' Balaam answered, 'You have been making a fool of me. If I had had a sword with me, I should have killed you on the spot.' But the donkey answered, 'Am I not still the donkey which you have ridden all your life? Have I ever taken such a liberty with you before?' He said, 'No.' Then the LORD opened Balaam's eyes: he saw the angel of the LORD standing in the road with his sword drawn, and he bowed down and prostrated himself. The angel said to him, 'What do you mean by beating your donkey three times like this? I came out to bar your way, but you made straight for me, and three times your donkey saw me and turned aside. If she had not turned aside, I should by now have killed you, while sparing her.' 'I have done wrong,' Balaam replied to the angel of the LORD. 'I did not know that you stood confronting me in the road. But now, if my journey displeases you, I shall turn back.' The angel of the LORD said to Balaam, 'Go with the men; but say only what I tell you.' So Balaam went on with Balak's chiefs.

Comments on the Story

Time out is taken in the saga of Israel's quest to the Promised Land for the comic drama of "curses foiled." We listen to the story of Balaam with outbursts of laughter and a serene trust in God's providence.

Having routed Sihon and Og in Transjordan, the Israelites settle down just east of the Jordan rift, on the steppes of Moab. From these arid highlands, the juggernaut into Canaan will be launched. For now, the people passively mill about in camp; the action on an overlook goes unnoticed.

Balak, a petty dictator in Moab, planned an attack on Israel's flank. Awed by their numbers, and more so by what storytellers were already saying about Israel, he hoped to enlist divine help—not to strengthen his cause so much as to weaken his foe's. Balaam, a holy man of considerable repute, is recruited. The Deir Alla inscription, discovered on a plastered wall of an eighth-century B.C.E. temple near where the Jabbok flows into the Jordan, names Balaam, proving his fame outside Israel proper.

Perhaps Balaam hails from Pethor, which is identified with Pitru on the river Sajur, a tributary feeding into the mighty Euphrates, just over ten miles south of Carchemish (in the vicinity of Abraham's homeland!). Looping around the fertile crescent, the trek from Pitru to Moab is about four hundred miles, three weeks of steady travel. Does he go back and forth four times? If so, the whole affair would span three months!

In the biblical world, a curse is not just ugly talk. The spoken word, especially from the lips of a professional like Balaam, was thought to unleash a terrible power. The very thought of an imported diviner invoking the wrath of heaven would wilt even the stoutest warrior. But just what is Balaam's specialty? In Mesopotamia and in the Bible, a distinction is made between a diviner (who foretells what will happen) and a sorcerer (who can actually manipulate what will happen). Balak needs and wants a sorcerer, but Balaam is patently unable to control the future. Did Balak simply make a colossal error, hiring the wrong kind of holy man? If so, he would be the butt of the joke, mockingly duped (as Pharaoh had been). Isn't it the case that, from Israel's perspective, no one controls the future but the Lord? Sorcery is bogus (Deut. 18:9-15). The true God is not malleable to the whims of even the most skilled operators on earth. Balaam was the best Balak could find to alter the course of history. But not even Balaam can thwart God's intentions.

148

Twice in the story, a three-step sequence heightens the drama. In the hilarious episode with the ass, the not-so-amazing Balaam is, to borrow Milgrom's matchless word, "lampooned." On his way to pronounce a curse over Israel's camp (without permission), Balaam is puzzled by his donkey's behavior. The ass swerves off the road, then mashes Balaam's foot up against a stone wall, and finally (with proverbially mulish stubbornness) lies down and will not budge. After her (yes, the holy man's mount is female) third thrashing, the ass miraculously speaks, upbraiding her rider. Only now does Balaam see the sword-bearing angel blocking the way.

The developing ironies are legion. Balaam is a seer (a see-er), but who sees the angel? Who is the real "beast"? Who is acting mulish? Whose mouth is filled with God's word? Balaam wishes he had a sword, but isn't a sword being brandished right before his eyes? Balaam could not look any worse. His pretensions are unmasked by a mere beast of burden. "Here was this ass, the most stupid of all beasts, and there was the wisest of all wise men, yet as soon as she opened her mouth he could not stand his ground against her" (*Numbers Rabbah* 20:14, quoted in Milgrom, p. 191).

The second buildup takes longer. Balak's first negotiators fail to secure Balaam's services. Balaam defers to the very God Balak hopes to confound! With great deference Balak ventures to the very fringes of his territory (northward to the southern bank of the Arnon river) to welcome this "honored" (well-paid) guest.

Once in camp, Balaam may practice his craft. Mesopotamian *baru*-prophets read omens, by oleomancy (discerning oil patterns in a cup) or hydromancy (water patterns), by hepatoscopy (liver reading) or necromancy (conjuring up dead spirits). Perched on a mountaintop (the "field of the watchers" was well-named, an "overlook" point near Pisgah, Moses' final destination), Balaam may be practicing astrology or even the well-known technique of discerning patterns in the flight of birds. Fastidiously, seven altars are prepared for the burnt offering of the most expensive of animals; no expense is spared. But Balaam gradually dispenses with his craft, receiving ever-clearer messages directly from Israel's God. Though Balaam's performance is 180 degrees from Balak's expectations, the Moabite chieftain stubbornly persists. Like Pharaoh, he is condemned for daring to defy God's purpose. Perhaps in Mesopotamian or Moabite religion god was thought to be fickle, but Israel's God stays the course.

The story of Balaam's "conversion" offered encouragement to Israelite hearers. Babylonian holy men must have loomed as impressive and awesome—over many generations. But the lampooning of Balaam and his inability to do anything but bless would create a sense of triumph, of superiority, of confidence. Before the Lord, all other powers ultimately shrink. Many wry phrases capture the essence of this dynamic: the friction in 22:37-38 and 23:11-12, the rhetorical question in 23:8, the remarkable debunking of Balaam's own profession in 23:23, and Balak's hilarious plea to Balaam in 23:25 ("If you won't curse them, at least refrain from blessing them!"); Balak's flattery of Balaam (22:6) is inverted by Balaam's praise of Israel's God (24:9). The storyteller will not want to miss the climactic, exasperated hand-clapping of the furious Balak (24:10).

Balaam looks bad only during the donkey incident, when he dares to move without the Lord's assent. Other texts censure him roundly (Num. 31:16; Josh. 13:22; II Pet. 2:15; Jude 11; Rev. 2:14). If we remove the vignette from Numbers, though, Balaam appears as a humble, obedient servant of the Lord (Mic. 6:5). It is finally Balak who is lampooned. By employing magic and force, Balak is comparable not only to Pharaoh but also to King Herod. In Balaam's fourth oracle, he utters a mysterious prophecy of a rising star, evidently a messianic vision. At the turn of the first century, Rabbi Akiba applied this "star" (*kokhab*) prophecy to the guerrilla rebel Simon bar-Kokhba. Of course, Christian theology understands Jesus as the rising star (Rev. 22:16). A glimmer of our story radiates through Matthew's account of the Magis' visit to Bethlehem. The star rises over the birthplace; isn't Herod's hysterical ploy to eradicate the light reminiscent of Balak's maneuver (and Pharaoh's)? The good news that rings loud and clear in all of these stories of kin is that the future of the people of God, despite harassment and even their own sin, is bright.

This future certainly does not depend on Israel's own good behavior. Immediately prior to the Balak/Balaam story, the people have faltered miserably (Num. 20:2-13; 21:4-9). Immediately afterward, we stumble across their most heinous, shameful idolatry yet—the Baal of Peor debacle in Numbers 25. Indeed, the Israelites in camp never realize that Balaam and Balak are peering down at them, planning their destruction, and they never realize that God has intervened to protect them. "The people are blessed without even knowing the danger of the curse" (Mann, 138).

For some fascinating parallels to the soothsaying of Balaam (e.g., Mohammed's curse before the battle of Bedr), inspired animals, and especially comets (which have accompanied the deaths of Julius Caesar and Attila the Hun, the Norman conquest of England, and even the apocalyptic fervor of the followers of William Miller in 1843), see Gaster, *Myth, Legend, and Custom in the Old Testament*, pp. 303-10.

Retelling the Story

Kathy was a manager in a large marketing firm. She had been working for the firm for about two years. She had an outstanding record and had been rewarded for her competence with appropriate compensation.

Things went smoothly between Kathy and her own supervisor for about two years. After that something happened that caused Kathy pain and consternation. A new employee was hired in the section Kathy supervised. She delegated hiring responsibilities to department heads who reported to her, because they would be supervising new employees directly. She rarely interfered with their supervision process unless there were problems.

One day Kathy's own supervisor asked her to investigate complaints about an employee who had been hired

> The ox has power, but that power is in its mouth. (The ox pulls up what it eats and sometimes nothing is left after it grazes, according to the rabbis.) Likewise, the power of Israel is in its mouth (its spoken prayers). (*Numbers Rabbah* 20.4, 13)

two weeks earlier, and Kathy agreed to do so. Her supervisor indicated that it had been reported that this new employee had an "attitude problem." Kathy asked her supervisor to be more specific about the particular offensive attitude. However, her supervisor said that she had enough information and that she needed to do what she was told. Kathy then felt more than a little concerned at her supervisor's attitude.

Kathy then met with the person who directly supervised the new employee. She pursued the leads that had been given to her by her own supervisor and tried to find out what the problem was with the new employee's attitude. Kathy was told that the new employee "just would not fit," that the employee did not associate with others or appear to be friendly. Kathy asked for more "specifics" about the new employee's attitude. However, the only thing she was told was that this new person did not fit. Kathy wanted to know about whether the person was performing the required tasks, and she was told that there were no problems with the new employee's job performance. When she realized that no one could be specific about the new employee's inability to "fit," Kathy told the new employee's supervisor that two weeks were not enough time to evaluate whether a new employee would work out or not. She told the supervisor to give the new employee more time and to try to keep a record of incidents demonstrating the "attitude problem."

Kathy then reported her findings to her own supervisor, who got very angry with her because she had not fired the new employee. Kathy reminded her supervisor that she had been told only to investigate the problem and that firing the person never came up in their conversation. Her supervisor said that she needed to "read between the lines" and then said that if she didn't fire the new employee, her own job would be in jeopardy.

Kathy was very disturbed and upset. She faced a real dilemma. She knew the policies of the firm. She knew that there were no grounds to dismiss the new employee. The new employee was already on a sixty-day probation that all new employees had to undergo. At the end of that period this employee could be let go without any questions asked. So she could not figure out why her

Balaam was the wisest of the wise men; yet, he was not as wise as his donkey. That is why God made animals without human speech, according to the rabbis. If they could speak our language, they would never have settled for being beasts of burden. In addition, they would have proven themselves far wiser than humans. For proof of this, just look at Balaam, who could not hold his own against the least intelligent of animals, the donkey. (*Numbers Rabbah* 20.15)

God's friendship is not like human friendship. Most people will drop an old friend when one who is smarter or wealthier comes along. Not so with God. God is a faithful friend to Israel, even though there are richer, smarter, and more powerful nations available. (*Numbers Rabbah* 20.20)

supervisor was so urgent to fire that employee. Why couldn't her supervisor wait until the trial period was over to let the employee go.

Kathy decided that she would talk the matter over with her pastor. Her pastor had preached several times on living out Christian ethics in the workplace. Kathy thought that her pastor could help her decide what she needed to do. She did not want to lose her job. But, on the other hand, she did not want to violate her own sense of Christian justice and fairness.

Kathy shared her concerns with her pastor, who agreed with Kathy. Like Kathy, the pastor could not understand why there was so much urgency to fire this new employee. The pastor said, "Surely, there must be something you have left out about the employee. There must be something wrong with this person that no one is telling you."

Kathy responded, "I don't think they know anything other than what has already been said. There is one fact that I have shared with you that comes to my mind, however. The new employee is African-American, but that should not matter. We have a nondiscriminatory policy." Kathy did remember, however, that her boss firmly disliked affirmative action and vowed never to hire anyone under compulsion.

After talking with her pastor, Kathy decided to follow her own instincts and conscience. She told her pastor, "I would be willing to lose my job over an important principle that is basic to my sense of fairness and Christian beliefs." She felt as if she needed to make a stand.

Wealth and Forgetting

Moses explains why Israel will lose the land if the people pursue other gods and violate the commandments.

The Story

You must carefully observe every command I give you this day so that you may live and increase in numbers and enter and occupy the land which the LORD promised on oath to your forefathers. Remember the whole way by which the LORD your God has led you these forty years in the wilderness to humble and test you, and to discover whether or not it was in your heart to keep his commandments. So he afflicted you with hunger and then fed you on manna which neither you nor your fathers had known before, to teach you that people cannot live on bread alone, but that they live on every word that comes from the mouth of the LORD. The clothes on your backs did not wear out, nor did your feet blister, all these forty years. Take to heart this lesson: that the LORD your God was disciplining you as a father disciplines his son. Keep the commandments of the LORD your God, conforming to his ways and fearing him.

The LORD your God is bringing you to a good land, a land with streams, springs, and underground waters gushing out in valley and hill, a land with wheat and barley, vines, fig trees, and pomegranates, a land with olive oil and honey. It is a land where you will never suffer any scarcity of food to eat, nor want for anything, a land whose stones are iron ore and from whose hills you will mine copper. When you have plenty to eat, bless the LORD your God for the good land he has given you.

See that you do not forget the LORD your God by failing to keep his commandments, laws, and statutes which I give you this day. When you have plenty to eat and live in fine houses of your own building, when your herds and flocks, your silver and gold, and all your possessions increase, do not become proud and forget the LORD your God who brought you out of Egypt, out of that land of slavery; he led you through the vast and terrible wilderness infested with venomous snakes and scorpions, a thirsty, waterless land where he caused water to flow for you from the flinty rock; he fed you in the wilderness with manna which your fathers had never known, to humble and test you, and in the end to make you prosper. Nor must you say to yourselves, 'My own strength and energy have gained me this wealth.' Remember the LORD your God; it is he who gives you strength to become prosperous, so fulfilling the covenant guaranteed by oath with your forefathers, as he does to this day.

If you forget the LORD your God and go after other gods, serving them and bowing down to them, I give you a solemn warning this day that you will certainly be destroyed.	Because of your disobedience to the LORD your God you will be destroyed as surely as were the nations whom the LORD destroyed at your coming.

Comments on the Story

Deuteronomy offers a fascinating biblical model for retelling the story. Compared to Exodus and Numbers, there is little action. Moses bends the ear with very, very long speeches. The Israelites are poised on the east bank of the Jordan, eagerly waiting to cross over into the Promised Land. To prepare them for life in that land, Moses, almost like a mother with her child on her lap, reviews what has transpired over the past forty years. The complete Exodus–Joshua sequence fills many pages, not easily told in a sitting; a hearer could miss the forest for the trees. In the encapsulations of Deuteronomy we see the sum total of God's work. The cumulative effect is staggering indeed.

Moses' retelling is not just interesting, or even profound. The story demands a radical decision (Mann, 147). The theological, homiletical interests of this narrator are evident in just a few phrases that interpret the ancient story. A casual reading of Exodus would lead one to believe that the Lord's intention out in the wilderness was that Israel survive and eventually arrive in the land. But in Deuteronomy 8, deeper motives are ascribed to the Lord in three verbs: *humble, test,* and *discipline* (compare Gen. 22:1; Exod. 17:7; I Kings 8:35; Ps. 119:71; Prov. 3:11; Hos. 11:3). A theologian may plumb these depths; the father/son analogy will ring negative changes for many hearers. But the storyteller must attend to Moses' interpretation. Consider verse 3: The people did not just get hungry; the Lord made them hungry—with the intention of feeding them!

Wryly, cagily, with a hint of "haven't you noticed?" Moses adds two fascinating details, not revealed in Exodus–Numbers, that the storyteller must not miss: (1) Their garments never wore out (in forty years of continuous wear!), and (2) their feet never "blistered" (REB) or "swelled" (NRSV)! Their sandals (miraculously) did not succumb to a forty-year trek through rocky desert (Deut. 29:5; Neh. 9:21). Rashi concluded that God made the clothes of the children grow right along with them. What wondrous love is this!

God's intentions are cogently unveiled in the first of two literary gems in this chapter. The matchless phrase at the end of verse 3 is clearly intended to include all of Israel. The REB's "People cannot live . . ." is not entirely off the mark, but the Hebrew singular *ha'adam* (KJV "man") is perhaps better reflected by "One does not live" (NRSV). God doesn't feed just to feed, but feeds (or blesses in other ways) in order to make possible and to invite persons into a relationship of love and fidelity. One might slip into the trap of injecting some physical/spiritual dichotomy here, but Israelite religion is unabashedly earthy

154

when it comes to human needs and hungers. The contrast is between self-sufficiency and God-dependency. God creates the world by God's "word" (Gen. 1; Ps. 33:6-9), and the manna is but one more reminder of the people's utter dependence on God. The storyteller may just dangle the saying, letting it hang in the air for hearers to ponder.

The second gem appears in verse 17: Never succumb to the perennial human temptation to lay claims, to take credit, to "boast" (in Paul's clever terminology). Were persons actually claiming that "my own strength gained me this wealth"? Or was this boast implicit in their actions and attitudes? In this early instance of the "diatribe" (used most famously by Paul), the wrongheaded are quoted and then reproved. A storyteller could exploit this very technique. The real test for Israel lay ahead. How will Israel handle the gift of the land? Will they be humble? Will they live by "every word from the mouth of God"? Or will they fail the test? Mann captures the essence of it:

> Affluence is not inherently evil, but it is inherently dangerous. The way to avoid an attitude in which materialism replaces allegiance to Yahweh is to remember the story of the wilderness journey, and especially the provision of manna. Israel's greatest treasure is not gold and silver, but the memory of a time of poverty that demonstrated God's love and humankind's dependence. (Mann, 151)

The land remains pure gift, but it is given only in fief. Will Israel "remember"? Or "forget"? Some scholars have disentangled an early usage ("forget" in the sense of taking credit for what the Lord has done) and a late usage ("forget" in the sense of ignoring the commandments). Both early and late, though, the Lord's deeds and the commandments are inseparably interwoven in Israel's common memory; forgetting either or their interconnection is sin.

Whoever put Deuteronomy into its final form used a "sandwich" technique, tracing a series of concentric circles, zeroing in on the gift of the land. Framing the broader Deuteronomy 1–11 narrative are two regrettable incidents, the Kadesh rebellion and the golden calf episode, grim warnings indeed when we recall that those indicted forfeit their taste of the land. Immediately flanking our story are chapters 7 and 9, which discount any illusions that the land is somehow deserved; 7:7 and 9:4-6 remind Israel that, if God rewarded merit, their just desserts would be the desert. In chapter 8 itself, statements of promise (vv. 1, 18), of divine guidance (vv. 2, 15), of "take heed" (vv. 5, 11) focus our attention on the climax, the land (vv. 7-9). This elaborate praise of the land does not settle well with the land of the patriarchs (it was famine that drove them into Egypt in the first place), or with the land that tourists visit today. Over centuries, despoliation has ruined much of the land, only recently revived via agricultural techniques. Perhaps God's intention even in the land "flowing with milk and honey" was that Israel have enough, always enough, but perhaps never much more than enough (v. 9). Surplus seemed to get folks into theological, societal, and political trouble!

In retrospect, we know all too well Israel's failure. Scholars claim the ability to discern at least three moments in which what we call Deuteronomy was thrashed out in retellings pointedly geared to the ancient storyteller's contemporary scene. When the famed "law book" was unearthed in the Temple rubble by Josiah's workmen (II Kings 22–23), the reading of the old, old story had a revolutionary impact on Josiah (even if on no one else). The origins of this "book" are shrouded in mystery, although the best guess fixes its composition in an aborted reformation of the northern kingdom prior to its collapse over a century before Josiah. The juxtaposed promises and warnings were preached loudly and clearly for the northern kingdom. But the words of Deuteronomy, much like the words of Amos and Hosea, fell on deaf ears. The fidelity required of those who would live in God's land was lacking. Consequently, a curse fell in the form of invaders, the dreaded Tiglath-Pileser and Sennacherib of Assyria.

So Josiah read Deuteronomy, not just from the perspective of Israel poised on the banks of the Jordan, but also with the horrifying memories of cousins and colleagues whose "forgetfulness" brought disaster. Hemmed in by Egypt and an even more menacing Neo-Babylonian imperialist state, Josiah hung his hopes on fidelity to the law. Too bad he was slain in his prime, only to be succeeded by men of chicanery and foolishness. Scholars believe that Deuteronomy was revamped once more in the wake of Jerusalem's political misfortunes at the hands of Nebuchadnezzar. The story explained clearly why the people found themselves in such a mess, and offered a dim, yet still flickering, hope in the darkness of exile.

The retold story in Deuteronomy 8 may be retold today by using the prism of scholarship on Deuteronomy. A storyteller may employ any of the various dramatic settings (the northern kingdom at dusk, Judea in the effervescence of Josiah's reform, or Jerusalem in ruins) in which the story spoke. "Remember the wilderness" takes great effort when, as in Josiah's reign, the economy is booming. But while trudging toward Babylonian captivity, "remember the wilderness" could not be more poignant. In a deep sense, each generation finds itself poised once more on the brink, with the same gifts, with the same temptations, with the same decision.

Jesus, of course, brandishes verse 3 to repulse the devil (Matt. 4:4). The same verse lurks in the background of the discourse of John 6. The storyteller is wise to recognize that these two pieces of furniture are in the room any time Deuteronomy 8 is retold.

Retelling the Story

The hardest part wasn't that he had to stay on this side, although he felt miserable standing here on the mountain and looking across at the rugged homeland, knowing that he would not be the one to lead them there. That wasn't the hardest. Not at all.

It was a beautiful sight, the homeland. Early in the morning like this he could see all the valley across the river, and even beyond, into the mountains almost as tall as the one he was on now. And there, in the valley, just the other side of the river, was the town called Jericho. Since he had first heard of its existence, he had sat up nights, planning how to overpower it. But now.

> One rabbi suggested that the reminder of all that God has done for the people left them with three distinctive characteristics: They became bashful, merciful, and benevolent. In some ways this is simply a reflection of the God they follow. (*Deuteronomy Rabbah* 3.4)

No, the hardest part was not that he did not get to enter the new land, although he had wanted nothing more for years. He wanted a piece of the land—just a small piece, large enough for his family and a few sheep. The years watching Jethro's flocks had been some of the best years he could remember, and he wanted to give that experience to his grandchildren. But there would be no piece of land, and there would be no flocks. But that was not the hardest.

What were people going to say? After all they had gone through together—from the now almost-ancient showdown with Pharaoh to the victory over the Amorites "just the other day," they had become a "people." And now he was not going with them.

Some would be saddened by the news. Some would be overjoyed. That had been the hardest thing about the journey. Not the desert, not the shortages—God had seen to it that bread was there for the taking daily. God even kept an eye on their shoes!

No, the hardest had been the people. By comforting one group, he had alienated another. So much time was spent in peace keeping that he had appointed others just to handle those headaches. Once the announcement was made that he was staying here, what would they do? Struggles for power, a fight for control. Would the new leader carry them into the land to claim it, or be satisfied to share some of it with those already there? Or, most frightening of all, would they turn around and go back to the brick yards? What would become of his people? But even that was not what caused the deepest pain.

> The later rabbis of the Hasidic movement said that the greatest danger of haughtiness came from being overly pious. (Plaut, p. 1392)

The hardest was *why* he could not cross the river. Why there would be no land and no flocks. Why, after all these years and miles and miracles, everything was suddenly up for grabs. Why? Somehow he had to tell them why. They had to know what had happened.

Every one of them had to understand that it simply made no difference who you were. It made no difference if you were an enemy king or a loyal servant. It made no difference if you were weak or strong, rich or poor. You could be the pharaoh over all of Egypt or even, yes, even Moses himself. No matter. If you do not follow the lead of God, there will be no homeland. Not for you.

Suddenly, Joshua walked up and stood next to his teacher. They just stood silently together for a moment, taking in the view. One of them would make the journey; the other would not. Nothing else needed to be said. Finally, Joshua lowered his head and said, "They're ready, Moses. Everyone is here, just as you asked."

The great leader sighed, put a hand on Joshua's shoulder, and together they walked back to the waiting people. The old leader took a long, deep breath and began: "Be careful to follow every command I am giving you today, so that. . . ."

DEUTERONOMY 26:1-11

Israel's Little Creed

When giving their offerings, Israelites are to recite the story of their people.

The Story

After you come into the land which the LORD your God is giving you to occupy as your holding and settle in it, you are to take some of the firstfruits of all the produce of the soil, which you harvest from the land which the LORD your God is giving you, and, having put them in a basket, go to the place which the LORD your God will choose as a dwelling for his name. When you come to the priest, whoever he is at that time, say to him, 'I acknowledge this day to the LORD your God that I have entered the land which the LORD swore to our forefathers to give us.' The priest will receive the basket from your hand and set it down before the altar of the LORD your God. Then you must solemnly recite before the LORD your God: 'My father was a homeless Aramaean who went down to Egypt and lived there with a small band of people, but there it became a great, powerful, and large nation. The Egyptians treated us harshly and humiliated us; they imposed cruel slavery on us. We cried to the LORD the God of our fathers for help, and he listened to us, and, when he saw our misery and hardship and oppression, the LORD led us out of Egypt with a strong hand and outstretched arm, with terrifying deeds, and with signs and portents. He brought us to this place and gave us this land, a land flowing with milk and honey. Now I have brought here the firstfruits of the soil which you, LORD, have given me.' You are then to set the basket before the LORD your God and bow in worship before him. You are to rejoice, you and the Levites and the aliens living among you, in all the good things which the LORD your God has bestowed on you and your household.

Comments on the Story

In many cultures, including those of ancient Israel's neighbors, the "first fruits," the season's initial produce from land or livestock, was thought of as especially sacred. *Reshît* in some contexts has the sense of "best" (see Exod. 34:26). Offering up such first fruits has figured in the worship of countless diverse societies. Does this guideline explain what went wrong with Cain's offering? Appropriately the lectionary targets this passage for Thanksgiving

Day. Perhaps it is only in our day that such "natural" blessings have come to be taken for granted. What an image: A poor, simple farmer gathers the first (not the last) of the produce into a basket and carries it to the altar. This most primal storyline may even be reenacted in the sanctuary, a class, or at home.

The earth is the Lord's (Ps. 24), and we are mere steward-tenants. Our text is genuine "torah," guidance for how to show gratitude to God. The law so understood is indeed "sweeter than honey, more precious than gold" (Ps. 19). As always, Israelite religion is characterized by tangibility. You can literally see, feel, taste, and hear it. The offering brings blessing upon the rest of the produce (Lev. 19:24-25). These gifts were essential for the expression of the worshiper and for the support of the sanctuary and its personnel.

But in ancient Israel, creation theology is always an understudy to the theology of God's acting and speaking. For Israel, it isn't just that by the grace of God plants grow out of the ground for our survival; the very presence of Israel in this particular land is a divine blessing.

A contrast is drilled into each generation's collective memory, no matter how sedentary and removed from nomadism or poverty: "My (great-great-great-great-great-great-great grand)father was a homeless Aramaean." While "Aramaean" is a bit obscure (Is the reference to Abraham? Jacob? Isn't this designation a bit anachronistic, since the Aramaeans made their debut on the world stage only in about the fourteenth century B.C.E.?), "homeless" is a provocative, on target translation of 'obed (NRSV "wandering"). Israel's ancestors were indeed landless, without "roots." No whitewashing of the "good old days" for Israel; the harshness of the Egyptian affliction was always constitutive of the current identity of the people. That we once were enslaved and oppressed makes all the difference in who we are, what we think of God, and how we treat others. The worshiper's address to God is direct: "You have given me these fruits." The personalizing of the ancient story is nowhere more vivid. The recitation in 5b-10 is replete with "my/us/we/our/I" pronouns when narrative context would ordinarily demand "their/they/them." Israel preeminently found its identity by identifying with the pair of generations that fled Egypt and entered the land.

Gerhard von Rad popularized the notion that verses 5b-9 represent an ancient creedal formulation of Israel's story. The phrase, "you must solemnly recite," is a formulaic Hebrew word pair ("declare and say") often used in legal and cultic contexts. While a vast array of stories has been encapsulated in these verses, we may at least ask why the twin rescues through the water (the Reed Sea and the Jordan) are omitted. This yawning gap might be comparable to the Apostles' Creed minus, say, the crucifixion and the ascension. We might even expect a cameo appearance of the tenth of the "terrifying deeds, signs and portents"—namely the slaughter of the Egyptian firstborn.

In any case, the theologically vital texts to hold in mind are the seemingly dull land grants in Joshua 13–19. God gives the land, not even in some generalized sense, but very specifically the land you and your family tend. Naboth faithfully refuses to sell his vineyard to Ahab and Jezebel, not to be stubborn or for investment purposes, but because the land is God's, and Naboth's family has been entrusted with its care.

Another small tension in the text has captured the attention of scholars. In verses 2 and 10 it appears that the worshiper puts the basket upon the altar in person. But in verse 4 the priest is injected as middleman. Has a later editor, eager to highlight the indispensability of the priests, added this? Don't pastors suffer from a congenital habit of striding between worshipers and God, saying, "I'll take care of this for you"?

Priestly prerogatives notwithstanding, it is the past, so fraught with difficulty and the sense of divine mercy, that alters ethical behavior in the present. Why care for the needy? Because you too were once needy (Exod. 22:20; 23:9; Deut. 5:13; 10:17; 15:12; 23:8; 24:17; 24:20). Not accidentally appended is the provision for the triennial tithe for the traditional triad of alien, orphan, and widow. Mann points out that "while other ancient Near Eastern law codes protected the widow and the orphan, only in ancient Israelite law was there legislation on behalf of the alien" (Mann, 152). Israel knew about being marginal, "homeless." In Israel, memory determines ethics. Indeed, *justice,* colored by Israel's story, is not when right and wrong are rewarded and punished. *Justice* is when the poor, needy, and helpless are cared for.

This text concludes the long section 12:1–26:15 that presents the law as being responsive to the history of God's care and deliverance (chaps. 1–11). Deuteronomy was put together long after Israel was fully sedentarized. Baskets had been offered for generations. But Deuteronomy's dramatic context portrays Moses delivering his lengthy peroration to Israel, poised on the brink of the Promised Land. Remarkably, the text suggests, "When you enter you will offer up. . . ." Israel is "in camp," preparing for battle; what a mundane, but utterly vital, directive for Israel just prior to entering the land.

In a profound sense, Israel never stops "wandering," being "homeless" (Lev. 25:23; Heb. 3–4). Each generation must in a sense emigrate once again; the Israelite cannot faithfully live in the "now" without squarely recalling the "when." As Mann again puts it so well, this text's imaginative setting "catapults subsequent generations back to a time and place 'beyond the Jordan.' Entrance into the land becomes a perennially potential reality" (Mann, 155).

Retelling the Story

Most good stories begin with "Once upon a time . . ." or "Back in the days of . . ." but this one doesn't. This story simply begins with a heartbeat. It is a *loud* heartbeat—so loud, in fact, that Isha is afraid that his poor heart may burst if it doesn't settle down soon. But the more he thinks about what he is doing, the more loudly his heart calls out.

The whole thing has taken Isha by surprise. Well, not the event itself, but his reaction to it. He has known this day was coming for a long time. In fact, since that first day he and his family came to this land he knew that before long he would be here, doing this. But he certainly had not expected it to feel like it does.

As he walks up the path, he wonders whether the others feel as he does. They are all here. There is Jerab, who owns the farm just north of Isha's. His basket is impressive, filled with sheaves of barley. He looks so composed.

> The Babylonian Talmud says that one cannot enjoy anything from the hand of God without offering a blessing in return. The prayer here is a reminder that God brought the farmer to the land and that God is present in the ordinary cycles of planting, growing, and harvesting. The first fruits are a blessing offered back to God from God's own bounty. (Marvin Wilson, *Our Father Abraham* [Philadelphia: Eerdmans, 1989], pp. 156-57)

"Blessings of a good morning be with you Jerab!" Isha calls.

"And also with you, good Isha," the neighbor replies.

Isha smiles. "And also with you," Jerab had said. But the way he said it! Jerab's voice was as shaky as Isha's. It is the voice their young sons use on the morning before the seder meal; so excited about what is to happen, but terrified that they might do something that might earn them a scolding.

At least he was not the only one. The others are just as nervous. Funny how something so simple can make an old man shake like a child again. Really, what could possibly go wrong? Carry in a few sheaves of the first barley cuttings, walk up to the big stone altar, lay the sheaves next to the base of the rock, recite a couple of sentences, and go home. Simple.

But every time he thought about how simple it was, he would remember how unsimple it had been just a year ago. His family had come from nowhere to somewhere. He remembered how it felt to come into a land after living so long out of one. He remembered making the journey that everyone had said could not be made. He remembered the bread from heaven and the water from the rock. He remembered the victories over stronger armies. He remembered.

And now, all he had to do was carry a few sheaves of barley up to a big rock altar, say "Thank you," and go home.

If only he could get his heart to quiet down a bit.

162

The Death of Moses

Moses dies in good health at the age of one hundred twenty, and Joshua assumes leadership.

The Story

Moses went up from the lowlands of Moab to Mount Nebo, to the top of Pisgah eastwards from Jericho, and the LORD showed him the whole land, from Gilead to Dan; the whole of Naphtali; the territory of Ephraim and Manasseh, and all Judah as far as the western sea; the Negeb and the plain; the valley of Jericho, city of palm trees, as far as Zoar. The LORD said to him, 'This is the land which I swore to Abraham, Isaac, and Jacob that I would give to their descendants. I have let you see it with your own eyes, but you will not cross over into it.'

There in the Moabite country Moses the servant of the LORD died, as the LORD had said. He is buried in a valley in Moab opposite Beth-peor; but to this day no one knows his burial-place.

Moses was a hundred and twenty years old when he died, his sight undimmed, his vigour unimpaired. The Israelites wept for Moses in the lowlands of Moab for thirty days.

The time of mourning for Moses came to an end. Joshua son of Nun was filled with the spirit of wisdom, for Moses had laid his hands on him. The Israelites listened to him and did what the LORD had commanded Moses.

There has never yet risen in Israel a prophet like Moses, whom the LORD knew face to face: remember all the signs and portents which the LORD sent him to show in Egypt to Pharaoh and all his servants and the whole land; remember the strong hand of Moses and the awesome deeds which he did in the sight of all Israel.

Comments on the Story

Venerable, hoary-headed Moses has spent his waning moments in an eloquent filibuster. The angel of death will wait no longer. Moses withdraws from the camp to a high place for a climactic moment alone with the God he first met eighty years earlier on another mountain. In the Ptolemaic worldview, if you went up topographically, you were just a bit closer to God. Moses' ascent has numerous parallels: Dante's purgatorial mountain spirals up to a restored Eden; in *The Faerie Queene,* Saint George is granted a view of the heavenly city from a mountaintop.

What can be seen from the top of Pisgah is a breathtaking panorama of the Promised Land. Mount Nebo, modern Jebel en-Nebu, soars over four thousand feet above the Dead Sea, whose northern tip washes against the mountain's southwestern foot. A spot called Ras es-Siyaghah, just across a small dip to the northwest, is usually identified as Pisgah; Ras es-Siyaghah affords the best view of the Jordan valley and the land beyond.

How are we made privy to this moment? One tradition claims that Moses wrote prophetically of his own demise. Another (Ibn Ezra) attributes Deuteronomy 34 to Joshua. This type of mountaintop survey was originally a legal act, in which tracts of land would be transferred. Compare the pertinent parallel in Genesis 13:14-16, in which the Lord and Abram scan the vast land to be given (and also the devil's proposed real estate deal with Jesus in Matt. 4:8). One cannot really see to the Mediterranean from Pisgah, so we have a symbolic sweep of all that will be given. Almost after the style of Egyptian execration texts, the land is summarily covered in zigzags, south to north (Gilead to Dan), zigging back down the Jordan valley, zagging to the west, zigging back around through the southern Negeb up to Jericho (just across the ford), then crazily zagging back south to Zoar. Until breathing his last, Moses is Israel's representative, signing the papers to the long-anticipated land.

Why does he have to die? Does he perish vicariously for the sins of the people (Deut. 1:37; 4:21)? Was it a picayune punishment for the mini-sin of striking the rock (Num. 20:12)? His untimely death was neither bad luck nor mere fate, but it was according to the incontrovertible word of the Lord (v. 5).

The poignancy of the moment cannot be underestimated. Mercifully granted a glimpse of his life's goal, Moses himself cannot make the crossing, only a few weeks away. Characteristically, the text offers no psychological portrayal of his feelings. In 3:25-27 we do read that he "begged" to be able to enter the Promised Land. Certain as we may be that his heart was swirling with joy, sorrow, gratitude, regret, or exasperation, the story trusts the reader, simply reporting the all-too-brief yet comprehensive glance across the tableau, and then the decidedly undramatic death. A last glimmer of adulation is noted: sight undimmed, vigor unimpaired, Moses' own "murmur" in 31:2 notwithstanding. A month of mourning was not too long at all (see Num. 20:29). The mantle had already been passed to Joshua (Num. 27:15-23). God's continuing care for Israel is demonstrated in a rush of wisdom upon the son of Nun.

Joshua will fill Moses' sandals, but there will never be another Moses. Verse 9 is precise: They listen to Joshua, and they do what the Lord commanded Moses! Joshua does not speak face to face with God so much as he implements what Moses learned face to face. The Pentateuch is rightly labeled "the books of Moses"; he is gone, and the sense looms that the burden from now on will fall on the people to remember Moses and his words. Weaned from the person of Moses, they must now walk with God themselves.

The Pentateuch thereby ends on a dour note. The storyline could more triumphally skip from Numbers into Joshua, yielding a happy ending to the trek. Deuteronomy seems an interloper, repeating what has gone before, but cutting us off before the climax. Yet, in Judaism, the Pentateuch, not the Hexateuch, bears the highest stamp of authority. The storyteller may wish to capture hints of the dynamic at work in this surprising breaking point. In a meaningful sense, Israel never came into the land. They came in, but their fidelity did not match God's gift. In just a few centuries they lost the land. For most of history, Jews have remained outside the land, sojourners, aliens, not yet home. The story presents each generation with the same choice offered to that first generation. We always wait, poised to receive God's gifts, challenged to live a life commensurate with those gifts. The opening chapters of Hebrews are but variations on this theme.

The mummy of the pharaoh of the exodus has been studied. Aaron's tomb has been visited in the isolated desert fortress of Petra. But mystery shrouds not only Moses' tomb, but even his death as well. No promontory or cave on Pisgah has spoken up for bragging rights. Did this holy man, who spoke face to face with God, die at all? The little-read epistle of Jude sparkles with several little jewels, one of which is the unexplained notice that the devil and the archangel Michael disputed over possession of Moses' corpse (Jude 9)! Philo, for whom Moses was practically god incarnate, claimed that Moses was summoned from the mountain to immortality. The Talmud notes that many believe Moses never died at all. Aboth de Rabbi Nathan (157) says that Moses was translated directly to heaven, welcomed tumultuously, clothed in light, beginning an eternity of studying Torah and interceding for Israel. In a cameo role in the Transfiguration, Moses lives a heavenly life alongside Elijah, who was snatched up from this earth aboard a fiery chariot.

But doesn't Deuteronomy 34:6 say that Moses was buried? The REB and the NRSV have followed an old tradition of introducing a passive ("he was buried") or a plural ("they buried him"), when the plain intent of the best texts we have is "he buried him." He who? Wasn't Moses alone? Isn't the Lord the implied subject of the verb? Moses was especially vouchsafed to the Lord's keeping. This mystery has the effect of protracting Moses' life, and more so his words. In the pseudepigraphal Testament of Moses (see James H. Charlesworth, *The Old Testament Pseudepigrapha* [Garden City, N.Y.: Doubleday, 1983], p. 933), Joshua, bidding Moses farewell, sagaciously declares, "All the world is your sepulchre."

Retelling the Story

The two of them were as different as night and day, but to see them standing there together you would have thought they were brothers.

165

The whole story is just too long to tell in one sitting, but I can tell you enough now to help you understand what you are seeing. Well, you will understand it as much as any of us understand it.

You see, the one standing there is a king. Actually, said to be the greatest king that ever was. A few years ago, the great king had a project that needed to be accomplished and decided it would be best to find someone to work "through" to get the job done. You know how things are with busy great kings.

So, as you have probably guessed, that's where the second guy comes in. He is not a king. In fact, when he got the call for an interview he was an escaped criminal working as a part-time shepherd down south. To be honest with you, if the great king worked with committees, this guy would never have been hired, but after some drawn-out negotiations the deal was made.

> Seeing that death was near, Moses told the people he had caused them great difficulty in bringing the Torah and the rule and regulations of their religion and asked them to forgive him, and they forgave him. Then the people told Moses that they knew the great difficulty they had brought upon him by being so "stiff-necked" and asked him to forgive them. Moses forgave them. (Plaut, p. 1585)

The two of them working together made quite a name for themselves. If we had the time, I could thrill you with tales of daring carried out by the great king and his partner, but I'll sum it all up by just pointing out that the whole experience goes to show that it's not always an easy thing to be the "front" man for a great king.

The two of them had their ups and downs. Part of the time things moved amazingly well. At those times the two of them worked together like twins. At other times it seems they pretty well got fed-up with each other, and if it hadn't been for the contract they had made, each might have gone his separate way.

But the result of all this hassle was that the two of them really grew to like each other. Even though it was always clear that one of them was a great king and the other was a whole lot less, neither had ever known before—or would again—the respect and friendship they felt for each other.

And so, there they stand. Shoulder to shoulder, saying things like, "Do you remember that time when. . . ?" and "Wasn't that something when. . . ?" You see, the project was over. Each of them had fulfilled his part of the contract, and there was nothing more for them to do together, but neither of them really wanted to say it outloud. Then quietly, the hired "front man" leans over, smiles, and dies. The great king holds him close and carries him down the hill. We are going to stay up here and let them have their time together. After all, that's the way it should be.

Moses asked God for a favor. Even though he could not enter the Promised Land as a human, would God allow him to fly over it like a bird or graze upon it like a cow? God's answer was no. But this must have been spoken with some sadness because, the rabbis say, God wept, along with the earth and heavens, when Moses finally died. (Plaut, p. 1586)

Spies in the Land

Joshua sends spies into the Promised Land who are taken in and protected by Rahab.

The Story

Joshua a son of Nun sent out two spies secretly from Shittim with orders to reconnoitre the land and especially Jericho. The two men set off and came to the house of a prostitute named Rahab to spend the night there. When it was reported to the king of Jericho that some Israelites had arrived that night to explore the country, he sent word to Rahab: 'Bring out the men who have come to you and are now in your house, for they have come to spy out the whole country.' The woman, who had taken the two men and hidden them, replied, 'True, the men did come to me, but I did not know where they came from; and at nightfall when it was time to shut the gate, they had gone. I do not know where they were going, but if you hurry after them you may overtake them.' In fact, she had brought them up on to the roof and concealed them among the stalks of flax which she had laid out there in rows. The messengers went in pursuit of them in the direction of the fords of the Jordan, and as soon as they had gone out the gate was closed.

The men had not yet settled down, when Rahab came up to them on the roof, and said, 'I know that the LORD has given the land to you; terror of you has fallen upon us, and the whole country is panic-stricken. We have heard how the LORD dried up the waters of the Red Sea before you when you came out of Egypt, and what you did to Sihon and Og, the two Amorite kings beyond the Jordan, for you destroyed them. When we heard this, our courage failed; your coming has left no spirit in any of us; for the LORD your God is God in heaven above and on earth below. Swear to me by the LORD that you will keep faith with my family, as I have kept faith with you. Give me a token of good faith; promise that you will spare the lives of my father and mother, my brothers and sisters, and all who belong to them, and preserve us from death.' The men replied, 'Our lives for yours, so long as you do not betray our business. When the LORD gives us the country, we shall deal loyally and faithfully by you.'

She then let them down through a window by a rope; for the house where she lived was on an angle of the wall. 'Make for the hills,' she said, 'or the pursuers will come upon you. Hide there for three days until they return; then go on your way.' The men warned her that, unless she did what they told her, they would be free from the oath she had made them take. 'When we invade the land,' they said, 'you must fasten this strand of scarlet cord in the window through which you have lowered us, and get everybody together here inside the house, your father and mother, your brothers, and all your family. Should anybody go out of doors into the street, his blood will be on his own head; we shall be free of the oath. But if a hand is laid on anyone who stays indoors with you, his blood be on our heads! Remember too that, if you betray our business, then we shall be free of the oath you have made us take.' 'It shall be as you say,' she replied, and sent them on their way. When they had gone, she fastened the strand of scarlet cord in the window.

The men made their way into the hills and stayed there for three days until the pursuers returned. They had searched all along the road, but had not found them. The two men then came down from the hills and crossed the river. When they joined up with Joshua son of Nun, they reported all that had happened to them. 'The LORD has delivered the whole country into our hands,' they said; 'the inhabitants are all panic-stricken at our approach.'

Comments on the Story

The ancient city of Jericho, today called Tell es-Sultan, was strategically important for Israel's entry. The story presupposes a walled city with a gate that would be closed for security by night. Rahab's house is said to be literally in the wall (*qyr*) of the wall (*hwmh*). We guess that this expression refers to "casemate" fortifications in which two parallel walls are built with perpendicular walls in between. Some of the rooms created would be filled with rocks and dirt, some used for storage, others as houses. Defensively such a wall system was designed to withstand a battering-ram assault. The story envisions Rahab living in such a home, albeit with a window to the outside. Such casemate construction may have been unearthed at Jericho, although precise identification and the dating are problematical.

Rahab must have had family (see Josh. 6:25; Matt. 1:5). A "prostitute" in Late Bronze Age Jericho is not quite the equivalent of today's streetwalker. Hebrew *zonah* describes not only sex-for-hire, but also sacred prostitution. In Canaanite religion, the liturgy often prescribed sexual activity. Far from being brothels, however, the sacred precincts were places where worshipers hoped by their own mating to prod reproductive activity among the gods (and hence, to elicit the climate for agricultural success). Rahab is not specifically designated as a "sacred" prostitute, though; and the gist of the story may indicate that her business was of a secular sort.

Why do the spies go to the prostitute's house? The question is left hanging. Boling (p. 145) humorously asks, "Where better to get information than a bar?" Tantalizingly the story reports no other actual reconnaissance; in Numbers 13 the scouting party executed a ballpark census, a broadly based survey of fortifications, clandestine fruit gathering. Infamous associations of military service and prostitution may lurk in the background.

Rahab, though, may be paradigmatic of what many scholars see as a socio-logical revolution coinciding with Israel's migration into Canaan. Evidently many marginal, disenfranchised, disadvantaged persons found the societal structure issuing from this new religion to be appealing, even liberating from the injustices of the Canaanite petty lords who grew wealthy at the expense of the populace. A storyteller would not be out of bounds to portray Rahab as even the first "convert" to a new society that (at least ideally) refrained from taking advantage of women and other oppressed persons.

What a surprise that the first to switch sides was a woman! Her grasp of Israel's sacred story is impressive indeed (vv. 9-11)—how ironic that the first teller of sacred stories in the book of Joshua is a Canaanite prostitute! As in Exodus, the curtain of hope is defiantly drawn back by civil disobedience. Shiphrah, Puah, and Rahab are women of mettle who hold no earthly king in awe, who do not shy away even from lying to undo the powers that be. The New Testament capitalizes on the role of women in the new "movement" to an astonishing degree. Though a prostitute, Rahab was remembered as an admit-tedly non-traditional model of faith (James 2:25; Heb. 11:31). Josephus and the Targum whitewash a bit by insisting that she was only an "innkeeper." Jewish lore imagined that she was the wife of Joshua and the ancestor of eight prophets (including Jeremiah, Ezekiel, and Huldah). She figures as one of only four women in Matthew's genealogy. Rahab, Ruth, Tamar, and Bathsheba have somewhat checkered pasts; yet, to such does the kingdom of God come!

How many stories hinge on a dramatic escape through a window? David became an outlaw from his father-in-law when Michal engineered a nocturnal escape through a back window (I Sam. 19:12). The newly converted Paul elud-ed assassination in Damascus via a basket ride out of a window (Acts 9:25; II Cor. 11:33). Did anyone back then think to call the basket a *tevah* (see com-ments on Exodus 2)?

Close attention to the sequence in Joshua 2:13-21 strangely enough finds the spies dangling from the window while they negotiate. Even more strangely, the ruse seems to violate the holy war legislation of Deuteronomy 20:10-20 as well as incidents such as those described in Joshua 7:1 and I Samuel 15. Yet, in Judges 1:23-25 a man who gives directions to spies is spared annihilation. We may even wonder why reconnaissance was needed at all, since the seizure will be miraculous, not military. Of course, the color of the thread is reminiscent of the sprinkling of blood on the door lintels during the climactic plague back in Egypt (Exod. 12:13).

Not coincidentally, Joshua sends out two spies. He knew something about reconnaissance himself; with Caleb he had spied out the same land forty years earlier, only to suffer the people's disbelief at the hands of the other ten spies.

The storyteller may profitably recall, though it is a minor detail, that Joshua, the ex-spy, sends only two spies this time.

Before Israel destroys Jericho (with the exception of Rahab, who has been granted immunity), a fortnight of ritual preparation must be completed.

Retelling the Story

She had been fascinated with the idea ever since the first time she had overheard its mention. Most people assumed she spent very little time "deep" in thought. It was probably their way of making those assumptions that made the new idea so fascinating to her.

She could not remember who she had overheard talking about it. It was some man, on some night. In her mind they all ran together. He had been talking with the others about preparations the city was making for the possible attack by a new group of people coming into the region. She half-listened as the men talked about such things as gate fortifications and securing the water supply. In fact, when they started describing the new people themselves she was getting up to leave the room to find something more interesting.

According to folk tradition, Rabab lived an immoral life from the time she was ten until the age of fifty, when she met the spies and became a follower of the God of Israel. This popular belief has it that she later married Joshua and became the forebear of nine prophets, including the woman prophet Hulda. (Ginzberg, IV, p. 5)

That's when she overheard it. It was said in passing. The only reaction from the group was a groan and a few sarcastic smiles. She hoped no one had noticed her reaction. The man had simply said that one of the most foolish behaviors of this group of wanderers was the way they treated their poor. It seemed that their God required them not only to protect the poor and outcast, but also to actually care for them and take them in. It was then that someone reached over and slapped her behind and demanded a drink, making her miss the rest of the conversation. But she had heard enough.

She had often dreamed of what it would be like to be taken care of. Not the way it was now. Now, if she was good enough, made them happy enough, they treated her fairly well. But she clearly understood who she really was. She was an outcast. Some women in the city were property. Some were "sacred" prostitutes, about as high up the social ladder as a woman could hope to climb. But she was far from "sacred." She was a "thing," or if the truth be known, probably a "nothing." She was treated however her customers cared to treat her. And she deeply hoped that none of them had seen her face when she had overheard their comments.

Tonight her mind is not on her work. She spent most of the evening in the kitchen, keeping bowls filled, letting the other "nothings" fill the other needs. If only dreams could come true. "Protected and cared for." She would do anything to have a share in that way of living. Anything.

In honest desperation she put down the bowl she was filling and looked out the window toward the east. She closed her eyes a moment, and using the only name for it she heard them use, said, "Oh great God of the mountain, if there is any way you would protect and care for someone like me. . . ."

> The Zohar says that there was as much difference between Moses and Joshua as there is between the sun and the moon. This gave rise to the folk belief in some communities that the man in the moon was Joshua. (Ginzberg IV, p. 4; VI, p. 171)

She was interrupted by a woman at the doorway. Dreams would have to wait. Two new strangers had just come to the door needing attention. Too bad. She would have to go back to work.

Crossing the Jordan

The people carry the Ark of the Covenant across the Jordan, and the water stops flowing, which allows them to cross the stream just as their forebears had crossed through the sea.

The Story

The LORD said to Joshua, "Today I shall begin to exalt you in the eyes of all Israel, and they will know that I shall be with you as I was with Moses. Give this order to the priests who carry the Ark of the Covenant: When you come to the edge of the waters of the Jordan, you are to take your stand in the river.'

Joshua said to the Israelites, 'Draw near and listen to the words of the LORD your God.' He went on, 'By this you will know that the living God is among you and that he will without fail drive out before you the Canaanites, Hittites, Hivites, Perizzites, Girgashites, Amorites, and Jebusites: the Ark of the Covenant of the Lord of all the earth is to cross the Jordan at your head. Choose now twelve men from the tribes of Israel, one from each tribe. As soon as the priests carrying the Ark of the LORD, the Lord of all the earth, set foot in the waters of the Jordan, then the waters of the Jordan will be cut off; the water coming down from upstream will stand piled up like a bank.'

The people set out from their encampment to cross the Jordan, with the priests in front carrying the Ark of the Covenant. Now the Jordan is in full flood in all its reaches throughout the time of harvest, but as soon as the priests reached the Jordan and their feet touched the water at the edge, the water flowing down from upstream was brought to a standstill; it piled up like a bank for a long way back, as far as Adam, a town near Zarethan. The water coming down to the sea of the Arabah, the Dead Sea, was completely cut off, and the people crossed over opposite Jericho. The priests carrying the Ark of the Covenant of the LORD stood firmly on the dry bed in the middle of the river, and all Israel passed over on dry ground, until the whole nation had completed the crossing of the Jordan.

Comments on the Story

Most of the year, the Jordan River isn't much of a river at all. A "meandering ditch," while not very romantic or picturesque, is more accurate. We wish we could pinpoint the exact locations of Shittim, Adam (possibly Tell el-Damiyek, just below the mouth of the Jabbok), Zarethan, and even Gilgal so we could target the exact spot of this miracle. The general area, though, was an obvious port of entry to the central hill country. Given what we know of the general area above the Allenby bridge, the greater miracle might be scaling the steep inclines on either side of the ditch, trees and brush clogging the way, rather than getting across the ditch itself.

But to comprehend verses 15-16 we must know that, while an easily fordable ditch most of the year, in the late spring ("harvest") the river is in flood. The huge swath cut through the overhanging cliffs indicates periods of massive waterflow over many millennia. So the picture is that the Israelites first step into the water of the flood plain (at many points more than a mile wide), but that the flow of the river (precariously dangerous, due to sudden variations in depth, to the crooked course of the channel, and to the swiftness of the flow) is stopped up before they proceed into the deepest parts. The water stands up in a "bank" (ned, meaning "heap," with the connotation of becoming gelatinized; ned also describes the walls of the yam suf in Exod. 15:8).

What dammed the water? History records instances of a bank collapsing upstream, temporarily stopping up the Jordan's flow. An earthquake precipitated such a landslide on July 11, 1927; the waters were withheld for twenty-one hours! Of course, the Jordan is not in flood in July. The story, though, has no intrinsic interest in earthquakes and landslides, but has its eyes open for the "mighty acts" of God. As in later battles, it is the presence of the ark that brings deliverance.

No military heroics occur here. Joshua gives orders, not as a brilliant tactician of guerrilla warfare but as a prophet-like mouthpiece for the genuine commander and leader, the Lord. Preparation, however, is necessary for the recipients of this miracle. Purification rituals may have included abstinence from sexual relations and foods, and washings (recall Uriah's restraint in II Sam. 11). Readiness will be crucial. This time, the danger will not be a chariot force pursuing from the rear. The peril lies ahead in the form of the same giants who had frightened off the original posse in Numbers 13.

How remarkable it is that Israel's twin stories of deliverance and occupation involve the parting of waters. The primal, almost mythological, sense of the danger and power of bodies of water might be exploited by the storyteller. Beyond recognizing historical ways to surmount physical barriers, Israel sensed a profound rescue from the most visceral sort of peril in these miracles. Perhaps this begins to explain the ongoing power of the story. In modern hymnody, crossing over Jordan has become a powerful metaphor for personal, political, and indeed eschatological hope.

Our text proper is only the central section of the fuller narrative that runs from 3:1 to 4:18. Even these two chapters are not easily separated from the whole story running from 1:1 to 5:12, which narrates a sequence of events that occupy exactly one week. Shrouded as the events are in the distant past, we catch glimpses of the primary context in which this story was first told. The scene draws to a temporary close with the provision for two twelve-stone memorials to the event. Stones are drawn from the river, to form the focal point of what will be the Gilgal sanctuary. Curiously, Joshua also makes provision for another set of stones in the river bed itself. The stones, reminiscent in hearer's minds of Stonehenge on the Salisbury plain in England, were to prompt the curiosity of children (see Deut. 6:2, 20).

This circle of stones (*Gilgal* means "circle") constituted an early worship center in which the story of the crossing was not just told but probably reenacted. We have a possible script for the reenactment. The drama would last a week, culminating in the Passover (5:10-12). The ark would be carried in solemn procession across the river once more; some scholars have even speculated that the river would be dammed upstream to recreate the miracle of the "dry bed," hardly a difficult feat.

The storyteller today may capitalize on Israel's very own habits of retelling and even reenacting their story. The people gathered to experience anew the primal saving events that were much more than once-upon-a-time. So, march around, carry a box on poles, get your feet wet!

Remarkable details in the story merit emphasis. After Joshua got busy early in the morning, the people "pulled up tent stakes" (the literal sense of *wayyis 'u*, 3:1). The focus is on "crossing" (taken from '*br*, which may explain something of the meaning of "Hebrew," '*bry*, those who "crossed over"?); the root occurs some twenty times in 3:1–4:18. A safe distance must be maintained between mere mortals and the divinely "charged" ark in order to avoid Uzzah's fate (II Sam. 6:6-9). The ark practically serves as the compass. The distance (2,000 cubits is just over one-half mile) is short, but the terrain is sufficiently steep and cavernous that getting lost is hardly out of the question.

Those in the procession do get their feet wet! The NRSV rightly includes the specification, "the soles of their feet." Those bearing the weight of the ark would experience a degree of sinking into the rich soil; mud oozing between the toes is hardly melodramatic. The rabbis delighted in whoever must have been the first one to get his (or her) feet wet in crossing the sea leaving Egypt. And that is no less so here. The story shares the marvelous detail that it is only after the people have actually stepped into the rushing current that the waters are restrained. A miraculous element in the story seems to be not just the withdrawal of the stream but the actual dryness of the river bed; those crossing may be said to be stunned, no longer sinking down into mud, but "standing firmly on dry ground in the middle of the Jordan." Even ditches do not dry very quickly.

175

Retelling the Story

They had peeked at it time and again as they made their way north through the mountains of Moab. Every so often there had been a wadi sloping down toward the great valley, and in the distance they could see the shimmering. At times it was a brilliant blue, bluer than the heavens themselves. At other times it was a dull gray; a fiery red; ever-changing. It was the constant change that helped make it so frightening. But, fortunately, it was always at the other end of some valley. They would not have to come near the water. Until now.

Some sources portray Joshua as a Jewish Oedipus. Nun and his wife could have no children for a very long time. When it finally became clear that his wife would soon have a child, Nun wept and mourned instead of rejoicing. When she asked why he cried, he told her that he had received a divine intuition that his own child would cut off Nun's head. As soon as Joshua was born, his mother left him out in the elements to die, so that he might not commit the terrible sin of killing his father. But Joshua was swallowed by a whale (like Jonah) and finally did decapitate his father (without knowing who it really was) on the orders of Pharaoh. Just as he was about to take his mother (again unknown to him) as his pay for the execution, God caused her breast to flow milk, and Joshua recognized her as his mother just in time. (Ginzberg IV, p. 3; VI, p. 169)

Now, it was right here in front of them. Almost a mile of water, flowing with the currents of flood season. To many people this would be of no concern. People lived in and around water all over the world. But not this people. This was a desert people. Give them a sandstorm or a nest of scorpions, and they would know exactly what to do. But here? This was the stuff of which nightmares were made.

At night, around the campfire, the old men told the already ancient tales of leviathan, the great beast that lived in the waters. As the stories were spun, from just outside the light of the fires they could hear the bubbling and splashing of the flood waters crawling by. It *was* a nightmare.

There were other stories. A few storytellers kept reminding everyone about the time another generation had walked right through the water, chasing it away while they passed on dry ground. But that was a generation ago, and this was now. Who knows what was hiding in that seething, murky flood in front of them? Besides, Moses led that group, and Moses was not here. They had Moses, and we had Joshua. We might follow Moses into the waters, but Joshua?

Joshua listened to all the stories. But he also listened to the Storyteller the others did not hear. It was because of this "hidden" teller of stories that Joshua took the chance he did.

As the priests leading the procession stepped near the water they stopped and looked over to see what Joshua was going to do. Moses at least had a big stick. He had at least pointed it at the water and commanded that it stand aside for his people. Joshua just stood there nodding his head for them to move ahead.

One more step would put them in the water.

In addition to stopping the water flow of the Jordan, God caused many other amazing occurrences to take place. One was that when the priests began to move out of the Jordan toward the shore, the ark began to move on its own, literally pulling the priests along behind it. (Ginzberg IV, p. 6)

Passover at Gilgal

After the Israelites celebrate Passover, Joshua has a visitor from God.

The Story

The LORD then said to Joshua, 'Today I have rolled away from you the reproaches of the Egyptians.' Therefore the place is called Gilgal to this day.

While the Israelites were encamped in Gilgal, at sunset on the fourteenth day of the month they kept the Passover in the lowlands of Jericho. On the day after the Passover they ate of the produce of the country, roasted grain and loaves made without leaven. It was from that day, when they first ate the produce of the country, that the manna ceased. The Israelites got no more manna; that year they ate what had grown in the land of Canaan.

When Joshua was near Jericho he looked up and saw a man standing in front of him with a drawn sword in his hand. Joshua approached him and asked, 'Are you for us or for our enemies?' The man replied, 'Neither! I am here as captain of the army of the LORD.' Joshua prostrated himself in homage, and said, 'What have you to say to your servant, my lord?' The captain of the LORD's army answered, 'Remove your sandals, for the place where you are standing is holy'; and Joshua did so.

Comments on the Story

The name *Gilgal* means "circle," so dubbed because of an ancient circle of sizable stones that must have marked a very ancient shrine. While not exactly of the grandeur of Stonehenge, this "circle" cannot be located with certainty. Just over a mile from ancient Jericho, Gilgal played a pivotal role in the days of Samuel (I Sam. 7:16). Within just a few hundred years, Amos and Hosea had to indict a pagan cult that had usurped Gilgal. Such circles of stones were common religious sites in the land. Gilgal was just one "circle" with a significant history for Israel (see Exod. 24:4; I Kings 18:31-35).

This story comes to us by an indirect route. We do not have a videotape of the original crossing and first Passover, but the liturgy of a much later worship setting in which the original was being retold for at least the hundredth time. In the misty recesses of Israelite pre-history, we may discern shadowy figures pulling stones up out of the Jordan River bed and fashioning a circular shrine some five miles along the way to Jericho. Shades of a festival at Gilgal, featuring the ark in solemn array, are dimly apparent as well.

But more than six centuries have passed before our story's ink was put to parchment. The time is Passover, the family-centered worship occasion. At Passover the youngest son rises to ask, "Why is this night special?" In Joshua 4:6, children are pictured asking the meaning of the circle of stones (see also Deut. 6:7-23). They are memorials to the obverse side of God's mighty redemption of the people. At Passover, Israel was rescued from Egypt, and, in appropriately divine timing, at Passover Israel was deposited in the Promised Land. The double significance of the Passover is hence preserved: The lamb sacrifice is a commemoration of the blood-stained doorposts as well as thanksgiving for God's gift of fertility in the land. Israel reenacts the dual deliverance, from Egypt and into Canaan, in a ceremony in which the River Jordan plays twin parts: as itself and doubling as the Reed Sea (too far away and in territory too perilous to frequent for a worship celebration). A seven-day course of remembrance may clearly be detected in the broader story of Joshua 1–5: three days of preparation (1:1–3:6), including the crossing itself (3:7-17); three days to set up the circle (4:1-24), including time for surgery and a brief convalescence (5:1-9); and finally the Passover. Jericho would succumb in the next seven-day period, filling out the prescribed time for Unleavened Bread. Amazingly, the manna stopped falling on the very Passover day on which Israel began to enjoy the fruit of the land. Again, the Lord provides just enough—no more, no less. "The miraculous help given in the wilderness is replaced by the equally great miracle which is constantly experienced anew by the devout Israelite (cf. Hos. 2), the spring harvest" (Soggin, *Joshua: A Commentary* [Philadelphia: Westminster Press, 1972], p. 75).

But if Joshua was written down during the generation that was going into Babylonian exile, then this story would take on weighty import. For a people about to leave the land, how heartening and encouraging it would be to recall how God long ago miraculously brought them home after a long wandering outside the land. The psalmist's question, "How shall we sing the Lord's song in a foreign land?" is answered, however partially, in Joshua 5. Two definitive marks will preserve Israel's identity even in a hostile land while another deliverance is awaited: circumcision (Josh. 5:2-9) and the Passover (Josh. 5:10-12). As children would ask about such curious traditions, parents could recount a story that was not once-upon-a-time, but was practically eschatological in the sense of rekindling a profound hope and brandishing a proud identity in a renewed Egypt-like situation that could be humiliating. It is little wonder that there was a desire to restore the often-neglected Passover observance in the days leading up to the deportation under Nebuchadnezzar (II Kings 23:21-23). Just as the opening chapters of Exodus sought to mock the pharaoh, so also this section (esp. 5:1) would spur late seventh-century Israelites to defiant determi-

nation in the face of the political reincarnation of Rameses II, the dreaded Nebuchadnezzar of Babylon. Evidence has mounted that this Lord can deliver
(Josh. 4:24; Exod. 32:12; the "melting hearts" of 5:1 reminds us of Exod.
15:13-17 and Josh. 2:10-11). A creative storyteller could invoke the specter of
Nebuchadnezzar's war machine threatening a hearty, faithful family, sitting by
night in a circle, eating the Passover meal, a parent regaling the children with a
timeless, yet timely, story about a long-defunct assembly at a distant place
called Gilgal.

A clever pun has come to punctuate the story. Gilgal (meaning "circle" or
even something "round," hence a sense of "rolling") has attracted a divine play
on words: "Today I have rolled away ("gilgalled") the reproaches of the Egyptians." A creative storyteller would be at some degree of liberty to rhapsodize a
bit upon this "rolling stone" image; a Christian narrator would not improperly
be drawn to the empty tomb scenario. Metaphorically, what is "gilgalled" is
the *herpat* of Egypt. *Herpat* is singular, meaning "reproach, disgrace"; the
whole complex of unjust afflictions in Egyptian servitude was too well remembered. Not surprisingly, the Targum (a later translation of the Hebrew Bible
into Aramaic) appended a plural ending, "reproaches" (a change uncharacteris-
tically adopted by the REB). Also possible is the suggestion that "roll away the
reproach" refers to a rite (see Josh. 24:23-24 and Gen. 35:1-4) in which other
gods would ceremoniously be put away. Moments of crisis and decision,
whether the departure from Egypt or the entry into Canaan or the forced march
to Babylon would pose most urgently the question of which gods would be followed and with what level of commitment.

Preparations are being made for battle, but the only marching is in a worship
procession. The only weapon being brandished is a flint knife for circumcision.
The only strategy session is the eating of a sacred meal. All is not ready,
though, until Joshua is surprised by a man. Both bravery and humility may be
inferred from his actions of stepping forward and then falling in obeisance
once the identity of the heavenly interloper ("captain of the army of the Lord")
is manifest. Psalm 121:1-2, I Chronicles 21:16, and Judges 7:13-15 offer
instructive images for the reconstruction of the scene. The storyteller needs to
piece together the "mosaic" (pun intended) of Joshua's portrait. He is surprised
by a heavenly visit. He poses Moses' own pre-massacre question (Exod. 32:26;
Boling fingers the famed "Who goes there, friend or foe?" from *Hamlet*).
Joshua, too, removes his sandals. While he will never radiate the glory as did
Moses, Joshua is summoned to serve the same role as an "earthen vessel" lead-
er/follower. The biblical Joshua is no Alexander mounting Bucephalus, no
Washington crossing the Delaware, no Rommel sweeping across northern
Africa. The hero is the Lord, brooking no rival.

Retelling the Story

Some things you just expect to have around forever. Even though you know it can't happen, you expect it just the same. Wives expect it of husbands, and husbands of wives. Children expect it of parents, and parents of children. Then, you wake up one morning and go to a wedding or a funeral, and there you are. You feel a mix of pain at knowing it is gone and foolishness at knowing you should have seen it going. That's how it was then, too.

They all wandered around outside their tents looking as if they were on an Easter egg hunt down at the city park. They looked in the easy places first, those places where they had always found pieces before, but as time went by they looked in new places. "Maybe it was inside the tents this morning, and we missed it!" Or "Maybe it landed over there on the other side of that hill!" And they would run off to see. One guy was even digging in the sand over there on the chance that the wind had covered it up, although that hadn't happened in forty years, but, "Hey, it has to be around here somewhere, doesn't it?"

> The angel Michael appeared to Joshua and accused him and the people of being so concerned with daily affairs that they were neglecting to study the Torah. Specifically, Joshua was so busy planning for war that he had not spent time in study, for which the angel gave him a stern warning. (Ginzberg IV, p. 7)

That's when it occurred to them. No, it didn't. It didn't *have* to be around here *anywhere!* They all came to the same realization at about the same time, all except for the guy digging in the sand, who just kept on digging, proving that some people wake up more slowly than others. They all just stood there, watching the guy dig, really hoping he would find it, but knowing with each scoopfull that he wouldn't. Then someone sighed, and they all went home.

The families were already gathered around the fires, waiting for the bread. When they heard the news, some of them ran outside to see for themselves; some of them grumbling that "if you want anything done right, you have to do it yourself!" But they all came back into the tent empty handed. It was true. There was no bread from heaven this morning.

Last night had been Passover. And, following the rules, they had eaten everything on the table, not leaving anything for tomorrow. It had been that way since they left Egypt, but it certainly felt different this morning. If only they could have known, they would have set just a few things back. But who had any idea that there would be no bread today? "What do we do now?"

It was later in the day, after the people had finally come to realize that if they wanted to eat they would have to go out and get their food from this new land, that Joshua came running up. "Hey, everybody! It is *wonderful!*" God is

181

Some say that Joshua's having to remove his sandals was not only a sign that the ground was holy but that it also indicated that he was in mourning for having neglected the Torah. (Ginzberg, IV, p. 7)

with us here, just as he was before!" They wiped the sweat off their brows and stared at him.

"Then where is the bread? If God is here, why can't we see the cloud anymore, and *where is the bread?*"

"But God *is* here. We are standing on holy ground! All this has been prepared for us—all the food, the water, the land for our animals. And God has sent the armies of heaven to lead us in!"

"Armies we got. It's bread for our children we need."

"But we have bread too! All we need or ever want. The land is full of fields of ripened grain. The hills have springs of water. The trees hold fruit and nuts, and it's all ours!" Joshua kept trying to convince them, "All we have to do is go get it!" But from the back of the crowd came the response, "I liked it better the way it used to be."

The Fall of Jericho

The army of Israel marches around Jericho seven times, and the walls collapse after the people give a great shout.

The Story

Jericho was bolted and barred against the Israelites; no one could go out or in. The LORD said to Joshua, 'See, I am delivering Jericho, its king, and his warriors into your hands. You are to march round the city with all your fighting men, making the circuit of it once a day for six days. Seven priests carrying seven trumpets made from rams' horns are to go ahead of the Ark. On the seventh day you are to march round the city seven times with the priests blowing their trumpets. At the blast of the rams' horns, when you hear the trumpet sound, the whole army must raise a great shout; the city wall will collapse and the army will advance, every man straight ahead.'

Joshua son of Nun summoned the priests and gave them instructions: 'Take up the Ark of the Covenant; let seven priests with seven trumpets of ram's horn go ahead of the Ark of the LORD.' Then he gave orders to the army: 'Move on, march round the city, and let the men who have been drafted go in front of the Ark of the LORD.'

After Joshua had issued this command to the army, the seven priests carrying the seven trumpets of ram's horn before the LORD moved on and blew the trumpets; the Ark of the Covenant of the LORD followed them.

The drafted men marched in front of the priests who blew the trumpets, and the rearguard came behind the Ark, the trumpets sounding as they marched. But Joshua commanded the army not to shout, or to raise their voices or even utter a word, till the day when he would tell them to shout; then they were to give a mighty shout. Thus he made the Ark of the LORD go round the city, making the circuit of it once, and then they returned to the camp and spent the night there. Joshua rose early next morning, and the priests took up the Ark of the LORD. The seven priests carrying the seven trumpets of ram's horn marched in front of the Ark of the LORD, blowing the trumpets as they went, with the drafted men in front of them and the rearguard following the Ark, the trumpets sounding as they marched. They marched round the city once on the second day and returned to the camp; this they did for six days.

On the seventh day they rose at dawn and marched seven times round the city in the same way; that was the only day on which they marched round seven times. The seventh time, as the priests blew the trumpets, Joshua said to the army, 'Shout! The LORD has given you the city.'

Comments on the Story

The story of the fall of Jericho is rife with problems. Somewhat in the manner of the search for ancient Troy, Jericho has long been a favorite of archaeologists, who through trial and much error have actually refined methodology at the expense of the mound itself. Since 1867, Jericho has been dug and redug by Charles Warren, Ernst Sellin, Karl Watzinger, John Garstang, and Dame Kathleen Kenyon. Garstang claimed in the 1930s to have found the biblical walls that tumbled, but Kenyon has dated them some one thousand years prior to Joshua's day.

Located near the spring es-Sultan, which spouts one thousand gallons of water per minute, and flanked on the east by what still is an oasis in the midst of a desert region and on the west by the massive Mount of Temptation and its monastery, Jericho is acclaimed as one of civilization's oldest cities. At over eight hundred feet below sea level it is the lowest. A Mesolithic settlement dates back to 9000 B.C.E. Neolithic walls and a twenty-five-foot high stone tower date to before 7000 B.C.E. Skulls have been recovered from perhaps 5000 B.C.E., but Kenyon found no trace of Late Bronze Age city walls. Were they in ruin when Israel got there? Or did a seismic disturbance prove to be the coup d'état for an antiquated wall that had already fallen into disrepair? Erosion has erased whatever definitive evidence that may once have existed.

Two facts stand out, though. First, bulinus truncatus, a kind of snail, has been found in the layers of rubble at Jericho. This snail hosts a parasite that causes schistosomiasis, a disease that manifests itself in ugly symptoms in one's private parts, as well as in depression and despair. Boling follows E. V. Hulse in tentatively suggesting that Jericho may have been so contaminated, explaining the fall of its kingdom, as well as offering a good reason for the holocaust of the site and the prohibition of its rebuilding. What other reason might there be to capture a town at a vital crossroads and then refuse to settle the town?

Second, to this day tourists are taken aback by the smallness of the mound that once was Jericho. While boasting a venerable history, Jericho was never large. The walled area was never as much as nine acres. Certainly its location, hovering over a fertile oasis that marked the readiest access into Canaan from Transjordan, was strategic. But its prominence grows, not from the greatness of Jericho itself, but from its symbolic importance as the first of all the victories in the Promised Land.

The story does not mention traditional warfare techniques for taking a walled city (scaling the wall, digging under the wall, battering the wall, siege works, or even the roughly contemporaneous Trojan horse). But at length the text describes God's instructions for the daily march, the blaring of the trumpets, and the sevenfold march and communal shout on the seventh day. Repetitively in the text, God tells Joshua, Joshua tells everyone else, and then they actually do it. How anti-climactic is the surprisingly brief notice in verse 20: "And the walls collapsed." The ancient storyteller had no interest in the theatrics of the cataclysm. Elaboration was reserved for the people's strict execution of the divine script for marching, blowing, and shouting, as well as for the utter obliteration of the city itself.

The marching, trumpets, and shouting have a liturgical sort of flavor. We may surmise that ancient Israelites, in their retellings of this event, performed maneuvers easily dramatized in even small Sunday school classes today. But what lay in the distant past (perhaps some ancient processional to and around the abandoned tell) is long forgotten. The trumpet (the *shofar*) was used in early Israel to muster the troops, as a signal to stop or start the fighting, and most likely in earliest worship. The ark's military role is somewhat muted here (compare I Sam. 4–5). Interestingly, Christian Crusaders tried the march/trumpet/shout method, albeit resulting in no "tumbling." Lacking any miracle, we may be sure that their blood-thirsty execution of the ban was not a holy act. Gaster even suggests that the horn-blowing and the shout fit into a cross-cultural pattern of generalized noise making, believed to send hostile powers on the run; many New Year's customs involve various and sundry makers of racket.

The "ban" (*herem*) is among the most troublesome of all idiosyncrasies in the Hebrew Bible. The law of Deuteronomy 20 insists that in "holy war" everything—animals, buildings, even the women and children—is to be burned. Perhaps this is a primitive oblation to a God somewhat misperceived as a warrior. Perhaps the after-effects of battle (such as bubonic plague or schistosomiasis) were so insidious that the razing and burning of the site were the only remedies. Isn't "holy war" an oxymoron? Even today, warmongers slaughter civilians, but a war crimes trial is in order for such atrocities. Are we not still embarrassed by the woeful history of killing perpetrated in the name of religion (e.g., the Crusades)? Or by generals of varied stripes who would piously pray for God to crush the foe? A storyteller must get in touch with these questions, for feelings and sentiments surely will rise to the surface.

The *herem* was not unique to Israel. Mesha, king of Moab (ninth century B.C.E.) even claims to have "utterly destroyed" Israelites in his own holy war on behalf of his god, Chemosh. As we recall that most of what the Hebrew Bible has to say about such destruction comes from texts not actually written until Israel had been in the land for centuries, is it that Israel came in retrospect to regret having not gotten rid of everything Canaanite, since they had let themselves be contaminated in their coexistence with pagan religion?

The severity with which the narrator viewed the ban, though, is evident in battle number two at Ai (meaning "ruin," aptly named, but nevertheless archaeologically problematical). Achan, in an act "perfidious" (REB) indeed, treacherously seized some booty, which was until modern times the only real payoff and motivation for soldiers. Militarily, all goes smoothly. The spies think the seizure of Ai will be a lark. But Israel's soldiers were killed, and (in a picturesque rendering) "the courage of the people melted and flowed away like water" (7:5 REB). Only after grave repentance, and only after a radical turning to the real hope for victory, is Ai in fact captured. Comments like that in 7:13 must have reverberated in the ears of Israelites over the centuries. The verse speaks profoundly even today to us modern-day Achans who harbor forbidden things.

Two more items: Rahab seems almost forgotten until verse 17b. The great promise keeper shields her house from the ban (in fulfillment of 2:14). Verse 25 may well point to an ongoing settlement of a "clan of Rahab" on or near the Jericho tell. Also, the dreadful curse of verse 26 lay in wait for centuries until finding a victim in Abiram and Segub (I Kings 16:34).

Again, in ancient towns, the majority of the population lived outside the city walls. Who was privileged to live within the walls? The wealthy, of course. Historically, persons have always lived in the oasis on the plain; the New Testament city of Jericho as well as the modern city are situated below the ancient walled city. Perhaps residents in the valley happily joined Israel in their march. If the walled section was largely deserted (as archaeology may indicate), then the marching could reflect an ancient custom of marking off claimed territory by such a symbolic tracing of its boundaries. An Egyptian ceremony called "the circuit of the wall" let a new pharaoh circumambulate a city wall as a segment of his inauguration (similar to cultures as far-flung as India, Africa, Thailand, and England; see the interesting details in Gaster, *Myth, Legend & Custom in the Old Testament,* p. 411). The modern theory of a gradual infiltration is therefore (curiously enough) consistent with this, the greatest of the "swift conquest" stories.

Some say that Joshua decided to take Jericho on the Sabbath, while others deny it strenuously. They say that Joshua consecrated to God the first city taken in the Promised Land, just as the first fruits of harvest are so consecrated. In any case, no evidence of walls has ever been found at the site of ancient Jericho. That is no surprise, say the rabbis, because God caused them to be swallowed up into the bowels of the earth. (Ginzberg, VI, pp. 174-75)

Retelling the Story

Siege.

Building walls around yourself can be a comforting thing until you realize that they keep as much on the inside as they keep on the outside.

It is a beautiful view from the walls of the city. To the west, just a mile away, stand towering red mountains. Their shear faces are pocketed with crevasses and caves, just perfect for hiding spies today and monks tomorrow. To the north is the aimlessly wandering Jordan River, while to the south is the vast mystery of the Salt Sea, or the Sea of Asphalt as we call it. To the east is the Jordan River again, and just beyond that the purple-shaded mountains of Moab. All put together, the view from the wall is one that puts you in a reflective frame, and standing here you find yourself speaking in big words and making resolutions to do more with your life. It is the kind of place that. . . . Wait a minute, what was that?

There, over east there, down by the river. Something moved, I'm sure. There! There it was again. It's a group, looks like soldiers. Maybe we should call the. . . . No, wait a minute. It's all right. It's just those crazy Hebrews again.

It is the funniest thing. For months we had been hearing about them. They have come all the way from the deserts in the south, beyond the sea. According to the stories, they have defeated great armies, gotten water out of rocks, and been fed by magical bread that floats down from the skies every morning. Well, I don't mind telling you we were getting scared. The nearer they came to us, the more we feared. The city gates were closed and sealed the day we got word of their arrival at Shittim, across the river. And the first day they launched their attack on us everyone was certain that we would be overrun. I have never been so afraid.

But it was amazing. Their great and powerful army, or so we had been told, marched right up to our city gates. There were rows of soldiers, followed by religious men carrying a shrine of some sort, and then another group of soldiers marching behind. Instead of attacking, as we had feared, they quietly walked all around the city and then went home! That's right—once around the city and gone. What's even stranger is that they have done the same thing for the past six days straight! The city guards are beginning to believe that the Hebrews are actually afraid of us. They are even talking about launching their own attack to drive the Hebrews away for good.

So here they come again. Right around the walls, just as before. It is funny how foolish some people are willing to look because of some God. Well, at least this time it is a bit different, I hear them blowing some horns.

I wonder what all the shouting is about?

> Rahab and all those related to her by marriage were saved from the destruction of Jericho. Some rabbis say that this was justified, because she did not belong to one of the seven nations that God had commanded the Israelites to destroy. Others say it was not justified, thus one of her descendants, Jeremiah, became the one who would prophesy the destruction of the temple and the exile. (Ginzberg IV, p. 174)

The People of Gibeon Trick Joshua

The inhabitants of Gibeon pretend to be from a far country to convince Joshua that it is safe to make a treaty with them.

The Story

When the inhabitants of Gibeon heard how Joshua had dealt with Jericho and Ai, they resorted to a ruse: they set out after disguising themselves, with old sacks on their donkeys, old wineskins split and mended, old and patched sandals for their feet, old clothing to wear, and by way of provisions nothing but dry and crumbling bread. They came to Joshua in the camp at Gilgal, where they said to him and the Israelites, 'We have come from a distant country to ask you now to grant us a treaty.' The Israelites said to these Hivites, 'But it may be that you live in our neighbourhood: if so, how can we grant you a treaty?' They said to Joshua, 'We are your slaves.'

Joshua asked them who they were and where they came from. 'Sir,' they replied, 'our country is very far away, and we have come because of the renown of the LORD your God. We have heard the report of all that he did to Egypt and to the two Amorite kings east of the Jordan, King Sihon of Heshbon and King Og of Bashan who lived at Ashtaroth. Our elders and all the people of our country told us to take provisions for the journey and come to meet you, and say, "We are your slaves; please grant us a treaty."

Look at our bread; it was hot from the oven when we packed it at home on the day we came away. Now, as you see, it is dry and crumbling. Here are our wineskins; they were new when we filled them, and now they are all split; look at our clothes and our sandals, worn out by the very long journey.' Without seeking guidance from the LORD, the leaders of the community accepted some of their provisions. Joshua received them peaceably and granted them a treaty, promising to spare their lives, and the leaders ratified it on oath.

However, within three days of granting them the treaty the Israelites learnt that these people were in fact neighbours, living nearby. The Israelites then set out and on the third day they reached their towns, Gibeon, Kephirah, Beeroth, and Kiriath-jearim. The Israelites did not attack them, because of the oath which the chief men of the community had sworn to them by the LORD the God of Israel. When the whole community was indignant with the leaders, they all made this reply: "We swore on oath to them by the LORD the God of Israel; so now we cannot touch them. What we shall do is this: we shall spare their lives so that the oath which we swore to them

188

may bring down no wrath on us. But though their lives must be spared, they will be set to cut wood and draw water for the community.' The people agreed to do as their chiefs had said.

Joshua summoned the Gibeonites and said to them, 'Why did you play this trick on us? You told us that you live a long way off, when in fact you are near neighbours. From now there is a curse on you: for all time you shall provide us with slaves, to cut wood and draw water for the house of my God.' They answered Joshua, 'We were told, sir, that the LORD your God had commanded his servant Moses to give you the whole country and to wipe out its inhabitants; so because of you we were in terror of our lives, and that is why we did this. We are in your hands: do with us whatever you think right and proper.' What he did was this: he saved them from death at the hands of the Israelites, and they did not kill them; but from that day he assigned them to cut wood and draw water for the community and for the altar of the LORD. And to this day they do so at the place which the LORD chose.

Comments on the Story

Israel's westward blitz has steamrolled Jericho and Ai. Strangely, almost illogically, Joshua 8:30-35 shifts Israel twenty miles to the north for the covenant ceremony at Shechem. In chapter 9 we get back to the thrust through the central hill country. Lying in Israel's path along the road from Jericho to the Mediterranean is a coalition of small towns, headed up by Gibeon.

Just over five miles northwest of Jerusalem, Gibeon (modern el-Jib) to this day is a picturesque rural village, a rocky knoll surrounded by farms, with threshing floors—a primitive feel. Visitors can peek down into a round stone shaft, ringed by a spiral staircase, no doubt the very pool by whose edge Joab and Abner fought (II Sam. 2:12-17). It was while dreaming in Gibeon that Solomon, with his sacrifices still smoldering, received the gift of wisdom from the Lord (I Kings 3:4-15).

Upon hearing about these invaders mopping up the Shechem valley so invincibly, Gibeon, with its compatriots Chephirah, Beeroth, and Kiriath-jearim, must have trembled in terror. Had they previously been loosely federated? Or did the Israelite advance galvanize them into a joint deterrence? Slender archaeological evidence indicates these villages were thinly populated in the days of Joshua. And how did the story (focused, as in the case of Rahab, on the demise of Sihon and Og; Num. 21) come to be known so widely and so quickly?

Their novel strategy was neither to fight nor even to try normal diplomatic channels. They embark upon subterfuge, trickery, the kind of ruse not unprecedented among the Israelites (Jacob and Tamar are noteworthy examples of such disguise and deception).

Verbally, they claim to be from "a distant country" (v. 6), "very far away" (v. 9). There is a grain of truth in their claim. The people of Gibeon are dubbed

189

"Hivites." Apparently, these Hivites (kin to the Horites or even the Hurrians?) hailed from the far north (perhaps Cilicia in Asia Minor, modern-day Turkey), although they had been in Canaan long enough to put down roots.

But Israel's diplomats come off looking either gullible or downright stupid. If they are from such a great distance, why bother to send a team to negotiate? The Hebrews are a bit suspicious, but they are too foolhardy to follow up on their hunch (v. 7). Almost hilariously, the Gibeonites dress up in tattered clothes and worn-out sandals. They gather up some meager food supplies— dry, moldy bread crumbs. What travelers could not secure some fresh bread? The narrator expects the hearer to recall that the Israelites still wore those miracle clothes from the wilderness (which did not wear out after forty years of daily wear; see Deut. 8:4; 29:5) and were well-fed during their long journey.

The upshot of the negotiation is that their nonviolent tactic works. Joshua gets hemmed into a predicament by his very own unnamed, unauthorized negotiators; they had no business finagling such a deal (see Deut. 20). The Lord had made it clear that for Israel to pursue any independent course of action is to court disaster. The negotiators are not said to have prayed or to have rolled the Urim and Thummim. But by the time Joshua discovers what's afoot, the promise has been made. He is then obligated to enforce it. "To spare their lives" (v. 15) includes more than refraining from slaughter; a sharing of pasture, water, and even provision of mutual defense would be entailed.

Like Cain, the Gibeonites live out a shadowy existence, partially under a curse of sorts, but still protected. Indeed, Saul (from nearby Gibeah, not Gibeon) treacherously violated the treaty; vengeance was had in the form of a famine and the morbid execution of seven of Saul's children (see II Sam. 4:2-8 and 21:1-9), a classic example of the father's iniquities being "visited upon" a later generation (Exod. 20:5).

The real shock of the story is the sorry fate ("to this day," v. 27) of the Gibeonites. We might expect the Hebrew principle of equality to prevail, but the Gibeonites are coerced into an inferior occupational caste. They are "delivered," but into a type of slavery, a repugnant and inexplicable perversion of Israel's covenant ideals. Tabernacle and later Temple worship required massive supplies of wood, and thus much manual labor (Deut. 29:11); considering the influx of pilgrims offering sacrifices at Passover, heaped onto the daily demand for fuel, timber consumption, and therefore "cutting" and "carrying" must have been staggering. Canaan indeed is becoming the slave of Shem (Gen. 9:25-26).

In chapter 10, the beleaguered Gibeonite enclave is successfully defended against yet another hostile confederation. Admittedly, if Gibeon had not struck a deal with Israel, Adonizedek's league would never have pounced! Nevertheless, the Israelite militia heroically rescues their cutters and carriers. Of course, the victory (the account of which is footnoted as being from the ancient storyteller's treasury, the "book of Yashar") is clinched from heaven. The Lord throws hailstones from the sky, and the sun even stands still over Gibeon (10:11-13).

These meteorological phenomena have been tackled by interpreters. A storm, rare in the middle of summer, would appear miraculous indeed; a driving hailstorm (even today) would lead one to invoke the gods. Was there an eclipse of the sun? Were the attackers, facing the east, blinded by the morning sun? Did a fortuitous juxtaposition of sun and moon strike fear into the superstitious hearts of these Canaanites who searched the skies so intently for omens? Was it the proverbial "long day"? The sun, worshiped as a god by the inhabitants of Gibeon, like the moon, is not divine at all, but a mere instrument in the hands of the true God. But the sun, halted by the hand of God in the midst of its daily jaunt across the sky, is a storyteller's jewel, a fitting dénouement to the sequence of events in the valley of Aijalon.

Retelling the Story

If it wasn't for the fact that it was just so incredibly funny, people probably would have been more upset about it. On the other hand, it was simply so frightening and revealing that no one dared to laugh about it. So most people just said nothing, and it soon became one of those experiences you just didn't talk about at all.

Over here, on the one side, we have this great group of people moving into their new homeland. With the help of that God of theirs, they have conquered and driven out everyone who has stood in their way. Very impressive.

On the other hand, we have this second group of people, who have just discovered that they are the next ones standing right in the way. They prefer to be neither conquered nor driven out, but this new God makes both seem pretty likely. The rules this God plays by are pretty clear. As God's people move in, there is no room for anyone else. You either move on or die. If ever there was the time for a brilliant plan, this was it. But just how do you go about fooling a God?

They found it was easier than they thought.

So these already-settled folks found themselves some of the oldest, most

It is said that Joshua offered the residents of "The Land" three options before he began his invasion. First, they could leave, in which case he would not bother them. Second, they could make peace, in which case he would make peace with them. Finally, they could prepare for war, in which case he would make war against them. If the Gibeonites had wanted peace from the start they could have had it, but they waited to see how fierce an enemy Israel would be. (Ginzberg, IV, p. 9) tired looking mules they owned and saddled them up. For provisions they packed up several loaves of bread from down at the day-old discount bakery shop and put their wine in some of the old canteens they had been letting the children play with. They picked out a handful of their best actors, dressed them in some old rags from the resale shop downtown, and lined them up in the town square for an hour or so of high-impact aerobics, just to make them look good and tired. Then, after throwing a few handfuls of dust over the whole collection of them, sent them on their way.

As they made the twenty-five mile trip, they passed the time by practicing their accents on each other. They also tested each other to be sure they had their story straight.

"Quick, Lemuel, how long we been traveling here?"

"Oh, my, we have been traveling now for—why just look here, when we started out our bread was fresh, and our canteens were just out of the boxes. How'd I do?"

> Though won by trickery, Joshua kept his word to the Gibeonites. This was to show how sacred was the word of an Israelite leader. Such a promise could be trusted even if it were gained dishonestly. (Ginzberg, IV, p. 10)

Now, each of the men had heard the stories about this new God. They each knew well that this parlor trick would not fool such a God, even for a minute. Their only hope was that these Hebrew people just weren't as sharp as their God was. So they kept practicing.

They should have gotten an Academy Award. What a performance! From the moldy bread to the dented canteens and resoled sandals, the Hebrews swallowed it hook, line, and sinker. They even made a covenant, with no loopholes, that as they took over the new land, they would never harm these friendly travelers from a distant land.

How they finally found out they were "had," we don't know. All we do know is that a few days later, when the Hebrew soldiers pulled another sneak attack on a nearby village, someone came sauntering out of the town gate carrying a piece of paper with Joshua's signature on it. Somehow they would have to share the land. But God had told them to drive everyone out and not to share with anyone. They knew that sooner or later they were going to have to ask God about this.

Sooner would have been better.

The Choice

Joshua presents the people with the choice between serving the gods of their ancestors or the God who brought them out of Egypt.

The Story

Joshua assembled all the tribes of Israel at Shechem. He summoned the elders of Israel, the heads of families, the judges and officers. When they presented themselves before God, Joshua said to all the people: 'This is the word of the LORD the God of Israel: Long ago your forefathers, including Terah the father of Abraham and Nahor, lived beyond the Euphrates and served other gods. . . .

'Now hold the LORD in awe, and serve him in loyalty and truth. Put away the gods your fathers served beyond the Euphrates and in Egypt, and serve the LORD. But if it does not please you to serve the LORD, choose here and now whom you will serve: the gods whom your forefathers served beyond the Euphrates, or the gods of the Amorites in whose land you are living. But I and my family, we shall serve the LORD.'

The people answered, "God forbid that we should forsake the LORD to serve other gods!' They declared: 'The LORD our God it was who brought us and our forefathers up from Egypt, that land of slavery; it was he who displayed those great signs before our eyes, who guarded us on all our wanderings among the many peoples through whose lands we passed. The LORD drove out before us the Amorites and all the peoples who lived in that country. We too shall serve the LORD; he is our God.'

Comments on the Story

Twin peaks, Mt. Ebal and Mt. Gerizim, flank the invaluable east-west corridor that cuts through the north central hill country of Samaria. Historically, control of this pass has been essential for trade and politics. From the top of Ebal you can almost see all the way to Jerusalem to the south, and the snow-capped Hermon in the north is visible; to the west is a vista toward the great sea and the long ridge of Mt. Carmel, to the east a cavity exposing the Jordan rift. Indeed, most of the Promised Land is situated within a thirty-mile radius of Ebal.

Nestled in the crux of the valley is ancient Shechem *(tell balata)*, at an ancient crossroad, "the uncrowned queen of Palestine." Excavations have unearthed a flourishing city from the Middle Bronze Age; a great fortress-temple (with walls as thick as seventeen feet) and a royal chapel fell into disuse around 1500 B.C.E. (not coincidentally the same era in which "a new king arose in Egypt who did not know Joseph"). Abraham had migrated there (Gen. 12); Jacob built an altar there (Gen. 33); Dinah was raped in Shechem (Gen. 34). Moving into the 1300s B.C.E., the famed Amarna Letters reveal a local prince, Labayu, creating havoc for the Egyptian overlords. The defunct temple was rebuilt on the "broadroom" design. It is difficult to escape the conclusion that a religion intimately associated with what we discern in the Bible was practiced in this temple.

Joshua 8:30-35 (an earlier covenantal ceremony at Shechem) claims that stones were plastered and written upon, standing obscurely enough as taciturn witnesses to the commitments made. Joshua read all the words of Moses in the hearing of the crowd. Judges 9 relates the devastation on Shechem wrought by the man who would be king, Abimelech. Much later, Jeroboam rebuilt the city; an east gate tower has been excavated from his work. Houses from the early monarchy may be seen; they were covered by four feet of debris, having lain in the path of the Assyrian army in 722 B.C.E. The Samaritans reinvested in the site, being at the foot of their holy Mt. Gerizim. A famed Christian image is that of Jesus and the woman at Jacob's well (John 4), apparently in the vicinity. Unfortunately, tourists are generally steered away from this region of the West Bank.

Labayu is even indicted for giving land to the "Habiru." These "Habiru" are not identical to what we think of as the "Hebrews." Evidently, these Habiru were poor, despised outcasts, some mercenaries, from many ethnic strands; today, sociologists have suggested with some justification that such persons in the margins may well have found the religion and community of the Israelites most appealing and indeed liberating. Historically it seems clear that there were poor, disenfranchised persons already dwelling in the land who jumped on the Hebrew bandwagon and became part of what at first was a loosely organized group of followers of the God of Moses. The parallel passage, Joshua 8:30-35, places native-borns and resident aliens across from one another. Natural barriers are shattered, as both are united in the bonds of their faith.

Shechem was the earliest religious center for the tribes of Israel after the exodus. Our text has all the earmarks of representing a ceremony that could be reenacted year after year. Israel's relationship with God, and its liturgical life, revolved entirely around God's deeds in the past. Sadly the lectionary has removed what Israel would regard as the very heart of the text. The creedal summary of the broad sweep of salvation history (24:2-13) is told in God's very own first-person speech. The love and persistence of the Lord are beautifully elaborated upon. Such a story must have heartened generation after generation of Israelites who came together each year (or in the most difficult times every seven years) at the old sanctuary at Shechem to remember, to retell, and to reenvision.

The literary craft is remarkable. The word *said* (*'amar*) occurs seven times; Joshua is named seven times; the people are referred to seven times; seven imperatives complete the picture. At this juncture, the full twelve-tribe organization was still inchoate; and yet, much as an American might say, "We fought the Redcoats at Bunker Hill," this liturgy, used over many centuries, could properly say that all of Israel was implicated. Perhaps in the presence of the ark ("before the Lord"), Joshua speaks as would one of the later prophets ("This is the word of the Lord"). It is often argued (with credibility) that the Israelite covenant was modeled in partial ways after diplomatic treaties well-known in ancient politics. The superior party (the suzerain) receives the allegiance of a vassal, motivated by the largess of the superior and the common needs of both. The panoramic recital of the largess calls to memory vital moments of gracious deliverance; how intentionally the story *in nuce* would guard against any boasting or delusions of self-reliance.

Verse 14 brings the narrative into the present with the pregnant *now*. The story is hardly mere entertainment. A decision must be made about this kind of story. The decision is not an intellectual one. The Septuagint added two little words to fit in to a later, more speculative, mind set: "For the Lord our God is God. He. . . ." The primal question is not "How many gods are there?" but "To whom will I be loyal?" The seriousness of the decision is heightened by the curses that the liturgy invokes upon the people should apostasy come. Joshua's swan song (chap. 23) is replete with dire warnings (see also 22:22-29). Joshua (with perhaps subsequent leaders or priests) makes the stirring asseveration, "I and my family have chosen; we shall serve the Lord." Whether a person can make this sort of decision for another, even for one's own family, is a matter for debate; even in Old Testament times, solidarity had its limits. (Ruth 1:16 dramatically recounts a different approach.) But cleaving to an exclusive relationship with this Lord is the last word when it comes to staying in and enjoying the land, spread so magnificently around Mt. Ebal.

The nagging threat to sharing in the bounty of the Promised Land was indeed "other gods." To "put away" such gods may entail a ritual renunciation much like what we read of in Genesis 35:2-4, when Jacob urges his extended household literally to bury all primitive figurine idols under the terebrinth at Shechem! The site has a centuries-old tradition as a good place to unload other gods. Strange indeed then is the Septuagint's addition to verse 30, which reports how the circumcision flint knives (from Josh. 5:2) were interred there.

Retelling the Story

"Hey buddy! Come win a stuffed animal for your lady there!"
"C'mon, step right up, three throws for one dollar!"

It has all the color of the midway at the carnival. Every hilltop has its priests, each calling for the folks to gather around his altar and "put their money down." Each one of them is different, and each one is the "best game in town!"

This one over here is for your crops. This priest offers a sure-fire way for you to have a tremendous barley harvest. Bow three times, leave a contribution, and it's yours.

And over here, the one with the long line. "Come up to the altar and spend some time with one of our little ladies!" Pay a visit to the sacred prostitutes, and your cattle will be blessed with bountiful offspring.

> Many sources say that it took the same amount of time to allot the land to the various tribes as it had to conquer it—seven years each. (Ginzberg, IV, pp. 16, 179)

There is one over here for trees, and one over there for your vineyards. "Gods for all occasions! Why take chances? Come and lay your money down!"

Of course, the greatest crowd is over there at the hilltop of Baal. The colored banners blowing in the breeze, the flashy dancers gyrating in front of the huge paintings of people being healed on the spot and of much-needed rain showers falling over fields of thirsty grain. Baal is the king of the midway. He has been here the longest and holds the best location on the midway, right at the end of the run, where the crowds all end up. But the crowds are down today.

Further down the midway, that is. It seems that something is stopping the crowds from coming to the end of the runway. The problem seems to be coming from that valley about half-way back toward the gate. It's not a good location, stuck between two mountains like that, but the folks who use it have been there for years. They seem to be a determined lot. Today, however, they are not only determined, they are popular!

As we make our way toward the crowd, the first thing we notice is nothing. Nothing! There are no flashy banners and no costumed, or uncostumed, dancers. There are no huge, painted images of rain or lightning or healings or anything, just a tired-looking old man, standing out on the stage, talking. He doesn't even have a "midway" kind of voice. What's that he's saying?

"I gave him Isaac, and to Isaac I gave Jacob and Esau."

Not much of a sales pitch, but look at how the crowd is eating it up.

"When I brought your fathers out of Egypt, you came to the sea."

Not a dancing girl in sight, but look at these people. Every so often there is a shout from the crowd. It's not a "Hey, Honey!" but a "Praise God!"

"Then you crossed the Jordan and came to Jericho."

Priests from the other hilltops are making their way through the crowd, trying to draw some away. No one is moving. Closer and closer they all push toward the stage and the strange old man standing upon it.

"But as for me and my household, we will serve the Lord."

Silence. Deep silence. The speech is over. The old man ends by telling them that it is time to either buy a ticket to the show, or move on down the path. "What's it going to be?"

And look at that! As people walk up to get their tickets, the old man argues with them. They want in, and he says they can't come in! Finally, after they plead and beg, he lets them enter the valley.

The people went to work farming after Joshua's death. They became so involved in planting and harvesting that they soon forgot Joshua and all he had done to help them obtain the land. As a result, God saw that the lives of the elders were shortened just as their memories had been shortened. (Ginzberg, IV, p. 16)

The other priests go back to their hillsides and their motionless dancing girls. No need to gyrate. There is no one to watch it.

I hope this valley thing is just a fad.

Index of Readings
from the *Revised Common Lectionary*

Index of Midrashim